C000090013

Cults

THE BATTLE FOR GOD

To Sally Evemy

To find a friend who will enthusiastically, and unpaid, work till the small hours, drive thousands of miles, check pages of text and listen patiently to the problems that have presented themselves at every turn, is rare indeed. To stay friends is a miracle. Here's to the next project?

Cults

The Battle for God

Shirley Harrison

with
Sally Evemy

Christopher Helm
LONDON

© 1990 Shirley Harrison

Christopher Helm (Publishers) Ltd.
Imperial House, 21-25 North Street,
Bromley, Kent BR1 1SD

ISBN 0-7470-1414-0

A CIP catalogue record for this book
is available from the British Library

All rights reserved. No reproduction, copy
or transmission of this publication may be
made without written permission.

No paragraph of this publication may be
reproduced, copied or transmitted save
with written permission or in accordance
with the provisions of the Copyright Act
1956 (as amended), or under the terms of
any licence permitting limited copying
issued by the Copyright Licensing Agency,
7 Ridgmount Street, London WC1E 7AE.

Any person who does any unauthorised act
in relation to this publication may be liable
to criminal prosecution and civil claims for
damages.

Typeset by Leaper and Gard Ltd, Bristol
Printed and bound in Great Britain by
Biddles Ltd, Guildford, Surrey

CONTENTS

PREFACE

ALL THE WORLD LOVES A SCANDAL, especially if sex and religion are involved.

For over 30 years the activities of the so-called 'Cults' have provided the tabloid press with both. Fuelled by the genuine heartbreak of families whose members have apparently abandoned them to join these movements, banner headlines have focused — often rightly — on the dark side.

The possibility that there might be any benefit from wearing a T-shirt proclaiming 'I'm a Moonie and I love it', or from chanting 'Hare Krishna', has been largely ignored. Yet, just as there are millions of men and women who find joy, comfort and security in one or other of the world's great religions, so there are many who find their spiritual fulfilment elsewhere.

Jesus said: 'seek and ye shall find.' I did just that. I went to look for the good — in order to assess the truth about the bad in those movements now branded 'cult'.

To use the Jesus Freaks' phrase of the sixties: 'I found it', though not all the time and not in all movements. I also found much that was bad, in equal measure, amongst the established religions. I came to dislike the word 'cult' and to realise how carelessly it can be used as a term of abuse.

I have continued to use it because it is at present the only immediately recognisable description of most of the fringe movements, but it is a concept I do not readily accept. 'Religion' is more often accurate, for this is where most — but not all — of the new movements really belong.

The Bishop of Woolwich once said: 'when religion goes wrong it goes very, very wrong.' Separating 'cults' in a spiritual ghetto, for possible extermination, will never eliminate the mistakes of religion. For a cult is not necessarily religion gone wrong.

It is true that some people need a clear reason why their loved ones have taken a different spiritual path from theirs and seek a target for their anger. It often helps to give that target a name — such as 'cult'.

There are others, more prepared to accept, to encourage individuality, within legal codes of conduct. Sometimes they are lucky and the family remains united, even enriched, by its diversity. Sometimes, they too are stranded, when the often stormy waters of religious enthusiasm appear to sweep their children, wives, husbands, siblings, out of reach.

I hope that widening the horizons, and setting the story in its historical context, may increase their understanding and ease, even prevent, their pain.

Dorothy:	'We want to see the Wizard.'
Guard:	'Oh . . . oh . . . but nobody can see the great Oz. Nobody has ever seen the great Oz.'
Dorothy:	'Well then, how do you know there is one?'
Guard:	'Because . . . because . . . he's . . . um . . . because, well if there wasn't a Wizard why would you be here?'[1]

There is no obvious link between the conservative little commuter town of East Grinstead, set amongst the wooded moorland of Ashdown Forest in Sussex, and its more sensual sister, San Francisco, in California.

There is nothing to alert the Brighton-bound motorist that the A22 from London could be the Scientologists' 'Road to Total Freedom'; little to suggest sinister rituals beneath the ethereally beautiful spire of the Mormon Temple.

Yet East Grinstead, like San Francisco, is a spiritual supermarket. On offer is a confusion of hope — or is it heresy? Within a five-mile radius you will find the British headquarters of the Church of Jesus Christ of Latter-day Saints (Mormons), the British heartland of the Church of Scientology, the country retreat of the shadowy Roman Catholic order Opus Dei. The Ancient and Mystical Order of Rosicrucians occupy a magnificent mansion high on the Forest, whilst the Anthroposophists' children at the Rudolph Steiner school, Michael Hall, float gently through the nearby village of Forest Row on the waves of the New Age.

The post office notice board offers almost as rich a range of alternative life styles as you can find in California. Druids dance where long ago Christopher Robin and Winnie the Pooh played at the Enchanted Place. There is also, they say, the highest concentration of witches outside Cornwall. Even the Baha'i faith, with its roots in deepest Iran, has settled nearby, and mainstream Christians of all denominations worship in idyllic rural churches.

Each claims to have unravelled the meaning of life.

But rumours are rife. Occasionally there is a shiver of unease, for as in a Hammer horror film no one is quite sure what *is* going on in Castle Dracula. The clergy cast a professionally quizzical eye, preach a sermon or two, but do little.

From time to time the national press arrives. Are Opus Dei practising flagellation? Are the Mormons polygamous? Is there Devil worship in the woods? Sometimes the events are, indeed, sinister and tragic, the truth behind them less certain. Why did a girl take her life? Why was a family made bankrupt by over-donating to its church? How could a daughter wish to sue her own father for trying to take her from her faith by force?

My own children grew up on Ashdown Forest. At the comprehensive school their paths crossed with young Scientologists and Mormons, just as they met Jehovah's Witnesses, Catholics, Baptists and Jews. We bought our live yoghurt from an organic Steiner Farm, danced around a maypole at their May Fair, invited Rosicrucians to dinner and lived to tell the tale! Sometimes the newcomers took part in the town carnival or played cricket on the green. We tended to take them for granted as part of the local scene and so, when sensational stories appeared in the papers, about Scientology in particular, it was hard, sometimes, to fit the people we knew into the framework of an 'evil cult'.

Years later, after my four offspring had passed, comparatively unscathed, through adolescence, I wondered what I might have done had they been drawn into such activity. Or, indeed, been Born Again.

I became curious to know more about these groups who, I read, had torn so many families apart.

They had mostly arrived on the tide of soul-searching that swept over from America in the fifties and sixties and, despite their vociferous critics, they took root and flourished, like the four-leafed clover which also thrives in the fields around East Grinstead. But their story did not, I now know, belong to East Grinstead or to America alone. Nor did it belong to hippy youth or even to our time. Religious independents are as old as humanity.

Since the Second World War, Africa, South America, Polynesia, the Far East has each witnessed a splintering of indigenous creeds and the arrival of foreign missionaries bringing 'new' ideas. In Britain and in the United States there were, among others, The International Society for Krishna Consciousness (Hare Krishna), who shaved their heads and chanted through the streets; the Unification Church (the Moonies) and the Beatles' Guru Maharishi, to join those who, like Jehovah's Witnesses and Mormons, were established well over 100 years ago.

In America 'Jesus freaking' gave rise to all manner of extreme breakaway Christian groups, some too extreme for British sensibilities.

The New Age movement and public longing for a more spiritual, better quality of life, fuelled the Western world with an enthusiasm for the Eastern values of meditation, yoga and holistic medicine. Many evangelical Christians view this as an insidious erosion of their faith by pernicious, heretical Hinduism.

Mostly, the roots of these rebels, whether they are called 'cults' or 'new religious movements' — NRMs, lay in mainstream religion. Some could trace their origins to ancient pagan wisdom and nature worship, though much of what they taught was a far cry from its source. There was also an alarming and continuing revival of Satanism, its tentacles feeling their way into public and political circles and sucking children into its black rituals.

Right or wrong, for better or for worse, it is easy for the television and other media to stimulate moral panic around the activities of these little-known movements. 'Cults' have always made good copy.

Now we are in the last decade of the century and are entering the Age of Aquarius; a time, we are told by astrologers, for balance, peace, tolerance and gentle feminine values. There are some who suspect that God is a Green.

With the former British Council of Churches having ecumenically contemplated Moonie admission to their ranks, Scientologists now owning ('infiltrating' if you are against them) many of the shops in East Grinstead and the established Anglican church being urged to stiffen its sinews and take on the 'challenge of the cults', perhaps now is the time to take stock.

For it will not be long before American-style tele-evangelism will be on tap in Britain. The satellite discs are in place to beam its frenzied emotion into our living rooms. The rhetoric and the bibles are at hand and the danger is that, far from peace and goodwill, we could be plunged into a go-go-go, holy ratings war.

All are embarked, like Chaucer's pilgrims, on a quest towards the year 2,000. Cultists, vigilantes, theologians, sociologists, psychologists, historians, the good and the bad jostling side by side, with parents often lost and anguished, as they chase each other's tales.

With such a motley company it is not possible fairly to introduce all pilgrims: some have, in any case, refused to speak, some threaten legal action if their presence is mentioned at all; others jostle for a prime place in the narrative.

My aim, as I set out, is understanding — not judgement. The very real and often dangerous areas of Satanism, and the perversions of child abuse, are too appalling and too complex to include because they demand the attention of a specialist investigation. Nor have I enquired into the far-reaching effects of the New Age gods — holistic health and psychotherapy.

I am spotlighting the few whose names are most often in the news and introducing some of the people in the industry that surrounds them.

It has been an emotional journey. Along the way I have listened to the stories of families whose lives have, indeed, been blown apart, who believe that the loss and sometimes even the death of their children can be laid at the door of the group they joined. Some of these stories are included here, though many of the names have been changed.

On the other hand, I have had conversations with elderly women, terrified by a new American fundamentalism of hellfire and retribution being preached from their Church of England pulpit; and I have heard from a young man who had a nervous breakdown after joining an Anglican community attached to a village church in the Midlands. I know a father, distressed because his son has gone into a monastery; I know a Scientologist who is content, if not happy, that *his* son is becoming an Anglican priest; and I know a Jehovah's Witness with an agnostic husband. There are no hard and fast rules about religion.

There has seldom been such a traffic jam on the yellow brick road to Heaven. The pilgrims are constantly changing but the rules of the road remain. The journey promises to be spiritually enriching for some, financially rewarding for others; often dangerous, always exciting.

Note
[1]From *The Wizard of Oz*, adapted by John Kane for the Royal Shakespeare Company.

ACKNOWLEDGEMENTS

THERE WILL BE MANY PEOPLE who are sad — even angry — that after all the time and courtesy they have lavished on me I have failed to support their cause . . . particularly the dedicated Christians and the heartbroken parents. But everyone — with few exceptions, has been generous and understanding of my aim. I thank them all. In particular I am grateful for the unstinting help given by Joy Caton of Deo Gloria Outreach, Ursula McKenzie of FAIR and Paul Booth of INFORM who have never failed at the end of a phone.

THE TRAVELLER'S GUIDE

'Now let us ride and listen to what I say.'

CANTERBURY TALES

PROLOGUE – The Pilgrims

18 NOVEMBER 1978 WAS JUST ANOTHER DAY. In London's Oxford Street children were waiting to shake hands with Father Christmas.

At 5 p.m., in the Christian community of The People's Temple, deep in the jungle of Guyana, 900 men, women and children were queuing too . . . for cups of Kool-Aid, laced with cyanide. Their leader the Rev. Jim Jones had given the go-ahead for a well-rehearsed mass suicide pact. First, parents syringed the liquid down their babies' throats. Then the older children and adults drank the rest – and an hour later they were all dead.

The horror sickened the world. *The Times* talked of 'the cocktail of death' and 'the frenzied fringe of religion'. Reports described bodies, dressed in their Sunday best, lying contorted in a grotesque tableau.

In America a Gallup Poll the following week found that 98 per cent of the population knew what had happened, a record equalled only by news of Hiroshima, and the attack on Pearl Harbour.

Yet, until a few months before 'Jonestown', the activities of The People's Temple had gone almost unnoticed. Jim Jones himself had, after all, been a friend of the former mayors of Los Angeles and San Francisco. In 1976 he had shared a stage with President Carter's wife, Rosalind, when she opened the Democratic Party head-quarters; he was one of the few guests invited to meet Vice President Mondale aboard his private jet.

The avowed aims of The People's Temple, which was founded in 1961, were to end oppression of the poor and eliminate class distinction. Its members were drawn largely from the poor, blacks, Asians and American Indians. Jones' wife, Marceline, who also died on that November day, had admitted he was not really a Christian and was using Christian fundamentalism as a way of attracting followers so that he could use them to further his Marxist ambitions. To the public, Jim Jones was an ordained minister of the Disciples of Christ and so he slipped through the net.

In the world outside The People's Temple, Jim Jones' star had begun to fade late in 1977. Former members alleged fake healings, physical beatings, exhausting work schedules, extortion and death threats to anyone who left. Despite all this, in 1978, 900 men, women and children followed him from San Francisco to the jungle of Guyana and were ready to die with him.

The reasons were complex and have occupied many academic books, but to ordinary folk the apparently willing 'martyrdom' of entire families is a terrible warning. Tragically prophetic were the words of Jeannie Mills who had been a follower and was found murdered just before the massacre — she had described her first impressions of The People's Temple. 'When you meet the friendliest people you have ever known, who introduce you to the most loving group of people you have ever encountered and you find the leader to be the most inspired, caring, compassionate and understanding person you have ever met . . . it probably is too good to be true.' It was.

Not long after, the Rev. Jim Jones said: 'We are devoted to a decision that it is better to die than be harassed from continent to continent.' So they died.

Four thousand miles away in Birmingham, England, on 18 November it was a thoroughly miserable day, grey, wet and windy. Major Joan Whitehead was banging her cymbals in a rousing performance of 'Bless His name, He sets me free' — the Salvation Army version of 'Champagne Charlie'. The unit was giving a concert to packed audiences to raise funds for a new night shelter in the City.

Over the county border in Northamptonshire a beautiful country manor was being restored by a team of enthusiastic young workers who were aiming to revive the community living of the first Christians. They had called themselves the 'Jesus People', and were energetic evangelical missionaries, in London and the Midlands. The 'Jesus People', or 'Jesus Fellowship', is a home-grown British movement which had been started in 1969, by Noel Stanton, a Baptist Minister for some years in the nearby village of Bugbrooke.

The People's Temple, the Salvation Army and the Jesus People were three vastly different, but Christian-based, organisations posing the question that lies at the root of much anxiety today: How can we know which of the New Religious Movements may follow the path of the Sally Army, which was itself reviled in the nineteenth century as a cult, whose members were stoned and even lost their lives, and is now a respected and well-loved force for good? Or which, on the other hand, will go the way of Jim Jones?

Could Jonestown happen again? Could it happen in Britain? Of course it could. There are always groups with that potential, for although crowd control and mass manipulation are well-studied sciences, the catalyst for genocide, or football hooliganism or religious hysteria may be impossible to detect.

Charisma is a dangerous responsibility. In their very different ways the Beatles had it, Hitler had it, Christ had it.

Ironically, the Jones brand of magnetism, which captivated an originally orthodox Christian community, represents the worst fears about today's breakaway movements. It is the fear that anyone, lured into their web, may lose all free will, for ever, to the control of a 'guru' or messiah.

That is why parents of all faiths, and of none, are devastated when their youthful offspring appear to become mesmerised by strange new 'gods' they themselves do not understand.

So it is sad that some of the NRMs have not been more concerned or caring for the agony of those bewildered families who feel they have been dispossessed. There has been a disastrous and often irresponsible lack of pastoral care.

The twentieth-century success of the ecumenical movement, the concept of unity in diversity, should have made it easier to break down the barriers between new and established movements and bring about improvements. In 1989 a Krishna devotee even helped to organise a multi-faith pilgrimage to Canterbury Cathedral attended by the Archbishop himself.

But alongside this there is a revived militancy, especially in America, where fundamentalist evangelism, upon which the country was founded and nurtured, has felt the need to fight back against what is seen as a soft option.

Dr Fazlur Rahman, of San Angelo, Texas, pleaded recently in *The Wall Street Journal* that entire systems should not be judged by the behaviour of the few. He was not talking of cults but of Islam, but . . .

'The wretched world of violence and oppression are not the realms of Moslems alone. Ferdinand Marcos and Augusto Pinochet are Christians. Some Jews in Israel use Biblical injunctions to preach and practise violence against Arabs; Hindus and Buddhists are at war in Sri Lanka. So are Hindus and Sikhs in India, Catholics and Protestants in Northern Ireland . . . Moslems, like everyone else, can be poor or rich, tolerant or intolerant, illiterate or scholarly, honest or dishonest. The majority are busy running their own lives, worrying about their own futures and those of their children.'

Intolerance encourages an intolerant backlash. 'Born-Again-Come-on-down-Christianity' is the other side of the coin that carries the image of the allegedly 'cultish' Children of God or the Church of Christ. Religion is the kingdom of intolerance.

There is a beautiful stately home, in West Sussex, which is one of the British bases of YWAM — Youth with a Mission, who are a well-established radical Christian movement.

YWAM was started 25 years ago, in America, just before the Jesus Movement, by a former Pentecostalist, Loren Cunningham. He saw that young people were turning radical and wanted Christianity to be in there too.

His plan was simple. He offered a training programme of three months theory and three months practical Christianity. His young people would be 'loaned' by their own churches and the cost of their stay with YWAM would be met through church funding, or the voluntary donations of friends and family.

The basic course costs £1,000 and the practical, which may well be abroad, another £800. In addition, there are teacher training courses, leadership schools and a Christian University in Hawaii.

World-wide there are some 7,000 full-time, unpaid staff, mobilising many thousands of missionary recruits. YWAM runs two charity ships, ministering as emergency medical and welfare services where needed. The ships have conference facilities for 400, and like everything else were bought and are run on donations.

Whilst training, students live, simply, in dormitories, sharing the running and maintenance of the house. They are taught to have 'Godly and Christian' character and that everyone has an obligation to spread the message.

At the end of the course, students either return to the world and, if they are lucky, pick up the work they left behind, or possibly stay on, as unpaid missionaries, depending on the time-honoured Christian principle of 'faith and fellowship' for their support. In practice this again means being subsidised by family, friends or church.

The cheerful literature, the smiling faces, the confidence, the methods all – on the surface – seem, to an outsider, much like those of the Mormons, or even the Moonies, especially since the YWAM leaders agree that there are many parents who 'would give anything' *not* to have their child a Christian. Divisions can be caused by religious commitment to any faith not shared by the rest of the family.

WHAT IS A CULT?

Since the word 'CULT' was first used in its modern sense, in the nineteenth century, it has developed a sinister, abusive ring and become a description for any non-conforming ideology, that is, for ideas we do not accept or understand. Cults are always 'them' and never 'us'. Historically, the word was used to describe any organised religious group. But in modern jargon it has come to mean a fashion, a trend, a popular activity which will not last. Vegetarianism has been called a cultish fad, Sherlock Holmes and Elvis Presley, cult figures.

The Shorter Oxford English Dictionary says: 'Cult – from Cultus (Latin) to worship or protect. A system of worship or devotion to a person or thing.'

The *Chambers Dictionary* is a little broader: 'A system of religious belief. An unorthodox or false religion. A great . . . often excessive admiration for a person or idea.'

No one ever considers their own religion a cult. Christian Scientists are offended to find themselves linked with the Unification Church, Jehovah's Witnesses will not preach to the likes of Scientologists. If you are a Muslim you regard the Baha'i Faith with disdain. If you practise Transcendental Meditation you are not following a specific religion at all. The Church of Christ believes that mainstream Christianity has departed from the teachings of Jesus.

The truth is that neither the word cult, nor the softer alternative 'New Religious Movement', can be applied to all these groups. Each is different. Very few are all bad.

The stories told by some former members are often genuinely heartrending; many mistakes have been made and there is so much misunderstanding. Families who feel they have lost their loved ones find small compensation in the fact they are alive, not tortured by drink or drugs and may even be quite happy. But such tragedies only represent a small part of the story. The problem is that fear feeds upon itself and by describing the agony of a few, rumours, which may well be false, are perpetuated. Mud sticks.

It is probably fair to say that belonging to most cults involves much the same commitment as devotion to any religious organisation (I do not say religious belief). No half-baked attitudes, no half-timing. It is much more than being a football fan. The danger lies in addiction. For addiction to God, or Theomania, as it has been called, has too often tended to create barriers, not bridges.

There are hundreds of Christian communities who live together and pool their worldly goods. In no way would they be considered cultish, and yet the strains of this way of life can be much the same as those in the more publicised, controversial groups.

Much of that publicity arose in the early days because some were over-enthusiastic in their proselytising and careless about the well-being of their often naïve young flock. There are fewer banner headlines today — but this has not reduced public anxiety. Today's concern is that some of the bigger groups are quietly plotting to take over the world and that there is hidden political motivation.

No one really knows how big is 'big'. Membership changes and numbers are often not available or even recorded. As with Christianity there are active and passive members. But it is probably true that numbers in Britain are far smaller at any one time than is feared — the most dramatic example being that of the Moonies. Actual membership in Britain is probably no more than 600!

Nevertheless . . . in almost every country, anxious, sincere people have banded together to confront the cults (see The Cultwatchers' Tale, p. 195). They are determined to monitor, discipline and possibly outlaw, what they believe to be a threat to society.

There are those openly fighting the Devil who, they believe, is using the vehicle of Eastern religions to undermine Christianity

There are also those who are concerned only with law breaking, the abuse of tax and charity laws and the protection of young people who, they insist, are deceitfully recruited.

These organisations act as a source of information and advice for those families who find themselves in trouble or become entangled with any suspicious minority. They accuse certain new religious and self-improvement groups of allowing their beliefs to generate anti-social, and often illegal, behaviour which is destructive of individuals and of families. Their complaint is not what cults say, it is the way that they say it.

Like Titipu in *The Mikado*, they each have a little list, from which, it follows, none would be missed! The problem with such lists is that it is unlikely that any cult group will ever be struck off. There is no allowance for change. Yet a group that begins well may go bad; a rocky start can improve. Any organisation may vary from branch to branch — the Hare Krishna movement in Dublin is not like Hare Krishna in Moscow!

The following then, are some of the best-known, and longest established of those organisations which have come to be known, perhaps unfairly, by their adversaries, as 'cults'. There are dozens more — the list is growing all the time. They are here because someone has expressed concern about a friend or member of the family who has thrown away a University course, or a brilliant career, to join such a group.

- **The Mormons**

- **The Church of Scientology**

- **The Unification Church**

- The Family of Love (formerly Children of God)
- The International Society for Krishna Consciousness
- Nichiren Shoshu (Soka Gakkai)
- The Jesus Fellowship (Britain only)
- The Church of Christ
- Rajneesh
- EST
- Transcendental Meditation
- WorldWide Church of God
- The Baha'i Faith

BASIC GUIDELINES

Concerned parents are usually given some basic guidelines by the cult information and advice network. This is their summary of what to expect. In broad terms it is sound — but over-simplistic, since clearly not all of these characteristics apply across the board to all the groups in question.

Where do they recruit?
- On the University campus
- In buses and on Tubes
- Door to door
- On the street

What do they offer?
- Instant friendship
- A caring community
- A goal in life
- A sense of personal involvement
- A chance to change the world
- A hotline to Heaven

Who joins?

- Almost anyone is susceptible, and no age is exempt
- More men than women
- More middle class
- More white than black
- 85 per cent of recruits have had a religious upbringing
- The homeless and jobless seeking a new family
- Singles and families

The need?

- Spiritual seeking
- A need to belong
- Food and shelter
- Adolescent independence
- Security
- A vehicle for energy and enthusiasm

By no means are all recruits from unstable or unhappy families. The 'changed personality' parents may see once the son or daughter has joined a new religion may well have been there, but un-noticed before. Young people feel sometimes unable to match their parents' dreams for them, feel guilty and inadequate and the 'cults' offer more apparently attainable goals.

The characteristics of the potentially destructive cult?

- A powerful leader who claims divinity or a special mission entrusted to him from Above.
- Revealed scriptures or doctrine.
- Totalitarianism and consequential alienation of members from family or friends.
- The use of indoctrination, by sophisticated mind-control techniques, based on the concept that once you can make a person behave the way you want, then you can make them believe what you want.
- Deceptive recruitment.
- Slave labour – that is, the use of members on fundraising or missionary activities for little or no pay to line the leaders' pockets.

- Misuse of funds and the accumulation of wealth for personal or political purposes at the expense of members.

- Exclusivity – 'we are right and everyone else is wrong'.

In addition to this are the sometimes serious charges against specific groups: sexual abuse of children, international arms or drugs dealing, political power games, bribery, theft and even organised murder.

The charge laid against their leaders is equally dramatic.

It is that they prey on their unsuspecting followers to satisfy greed for political supremacy, personal power or even world domination and the elimination of Jews, blacks and Communists in particular.

What happens?
The first step along the way is killing with kindness. Not bad in itself. Not good if it is only a means to an end, if friendship is purely a hook to catch converts.

Love-bombing
This is the peculiarly American trait of friendly over-kill; Europeans are over-whelmed by servers in any restaurant, pouring it out with the maple syrup. To speak of love-bombing by religious groups is possibly to misunderstand the fervour, the passion, with which youth tries to convey its message — especially in the States. Sickly and overpowering it may be to some, wonderfully welcoming and reassuring to others. But the NRM's in all countries have been accused of adopting 'user-friendly' techniques as a way of undermining a recruit's willpower and eroding common sense to prepare the way for the next stage.

Brainwashing
The vivid word 'brainwashing', or thought reform, was first used by an English journalist, Edward Hunter, in 1951 as a translation from the Chinese *Hsi-nao* or 'wash brain', and means 'purify thoughts'. It was his way of describing what happened in Korean war camps when American prisoners were induced to change their minds about the evils of Communism.

The word has now become one of the most dramatic rods with which to beat the 'cults'. It is brainwashing which is the alleged infringement of civil liberties most cited by critics.

The word implies disapproval. Someone whose ideas have been changed, or even affected, in a way we do not agree with, has been 'brainwashed'. If we are in accord with the result of that change of mind or heart, then they have been 'persuaded'.

No one really believes that recruits to the Moonies or even the Children of God are, like Korean prisoners, held by physical force. But it is believed that restraint is achieved, just the same, by subtle psychological methods of mind control. It more nearly resembles the subliminal effects of a Madison Avenue advertising campaign.

Flo Conway and Jim Siegleman said, in their book *Snapping* (Delta 1976):

'America is gripped by an epidemic of sudden personality change. The techniques used by cults and therapies permeate every level of society from Government and business to daily social interactions. Yet most of us have little understanding of the extent to which we, ourselves, not only our beliefs and opinions but our individual personalities, may be shaped or changed by those around us and by the things we experience every day.'

'Snapping' is one of the buzz words in America. It describes what happens when an individual undergoes a dramatic personality change, through enlightenment, cosmic consciousness, conversion, re-birth, becoming 'clear' or any of the thousand and one transformational processes on offer today.

The process is not new. John Wesley described it as a way of holding a convert to Christ, for ever.

Psychiatrists who are critical of brainwashing say that use of such techniques destroys any possibility of individual choice. The power of rational thought is undermined by low protein diets, increased blood sugar to befuddle the brain, lack of food and sleep, disorientation, isolation from familiar surroundings and information overload. Those parents who are in touch with their children complain that they have become glassy-eyed, distant, robotic and apparently incapable of even explaining their new religion (perhaps they should try explaining Christianity over supper!).

What happens to potential recruits depends greatly on their state of mind and personality at the time they join the movement. The lonely, unhappy adolescent *can* be more vulnerable because he cannot handle the overload of new experiences.

It is a question of chemistry. For the majority, the experiment is short-lived and does little damage. Turnover in most cults is very fast and of those who stay on, most eventually leave of their own accord, with no lasting ill effects; some even become dedicated members.

But for a few — and these are the tragic victims — the experiment is disastrous and even leads to death.

Dr Elizabeth Tylden is one of the few British psychiatrists who has made a detailed study of 'cult' behaviour. She believes that what happened to some of her patients has been the result of the ineptitude, rather than the evil design, of the 'cult'.

But she has learned that you cannot generalise; that all cults are not religious, that therapy and self-improvement groups may also put intolerable pressure on some people. Each case must be taken individually. Her main concern is over any organisation with global aspirations, and any organisation that exploits its members. She does not put 'cults' in a bracket of their own. 'I have a patient whose parents are convinced that her orthodox church organisation is cultic and I have seen some appalling pressures caused by the House Church movement,' she says.

'The leaders are, so often, amateurs, using techniques such as chanting and meditation that they really do not understand and which should only, ever, be suggested for people with balanced, healthy minds to start with, and only then after careful preparation. On the other hand I have had drug patients who have been helped by the Sufis and by TM.

'It is well known in all contemplative religions that people who practise extreme patterns of meditation need to be extremely mentally stable. Some people whose perception and behaviour have become highly eccentric as a result of heavy religious exercises, are regarded in the Hindu religion as Holy men, and in our culture as mentally ill.

'The mechanisms used by many cults to recruit are designed to produce an obsessional state — and in certain susceptible people that obsession conflicts with their previous mores.'

Dr Tylden is angry that some 'cults' (not all) try to become an alternative family, encouraging their members to reject their parents. 'Can you be regarded as functioning normally if you reject parents who are screaming for help?' she says. 'How dare these cults attempt to replace true parents and then, when the member is sick or becomes depressed, drive them out. How dare they! This is torture.'

Contented cult members do resent the implication that they are unbalanced or even in need of psychiatric help.

But she feels that psychiatrists are not treating the ex-cultist correctly. 'I want them to realise that drugs are not the answer. They need tranquil discussion. I am also against de-programming — two wrongs do not make a right and de-programming is worse than the original indoctrination'.

The trouble is that many people who become obsessed, by anything, seem to *need* that obsession. They are obsessive by nature. This is why ex-cultists tend to become obsessively vitriolic about their former faith.

Dr Tylden says: 'The cult member, like the addict, very often looks the same but speaks, and behaves, quite differently . . . we now know that far more drug addicts than we once dreamt of do get better — hopefully, this is true for cultism.'

The rarified and all-demanding atmosphere of the cult club can lead to institutionalisation, which harms the ability to relate naturally with the outside world.

In those groups which revere celibacy, everyday human contact becomes difficult, especially with the opposite sex.

Those where sexual freedom is practised can have much the same result.

Many people cannot cope with the hypnotic effects of constant chanting which can, in some cases, induce a state of uncontrollable trance.

Sometimes there are physical problems — paranoia, confusion, even hallucinations. Sick people are a problem to many movements who have no facilities for coping.

With no home to go to and no job or money, fear of the outside world and loss of God's love prevent some from eventually making the break.

A few years ago Canadian television made a film, *Captive Minds*, which looked at the training schedule of recruits to the United States Marines, the Jesuits and the Unification Church. They were the same!

Trappists and Jesuits change their names, like the Krishna devotees. They live in communities, like the Moonies, often separated from family. Many Roman Catholic Orders strictly control the environment of their novices, putting them on a rigorous daily routine, punctuated by the ringing of bells, maybe 40 times a day. Meditation is an accepted practice, chanting is a part of the ritual. The Jesuits use silence to induce a state of susceptibility.

In the Marines everything that encourages individuality is stopped, the environment controlled. The Marine wears a uniform to be anonymous, hair is short, equipment identical; there is much shouting of commands in situations of stress, physical exhaustion and the fear of brute force.

Trained to react without thinking he comes to believe there is no greater glory than dying as a Marine.

Of course, a would-be priest or a Marine volunteers. There is then a lengthy period of preparation before he is accepted, whereas a cult recruit is often enticed, unsuspecting, by a missionary, and may not fully realise the long-term implications of his actions. At the time of greatest susceptibility — maybe home-sick and alone — he commits himself from within the group, rather than making an objective decision whilst still in contact with the outside world.

Politicians, church leaders, advertising moguls all make use of such methods and may call them by a variety of names, such as convert or reform. *Roget's Thesaurus* lists a few more; entice, seduce, tempt, influence.

Change soap powder and you are persuaded; become a Christian, you are converted. Join Scientology and you are brainwashed.

In the nineteenth century, according to the American church scholar, Leo Pfeiffer, a 'Nunnery Committee' was appointed in Massachusetts to report on 'such theological seminaries . . . nunneries, convents . . . and other institutions as it may deem necessary.' This reflected the widely held belief then that 'young women did not voluntarily commit themselves to serving their religion as nuns but were the victims of physical duress or "mind control"'.

Yet despite this, it was over 'brainwashing' that the Unification Church lost its action against the *Daily Mail* in 1981 to the tune of £178,000. The Moonies had charged the *Mail* with libel in its sensational story of a family who 'rescued' their daughter against her will from the clutches of the church. Expert witnesses were wheeled in by the church from all over the world to testify that there was no coercion — to no avail.

Margaret Thaler Singer, professor of psychiatry at the University of Berkeley, San Francisco, said that 'love-bombing and deception work much more rapidly than the gun at the head or torture'.

In summing up, counsel for the *Daily Mail*, Lord Rawlinson, listed the methods which, he said, 'created monsters', and reminded the jury that the witnesses included five broken families, six nervous breakdowns and 24 people with careers destroyed. He called it a 'very evil system'.

Both the daughter and her sister testified *against* the *Mail* at the trial and later re-joined the Church!

The Moonies objected to another *Daily Mail* story in 1985: 'Crazed former Moonie turned killer', which told of a 'tormented ex-Moonie who . . . killed a man in a crazed human torch attack'. The man had never joined the Moonies and was already having psychiatric treatment. The Press Council said the *Mail* story was not justified. No apology or correction ever appeared.

A few years ago the respected Second Chamber of the Dutch Parliament set up a Special Committee on Sects. It recorded: 'the allegation that new religious movements use coercion when recruiting and then subject members to forms of conditioning has not been confirmed by our study. As a rule, membership of a new religious movement is the outcome of carefully weighed choice.'

Dean Kelley, of the American National Council of Churches, has said: 'It must be questioned whether such an exotic new explanation is needed. Most of the behaviour changes described can be adequately accounted for by the age-old phenomenon of conversion.'

The differences between conversion to any religious extreme are hard to understand. To the agnostic by-stander, there is not a lot to choose between passing out in an emotional frenzy at a Jimmy Swaggart rally, a Rajneesh discourse or a Jesus Army 'Burn Out'.

Yet the brainwashing issue has also become a platform on which a number of sociologists and psychologists have made a name for themselves, both for and against. It has been at the core of the dozens of legal battles fought by parents, especially in the United States, in which the 'cults' have often defended themselves successfully.

'Brainwashing' is the only dignified excuse hurt families can offer when they explain to friends and neighbours what has happened to their child. It passes the buck.

THE HAPPIEST DAYS?

To a large extent an adult's decision to join any of the new movements is personal: whether or not relatives feel it has been forced, it *is*, usually, a question of choice.

Children have no such choice. The Moonietots or Krishnakids are there because their parents are converts. They want their little ones to grow, spiritually, in the light of what they have learned. At worst their offspring may become stranded misfits, sacrificed to their parents' fanaticism. At best they may grow to become happy believers too or leave to make sense of life in their own way.

Several of the new movements have been long enough established now to have woven the education of their own young into their systems, although it is early days yet to judge the results. One or two are supporting thriving universities.

To the outsider these schools provide yet more fodder for rumour and their very existence is a threat to the young personalities. But are they, in fact, so very different from the very controversial free expression methods of A.S. Neill at Summerhill, the liberal, drug-troubled Bedales where Princess Margaret's children went, or the cold shower routines of Gordonstoun?

The teenagers of the sixties and seventies are now parents of teenagers them-selves. The second generation is moving through its own rebellion, and it's hard to say yet how they have been affected by their upbringing. They could return to traditional patterns of belief . . . they may break away and start their own. You will find in most groups — in families of Anglicans, Catholics or atheists — young people following similar patterns of acceptance and rebellion.

There is a markedly varied attitude towards children in each of the groups we met. There are those who use them, if unintentionally, as a means of boosting numbers; others, like The Jesus Fellowship, who encourage celibacy. All would profess a love of children and a wish to care for their spiritual and physical well-being.

The form that that care takes varies from a 4 a.m. jump start to the Temple, if Dad is a Krishna devotee, to bedtime romps if you've been born into the Family of Love. Moonie children all attend ordinary schools — there is no separate Moonie education. The children of Rev. Moon have been pupils in American schools and have, apparently, suffered a fair degree of harassment themselves.

In most cases, the parents' personal formula for the rearing of their children is untouchable by law, and there is an elusive borderline between what is socially unacceptable, and actually illegal.

But where adults are living in a community and children tend to be isolated from contact with the outside world, rumours begin to fly. Sometimes, with reason, there is real concern.

The Family of Love, for instance, has no base. Its members are mostly in hidden communities and so its children do not go to school at all. They are taught by members of the group and rarely, if ever, mix with other children. Finding them, let alone observing their educational standards, seems to have proved a problem for hard-pressed education authorities.

The rules governing home tuition are loose and often difficult to enforce.

Discipline is necessary — even corporal punishment, however distasteful to many, is woven into the life of our public schools. But physical and sexual abuse is notoriously difficult to locate and root out.

In Britain and America, experts are increasingly alarmed at the amount of child abuse. The Los Angeles Police Department has a special section to investigate reports of Satanic ritual and even alleged animal and human sacrifice.

In Britain, the founder of Childcare, Diane Core, claims personal knowledge of children participating in suburban Satanism.

It is a subject too sensitive to be dealt with as part of such a general study as this. It calls for an independently researched book, for it touches all strata of society and many people in high places.

Most sex offenders have a strongly religious background and, whereas within the established churches there are some safety valves which help to diffuse the intensity that produces paedophilia, smaller groups tend to create loyalty struc-tures which increase it. The House Church movement, for instance, has much to commend it but, according to the child watchers, it also hides some very unsavoury activity.

The horror stories, particularly in America where there are so many little-known organisations, speak of small children abandoned and neglected. Lack of health care and poor diet are common, as is excessive punishment to the point of cruelty.

Even where specialist education is provided, not all group members take advantage. There are only 60 Rajneeshi boys and girls at Ko Hsuan, in the hilly peace of Chulmleigh, Devon, and thousands taking whatever their local authority offers.

Learning about Greenfields School, down a lane outside East Grinstead, where the children of Scientologists are set off on the road to total freedom is as diffi-cult as defrosting an iceberg. It is an independent charity and so is free from statutory regulations.

But, as with all independent schools, so long as parents are willing to pay — and with a huge organisation like the Church of Scientology there is a captive audience — there is little outsiders can do should problems arise. It is simply not their business.

It is not possible to prosecute a school because its philosophy is unusual.

BIG BROTHER'S WATCHING YOU

On 22 May 1984 the European Parliament adopted by 98 votes to 28, with 27 abstentions, a resolution on 'new organisations operating under the protection afforded to religious bodies'. This resolution was brought about through the work of Richard Cottrell, former MEP for Bristol and Bath, and his researcher David Wilshire MP.

Five objectives were listed: (1) To respond positively to public concern about the activities of cults. (2) To respect freedom of religion. (3) To focus attention on practices arising from religious beliefs. (4) To stress the international dimen-sion of the subject. (5) To protect the EEC's labour and social laws.

Four proposals were put forward: (1) An exchange of inter-States information on charity and tax legislation; legal status; social consequences; missing persons; abuses of personal freedom; help for those seeking to leave the cults; stopping up of legal loopholes. (2) A proposal to establish a data-pool on cult activity. (3) A Voluntary Code of Conduct. (4) A proposal for a common approach.

The Voluntary Code of Conduct suggested:

- People should be 18 before making a long-term commitment.

- There should be a period of reflection.

- Student recruits should be allowed to finish their education.

- Recruits should be free to leave, and seek medical or legal advice.

- Cults should agree to operate within the law.

- Cults should not take advantage of foreign visitors.

- Cults should own up to who they are and what they believe in.

- Cults should tell enquirers where members are.

- Cults should permit proper rewards for work done by members.

- Cults should provide return travel for members sent abroad.

- Cults should pass on all messages and phone calls to and from families.

- Cults should respect the rights of children of members.

This seems reasonable on the face of it — once you have agreed on what is a cult!

The resolution has never been ratified, despite strong pressure from organisations like Asociación PRO-Juventud at their International Congress on Cults and Society in Barcelona in 1987. All major British and American anti-cult groups were present. There has been objection to it from many mainstream bodies, including sections of the Roman Catholic Church, the Dutch Council of Churches and the French Protestant Federation.

The British Council of Churches (itself only founded in 1942) said 'no technically acceptable criteria exist on the precise dividing line between churches and sects. At what stage can a religion no longer be called new?'

In other words, at national or international government level no one is anxious to point the finger.

The philosophy of the BCC is that of 'jaw jaw rather than war war'. In a letter to all British MEPs, it said: 'The BCC is acutely aware of the great distress caused to families and individuals by the activities of certain religious groups. We believe that the British churches must have a pastoral care for such people based on an informed understanding of the beliefs and practices of such groups . . . and we reaffirm our conviction that an important matter of the freedom of religion is at issue.'

They expressed fear that the resolution could be used by individual member governments as a basis for punitive legislation against any church. The common law existing in each of the member countries was, they declared, adequate to deal with the problem.

The fur then began to fly.

In America, The American Family Foundation Conference on Cultism was convened, at Wingspread in Wisconsin, in 'a spirit of free and rational enquiry'. There it was reported that cult critics were being charged with atheism, fascism and even plotting the genocidal extermination of all religious believers.

On the other hand, the BCC was also swamped by abusive and often hysterical calls, mostly from within the evangelical lobby. The then secretary of the Committee for Relations with People of Other Faiths, the Rev. Kenneth Cracknell, was accused of being a secret cultist and the BCC itself a bunch of subversive left-wingers.

In a speech in Germany, later in the year, David Wilshire stressed the confusion between civil and religious liberty, spiritual and political affairs.

'We are told by the cults that religion has nothing to do with politics. If you believe that, you misunderstand politics and history . . . much of Europe today derives either from action or resistance done in the name of religion. There is no reason to suppose that passions aroused by religious issues in former centuries will subside simply because cults say they should.'

Before the French revolution, according to Dr Tylden, 15 per cent of psychiatric hospital admissions were due to 'religious insanity'. After the Revolution it was reported that only 1.35 per cent of admissions were for religious insanity, the rest being due to 'political excitement'.

We expect our spiritual leaders, our gurus, whether establishment or fringe, not to betray our trust. We are more cynical about politicians and have come to suspect them all of duplicity and dirty tricks. But there is often not a lot to choose between them; their worlds are, indeed, inextricably entwined. When Roman Catholic Jack Kennedy, for instance, became President of America, the shadow of the Pope loomed over non-Catholics in the country.

It is most unlikely that within a powerful organisation like the Unification Church, which has a strong anti-Communist stance, there is no political string pulling somewhere in the world.

Even so, there is no room for hypocrisy, for there is many a prostitute paying rent to the Anglican church, many an unsuspecting Catholic buying contraceptives from a company in which the Vatican allegedly once had shares (*In God's Name*, by David Yallop (Corgi 1985)). These days, when Heinz the Beanz people own Weightwatchers slimming clubs, it is hard to be sure who is holding the reins and in whom we can safely trust. In times of the hard and soft sell, even religion is packaged to attract buyers.

This materialistic climate has encouraged a number of attempts by the cultwatchers to introduce a system of quality control which could be applied to the new religious movements.

The situation in the USA is very different from that in Europe.

In some American States, parents and ex-cultists have sued, under a trades description act, because a religious group had failed to produce the goods offered in its brochures. An individual who is damaged by a cult can bring a civil suit and ask for awards that can be very substantial. There have also been cases where parents have sued for custody of their offspring. This has meant the destruction of some smaller groups and has resulted in the extreme paranoia of others.

Such tactics have been strongly opposed by those who also oppose the Cottrell Report on the grounds that religion is being diminished to the status of a consumer durable.

In Britain there is constant anger at the apparent abuse by some religious groups of their charitable status.

The Secretary of State for the Home Office presented a White Paper to the

British Parliament in May 1989: 'Charities; a Framework for the Future'. It seems to accept the need for overall vigilance of all religious groups rather than the specific targeting of 'cults'.

'The present position is that any religious body is entitled to charitable status (and so tax benefits) so long as its tenets are not morally subversive and so long as its purposes are directed to the benefit of the public.'

But the paper does recognise the difference between the *objects* of a group and its *conduct* and the consequent frustration which leads to frequent demands for a change in the charity laws. Even so, the report concludes: 'The existing law is adequate. What is needed now is the determined pursuit of evidence in order to justify the bold use by the Commissioners of their powers of investigation and remedy.'

Wrapped up in all the legal language is confirmation of what most parents believe — that the price of freedom is not only eternal vigilance but social responsibility, too. Every organisation, every religion — great and small — has to toe that line.

However, achieving such responsibility is rarely, if ever, the role of governments.

Jack Gratus says in his book, *The False Messiahs* (Gollancz 1975): 'It would seem, that no matter how successful or otherwise our social, political, economic or religious institutions have been, there will always be men and women in doubt, despair, anxious . . . without a sense of future . . . some accept their lot . . . others find answers in themselves alone or through the help of priests or doctors. A third group, smaller than the other two, find their answers in an individual whose needs are as their own. They call him 'Messiah'. He encloses the world for them, makes it smaller.'

We should be wary of messiahs: the men who mediate between God and mankind. More public awareness in Germany during the 1930s would have been a good idea. Of his young people, Hitler said: 'I want a powerful, masterly, cruel and fearless youth . . . the freedom and dignity of the wild beast must shine from their eyes.'

For better and worse, new religions always reach the parts that others do not reach. At least, in the short term. Were they not available, where would all those nature-worshipping disciples, sanyassins and devotees turn? There are always people in need of spiritual sanctuary.

'Each culture tries to fix its visionary moment when it was transformed by a new conception either of nature or of man,' says Professor Bronowski in his inspiring book, *The Ascent of Man*. 'But in retrospect, what commands our attention as much are the continuities, the thoughts that run or recur from one civilisation to another.'

Ideas have a habit of being recycled, generation after generation. After all, who was it who said: 'I have not come to bring peace but a sword. I have come to set a man against his father, a daughter against her mother, a son's wife against her mother in law . . . no man is worthy of me who cares more for father and mother than for me'?

That was no Moonie, that was Jesus.

As long ago as 1785, when the American Declaration of Independence aimed to end intolerance, there was an outcropping of bizarre movements. The 'Know Nothing' party actually gained control in some States on a declared manifesto of 'anti-Romanism, anti-Bedinism, anti-Pope's Toeism, anti-Nunnerism, anti-Winking Virginism, anti-Jesuitism and anti-the-whole-Sacredotal-Hierarchism-with-all-its-humbugging-mummeries'.

By the same token, this freedom, which we must cherish, permits the Rev. Ian Paisley to issue a booklet which accuses the World Council of Churches, whose members include the Church of England and the Baptist Union, of being 'Doctrinally unBiblical, basically unProtestant, ecclesiastically unClean, practically unChristian and Spiritually unTrustworthy'!

To attempt to classify all NRMs, 'evil' or not, under the one banner, or to put a wall of fire between them and mainstream religion, is dangerous and will achieve nothing. It ignores their diversity, their origins, what they offer and how they put across their message. It ignores history.

WHAT IS A FAMILY TO DO?

The soundest, roundest advice for friends, helpers and families can be summarised from *The Cults Experience*, by Gordon J. Melton, published by Pilgrim Press, New York.

1. You are not helpless. Although it is tempting to believe the worst, your child is probably not a zombie . . . Such a decision by a young adult is one that should (indeed, is probably designed to) get your attention. It is not a time to become hysterical but to focus thoughts and energies.

2. Present no ultimatums and do not intimidate. Parents tend to indulge themselves in tantrums, forgetting that their power to influence, in this way, is limited at this critical point, if not non-existent. The most important asset you have in the coming months or years is to keep the lines of communication open.
   If communication has already been severed:

3. Research the group concerned from objective, scholarly sources. The new 'language' your child is using may be easier to interpret than you think.

4. Show interest and willingness to discuss. Conversation should be honest but not hostile. Show respect for their right to engage in such an endeavour. This may be a desperate move to overcome a sense of failure. It is dangerous to attack faith — however strange it is — when the believer has shown signs of discouragement in facing life.

5. Do not communicate the idea that the young person is deviant or defective or a total disappointment: 'Any child of mine would know better than this,'

'I am worried sick about you,' 'Anyone who gets in to this has to be crazy.' Teach a young person they are a loser and a loser they will become.

6. Communicate confidence in the person's ability to find his way and learn from experience. Be positive. 'Whatever our differences now we will continue to love each other.' 'I recognise your wish for your own life style. I may not agree with you but you must be getting something out of it.' Options for the future should be left open.

7. Do not turn automatically to your doctor. Joining a group does not always mean a need for psychiatric care.

8. If there were genuine signs of psychological problems before joining, consult a family therapist. Religious conflict within a family is usually a pointer to problems elsewhere. With family therapy everyone can be involved and the 'cult' recruit is not the focal point. It is a family issue.

9. Be honest with yourself. Try to understand the difference between fear for the child's welfare, and disappointment at their rebelling.

10. Remember the normal traumas of growing up. Reading and discussion with specialists will make you more compassionate.

11. If you cannot find your child, seek help to re-establish trust. You will not re-establish trust by de-programming or kidnapping.

12. Seek an independent mediator.

13. If your child remains in the group but returns home do not act as if a flying saucer had landed in your living room. Be natural, whatever they wear or do. Beware overpraising the siblings who have remained at home.

14. If the child decides to leave, respond positively. Most members do leave of their own accord. Don't be afraid to offer limited financial or moral support and as soon as possible encourage them to leave home and stand on their own feet.

Addresses

There are non-aligned, or objective, organisations who will help anyone in trouble. For those who want to break away from their present beliefs and are afraid of facing the world, talking may help get things into perspective. For families who have been torn apart, a third party may re-establish contact and build bridges without anyone losing face.

The Centre for New Religious Movements, Kings College, London University, Strand, London WC2

Childwatch, Diane Core, 60 Beck Road, Everthorpe, Brough, North Humberside, tel: (04302) 3824

Relate (consult the Citizens Advice Bureau for the address of your local branch)

The Committee for Relations with People of other Faiths, Church House, Lower Marsh, London SE1 7RL

For other addresses, see The Cultwatchers' Tale (page 195ff.)

GOD'S TALE

AT ABOUT THE TURN OF THE FIRST CENTURY AD, Jewish families in the villages around Jerusalem were uneasy about the recruiting methods of a small, but persistent religious cult. The old folk could remember their parents warning them about a rebellious young teacher called Jesus who had been crucified for subversion. But his death had not seen the end of the affair and for many years afterwards vigorous teams of His disciples continued converting new followers to 'Christianity'.

Christianity was a controversial movement within Judaism — Jesus, after all, was a devout practising Jew. Then, as now, it was the high-pressure techniques used to sell religion which divided families. Then, as now, there was no way of forecasting that any particular cult would settle down, grow, adapt its ideas and become, as Christianity did, one of the world's great faiths. The fears of ordinary parents for the well-being of their young, who might be tempted by Christian promises, were as real then as is today's concern about 'brainwashing' cults.

Rumours arose, based on fear of the unknown and the threat to established ideas.

The pagan philosopher, Celsus, commented about AD175; 'In private houses we see workers in wool and leather, fullers and the most uneducated and rustic people, (Christians) who dare not utter a word in the presence of their elders and wiser masters. Yet when they get hold of the children, privately, and any woman as ignorant as themselves, they pour forth these wonderful statements; that they should pay no attention to their father or teachers but only to themselves . . . and that if the children do as they say they will make their home happy also. With words like these they win them over.'

David Christie Murray says in *A History of Heresy* (New English Library 1976): 'To the modern Christian that sect was right and world-wide Jewry, wrong. To every founder of a heretical sect, the same hope must appear, that time will prove him right, and that the established churches be in error.'

The roots of heresy, sect or cult are inextricably entangled with the roots of religion. They feed on the same soil — and have an equal right to life, because one man's religion is another man's heresy.

Whether God created Man in His own image, as the Jews believe, or Man created God in *his* — as a comforting way to avoid answering the unanswerable mysteries of life and death, spirituality is as fundamental to the human race as food, drink and procreation.

It is in the organisation and practice of that spirituality into religion that things so often go badly wrong.

To take God's eye view of man's spiritual journey thus far may help to put our fears in context, to understand how to guard against the dangers that arise if religious ideology runs amok, and to appreciate at the same time the value of diversity.

THE UNIVERSAL GODDESS

To begin at the beginning. If — as is possible — the bleak, heaving East African land-scape near Lake Rudolph in Ethiopia was the birthplace of humanity then here, in fact, should have been the setting for the Garden of Eden — unless you are a Mormon and believe that Independence, Missouri, was the place!

Somewhere around two million years ago, the ape-like creatures who preceded man here gradually changed as their spines unfurled. We know of these changes because skeletons remain as physical milestones along the evolutionary path. What we cannot measure is the evolution of man's spirit. All that remain to mark that progress are a few artefacts which mirror man's vanished soul . . . or, more accurately, his belief in the existence of his soul from the start. The provisions with which he buried his dead reveal that he was already far removed from the rest of the animal world in his hope for the existence of life hereafter.

Itinerant communities developed their own localised explanation of why they had been born and why they would die. Gradually, from beneath this protective concept, all manner of sometimes strange, and often competitive, gods and goddesses emerged in different parts of the world.

With the end of the last Ice Age, about ten thousand years BC, the formation of more settled community life and the development of agriculture in Europe and Asia, the earth itself began to be symbolised as a living body from which all life came and to which all life returned.

The earliest 'God' may well have been a woman — an idea probably arising from the reverence for the mother figure and the woman's supremely dominant role in creation. She was 'Mother' — a goddess — with whom to live in harmony and treat with wisdom. Dependence on natural order and the seasonal cycle developed an intuitive sensitivity, and the universal Cult of the Earth Mother was basic in its uncom-plicated vision of a wholeness of which humanity is a part — not apart.

Over many centuries the process of creation, birth and death became ritualised and in America, New Mexico, Mesopotamia, Crete, India and, eventually, in Britain, religion was made tangible by basic symbolism. Very often this was sexual and erotic.

The link between religious fervour and sex was understood from the beginning, even when it was not acknowledged. The sexual road to religious ecstasy is universal — from the nuns who 'marry' Christ, to the Hindu temple prostitutes. The phallus and the fertility symbol appear throughout religious ceremonial.

That eroticism has been interpreted in the art, architecture and ritual of Tao, Hinduism, Buddhism and, eventually, Christianity; less so by Islam and Judaism although Judaism has traditionally honoured its women in the most profound way of all — 'Jewishness' is inherited through the female line.

The original religion, nature-worship, sometimes called pantheism, with its many sensual connotations, endured long into the civilised world; in fact it never really died.

The profound link not only between mankind's sexuality and his religion but also his religion and nature is clearly identifiable, even in the Christian church.

In our urban sophistication we admire such few remaining primitive communities as the Aborigines, and our envy of their instinctive direct harmony with the life force, whatever it is, is fuelling a revival of nature-worship and even witchcraft today.

The growth of the gentle, holistic approach to medicine, the ecumenical movement, the 'Green'-ing of Europe, even the peaceful yearnings of perestroika, may have a practical, commercial, political base; no matter, they also mark a widespread wish to be a part of a new sensitivity.

HINDUISM

Hinduism was probably the first 'new' belief system to become organised and to endure as one of the world's great religions. It is much misunderstood in the West because of its apparently idolatrous array of gods and goddesses. The word 'Hindu' has been coined in recent years by Westerners to describe a religious, social, economic and cultural way of life which the Indians themselves do not regard as a religion but as an 'eternal order', a complete way of life, based on a belief in reincarnation.

Hinduism had no founder. It emerged from the highly developed Harappa civilisation, which lasted along the Indus valley from about 3000–1700BC. The Harappa cult of the Earth Mother was absorbed when the Aryans invaded India from Russia and Central Asia, bringing with them a sacrificial system known as Vedism or Brahmanism — a male-dominated polytheistic (many gods) religion.

Internally complex, with a rich literary and philosophical tradition, its incredible variety of regional beliefs and practice provides a way of life today uniting 647 million people world-wide. It is doctrinally tolerant, placing more emphasis on right living than on ritual.

The many millions of gods and goddesses adopted for local worship by individual families are said to be representations of the Brahman, the One and All. The God Vishnu, one of the three most important creator deities, is probably the most popular. Vishnu, it is believed, has been incarnated ten times in order to save the world from destruction.

One of these incarnations was as the Lord Krishna, in about 3000BC and it is Krishna, of all the gods, who has become most familiar to the Western world through the singing and chanting of devotees from the International Society for Krishna Consciousness, or the Hare Krishna movement (see p. 104).

But it is not only the Hare Krishna movement whose roots are entwined in Eastern tradition. Transcendental Meditation(see p. 93), Maharaji (see p. 185) and even the renegade Rajneesh (p. 147) who admits allegiance to no one, share ancient Eastern origins, with their emphasis on the spiritual tools of Tantra, of meditation and on yoga, and on the charismatic quality of individual 'masters'. From Hinduism have come our Western buzz words — mantra, karma and guru. There are 150,000 practising Hindus in Britain.

Information from: The Institute of Indian Culture, 4A Castletown Road, West Kensington, London W14 9HQ.

TANTRA

Tantrism is a school that developed both within Hinduism and, later, Buddhism. It taught that the universe is divided into male and female forces who hold it together by blending with each other. There were various ways for an individual to experience union with the gods, one of which was ritualised sexual intercourse.

This idea has, not surprisingly, provided a theological base for a number of free-thinking groups and, although serious in intent, lends itself to perversion and degeneracy. Many of the free-expression, liberating techniques of crying, laughing, shouting — often in the nude — used by followers of Rajneesh in Poona, for instance, owe much to Tantrism.

YOGA

In Eastern terms Yoga is the yoking of the mind to Brahman (God); the word means unity. It is a physical and mental discipline which, in its highest form, can enable the yogi to transcend the body, to cut off all senses and become one with 'Brahman'.

In the West we know of music hall turns, in which the yogi can lie on a bed of nails or walk on hot coals; and, of course, many a village hall and civic centre has its classes in yoga, where the emphasis is on beneficial basic exercise rather than on spiritual experience. It has become more a fashion than a cult and is available to anyone, whether inside or outside a religious group.

Western yoga is an uneasy transplant of ancient Oriental disciplines on to an alien way of life. There are many different methods — each suited to individual needs. There is probably more danger of a dislocated bone than a broken mind, although Christian anti-cultists attack its self-centred, not God-centred, approach.

TAOISM AND CONFUCIANISM

Legend says that around 2,500 years ago an old sage called Lao-tze, on his way to die in the wilderness, was stopped by the Keeper of the Han-Ku Pass in North West China. The Keeper begged him not to go without leaving behind his wisdom for others. The words the old man wrote on bamboo tablets are now known as the Tao Te Ching. Tao means road . . . following the Tao means working with universal energy and its natural laws.

At about the same time, the philosopher K'ung Fu-tze (Confucius) was teaching a new code of conduct which became a religion and a way of life throughout China and, eventually, in Korea, Japan and Vietnam. Although the common goal of Taoist and Confucianist was individual and political harmony, their approach was very different. Confucianism was rational and rigid, emphasising obligations and good deeds. Taoism was humanist, more mystical and based on unlimited love and compassion.

If Confucius saw man's way to harmony through material order, the Tao remained to care for his soul and it is Taoism, not Confucianism, which has had such a deep impact on much New Wave thinking. It is largely through the Tao that we have learned of the balance of Yin and Yang, the interconnected forms of energy which are life itself. These are sometimes described as the 'shady side and the sunny side of the mountain'. The sunny side — Yang — is positive, active, physical, scientific, hot and masculine. The Yin is negative, cool, thoughtful, intuitive and feminine. The ideal is to perfect a balance. It is a difficult concept for the Western mind to grasp.

In many ways, the Tao is a book whose time has come — its pagan message matches the growing awareness of a need for conservation and ecological sensitivity. Unlike books such as the Bible, the Koran, or the Upanishads of Hinduism, the Tao has no sponsoring religion (though there are a few Taoist monasteries in China), no leaders to promote it; its philosophy seems to be spreading by remote control and innumerable, often poor, translations through Western book shops, health centres and wholefood suppliers.

BUDDHISM

The peaceful, passive nature of Buddhism has touched many a twentieth-century Western soul but Buddhism is no soft option and its teachings are extraordinarily elusive and complex, because they do not bow to any central authority and its large number of sects interpret them in their own way.

Siddharta, the young aristocrat who was to become the Buddha, was born about 560BC in North East India, into a society that was dominated by Hindu Brahmin priests. At the age of 29 he abandoned his wife, family, power and privilege and went in search of truth. That quest took him through a series of temptations and renunciations until eventually he received Enlightenment and proclaimed the gospel of salvation — 'Dharma' — around which Buddhism centres. Dharma shows the path to Buddhahood or Nirvana — Enlightenment.

The gods, or God, play no great part in Buddhism which has its own interpretation of reincarnation leading to an intensely personal quest for Enlightenment. The conception of an all-powerful Creator is seen as a barrier to full spiritual growth and as a failure to take responsibility for oneself. The reason for doing good, or being good, is not the hope of salvation or self-interest.

For the first time since it arrived in China to confront Confucianism 2,000 years ago, Buddhism faces a new cultural challenge — that of expanding into our totally alien society. In order to meet that challenge there are a growing number of Westernised Buddhist groups, such as the Friends of the Western Buddhist Order (FWBO). These are attracting fugitives from the materialist world and have broken away from mainstream Buddhism.

FWBO, Lesingham House, Surlingham, Norwich, Norfolk, which claims to be a free association of committed Buddhists, was founded by an Englishman, Dennis Lingwood, in 1967. He was a priest, Sangharakshita, but his criticism of certain Buddhist practices, and his radical teachings were frowned on by the British Buddhist establishment. The FWBO aimed to work out traditional Buddhist principles, in the lives of individuals, responding creatively to opportunities and challenges encountered in an environment new to Buddhism.

One of the fastest growing movements, and one which causes concern to international cultwatchers, is Nichiren Shoshu, a Buddhist sect founded in the thirteenth century, (see p. 161) and in particular its lay society — Soka Gakkai, which means Society for the Creation of Value.

There are 29,000 practising Buddhists in Britain.

Information on mainstream Buddhism from: The Buddhist Society, 58 Eccleston Square, London SW1V 1PH.

ZOROASTRIANISM

Zoroaster was Iranian and was possibly the first prophet in the history of religion. He was certainly the first to teach a belief in the two judgements of Heaven and Hell and the resurrection of the body. His dualist faith was developed from the existing Vedic Hindu religion of Iran. For over 1,000 years Zoroastrianism was the faith of three world empires and was finally defeated by Islam in the tenth century AD. At this time some believers escaped to India where they were called Parsees.

It is an optimistic religion, with strong moral ideals and a belief that evil will be overcome. Once initiated the follower has a religious duty to fight evil in all forms. It has influenced Judaism, Christianity, Buddhism and Hinduism because of its position on the East-West trade routes.

Nowadays numbers are small — there are about 3,000 practising Zoroastrians in Britain.

Information from: The Institute of Indian Culture (address as before).

JAINISM

Jain theology is atheistic. It is traced back to the life and work of Vardhamana Mahavira, who lived in Eastern India between 599–527BC. Jains believe there are two realities — eternal souls (jivas) and eternal, non-living material elements (ajivas). Humans are trapped in cycles of reincarnation because their jivas have become attached to ajivas by soul energy, or karma. The aim is liberation by living austerely and so reducing karma. They are vegetarian and strictly non-violent, rejecting ownership of property including clothes (they wear robes in public). To avoid killing any creature, however small, they will, on occasion, walk sweeping the floor ahead of them and wear face masks.

There are about 3¼ million Jains in India; numbers in Britain are not known.

Information from: The Institute of Indian Culture (address as before).

JUDAISM

In about 2000BC, a man called Abraham had left the declining city of Ur of the Chaldees to travel south and settle in Canaan, the land 'of milk and honey'. Here he was to found a great nation. Abraham was the father of Jacob (later named Israel) head of the Israelite tribe and grandfather of Judah.

The tribe of Judah was based in the south of ancient Palestine and it is from them that most of today's sons of Judah — the Jews — are believed to descend. Their God, Yaweh, was a tribal god, and not until Moses heard the Ten Commandments on Mount Sinai in about 1235BC did the concept of one God for all mankind really begin to take a hold.

It was a slow transition. From a variety of unstable, divided beliefs, unified only by certainty of a unique relationship between themselves and God, Judaism developed to become the strictly codified system into which Jesus was born. By that time, mainstream Jewish religion had survived many hundred years of onslaught by all manner of upstart cults within and around it, just as the Jewish race itself was to survive persecution after persecution in the centuries ahead.

Compared with Hinduism or Islam the Jewish community is small. There are 108,000 practising Jews in Britain. Jewish youth appears to be particularly susceptible to the evangelising zeal of new religious groups. Judaism is one of the few world religions that does not believe in proselytising — in fact it is forbidden.

Perhaps, because of its history of persecution, it has strong defence organisations and lays the blame for much of today's cult militancy at the door of Christianity.

Information from: The United Synagogue, Woburn House, Tavistock Square, London WC1H 0EZ.

EARLY CHRISTIANITY

When Jesus was born, the Mediterranean was bubbling with religious unrest. Judaism had fragmented into cultic groups and the Roman Empire was awash with a vast repertoire of gods for all seasons.

The long established orthodox religion of the Romans was an adaptation of that based on the ancient Greek gods of Olympus — and it was floundering.

There was a rootless wandering betwixt and between faiths, a searching for a new meaning to life.

When St Paul began his travels in the first century he was deeply interested in the contemporary cults. He knew all about Mithras and Isis and, like most early Christians, had no problem in adapting the established ideas to his new faith. Isis was worshipped as one part of a trinity — Osiris, Isis and Horus representing different facets of the one god — and her influence extended through India into Western China. Isis's temple images were those of the Queen of Heaven — with the baby Horus in her arms. Candles were burned before her, celibate priests waited on her altars. The hymns of the day sang of eternal life. Isis and Osiris live on today in many occult and pagan organisations and also within the masonic orders, who have adapted much of its symbolic ritual (see Stephen Knight's *The Brotherhood*, Grafton 1985).

Paul preached that Jesus, like Osiris, was a god who died to rise again, and give men immortality. Christianity needed a female figure and so the Virgin Mary became the Christian Isis. Many other external trappings of the Mithraic and Egyptian cults were adopted as the religion established itself . . . the shaven priest, the ritual offering of blood, the altars and the chanting and also many of the theological ideas. Much of Jesus's own Jewish faith, based on Old Testament law, was adopted lock, stock and barrel.

However important, revolutionary and necessary were Christ's teachings of love and compassion in those harsh, often cruel, times, it was the command that His followers should carry His words far and wide that marked a vital and histori-cal difference.

We are talking at first of peaceful propaganda and conversion, which many of today's Christian-inspired cult groups claim to be reviving when they knock on our doors, or beam at us on the buses. The doctrines they preach may find their source in any one of a dozen early splinter groups.

One of these was the Gnostics who were closely linked with Christianity but whose underlying philosophy was that knowledge is the way to salvation — those who are worthy will receive this knowledge from a redeemer. They believed that the material world is evil, while the spirit world is good and that they owed their existence to two different creators.

The Christians never were the golden, be-haloed saints of medieval painting. They came from a motley cross section of Middle Eastern society, as good or as bad as any other, arguing about their newly discovered faith and how best to follow it. Most were neither academic, nor especially holy. Many were poor and grappling with hardship; they had to earn a living, bring up their children and cope as best they could. Not surprisingly, after Christ's death, as his teachings spread to the Gentiles (non-Jews) there were even more breakaway groups, each trying to make the new ideas suit the framework of their own lives, each with its own leader.

Some of these challengers of the mainstream were considered heretical. The terms 'cult' and 'heresy' were very often synonymous — because Christian heresy was frequently a minority's attempt to make extreme doctrinal changes in the established religion of the time.

The cult of the Saints, for instance, developed a very skilful blend of com-mercial opportunism, genuine devotion and a merging of revolutionary ideas with the old.

In the cult of the Saints, for the first time, the bodies of Christian martyrs, or some part of them, became a focus of worship — and a thriving industry developed around them. Cathedrals flourished; candlemakers, stonemasons, gilders — all made money on the public's belief that contact with such relics brought them into contact with God.

Contemporary records have described how: 'They collected the bones and skulls of criminals who had been put to death for numerous crimes . . . made them out to be gods and thought that they became better by defiling themselves at their graves.' Bodies were dug up and dismembered in the fevered, hysterical desire to be in contact with what was, naively, thought to be holy (Peter Brown, *The Cult of the Saints,* SCM Press 1981).

Today, there are about 6 million church members in Britain.

Information from: The British Council of Churches, 35 Lower Marsh St, London SE1

SHINTOISM

Shinto is the indigenous religion of Japan and was the state religion until the end of the Second World War. Its name is derived from 'shin tao' — the way of the gods — and it arose in the eighth century AD as an alternative to Buddhism. It is concerned primarily with nature worship and the benefits of this world, stressing the importance of morals and ethics. There are innumerable gods, the chief being the Sun from whom the Mikados (Emperors) are believed to be descended. Priests are not celibate and there is almost no formalised worship although Shinto temples can be seen everywhere.

Information from: 4/12/26 Shibuyaku, Higashi, Tokyo.

ISLAM

'Do not be the aggressors for God does not love the aggressors . . . belief is an affair of the heart between you and God. Let him who wants to disbelieve, disbelieve,' says the Koran.

Islam is a part of the daily life of 12,000 million people — one-fifth of the world's inhabitants, and is the largest of its religions. The great majority of Muslims are saddened and angry at the way in which the violent Middle Eastern politics of a minority have discoloured the international reputation of their religion.

Muhammad was born around AD570 in the prosperous town of Mecca, which controlled trade between Syria and the Yemen. In 595, when he was a merchant, Muhammad married a much older, wealthy widow who bore him several children. Then in about 610, on his annual monthly retreat, he experienced his first call to become a prophet. From then on, throughout his life, he received revelations which Muslims today universally believe are the direct words of God. These messages form the Koran, which has remained intact in its original language and, so, pure.

The Koran demands complete submission to the will of God. When Muhammad died in 632 there was a split over who should be his successor. The largest group, 90 per cent, the Sunnis, believes that there should be no inherited succession — that Prophetship is God's decision and therefore anyone should be eligible to lead Islam, according to suitability.

The Shi'ites, who form the remaining ten per cent and are based mainly in Iran, Iraq, Yemen, Algeria and Pakistan, say that Muhammad decreed continuity within his family before he died. They appointed his son-in-law, Ali, as his successor, to be followed by directly descended leaders, or Imams. In time these Imams, like Ayatollah Khomeini in Iran in the 1980s, became all-powerful. It is fair to say that today the Sunnis regard the Shi'ites, with their revered charismatic leaders and expectations of a mahdi who will restore Islam to its original purity, as a cult movement.

Smaller still, and known mainly for its famous leader, is a sub-sect, the Ismailis, a prosperous and influential merchant-class group based in India and East Africa. Their Imam is the Aga Khan, who is believed to be of sinless perfection.

One of the most active of a great many breakaway Shi'ite organisations is the Ahmadiya Movement, which has 12,000 members in Britain, and has claimed that it was its curse which caused the death of President Zia of Pakistan. The movement was founded 95 years ago by Hazrat Mirza Ghulam Ahmad in India. He claimed to be the 'Mahdi', or Promised One, and taught a fundamentalist approach to Islam. According to Sunni Muslims, they too are a cult. Mr Ahmad died a broken man, but the Ahmadiyyat say they have a following of ten million people world-wide, representing a 'revived, resurgent, invigorated Islam'.

Islam, like Judaism, seems to have spawned fewer Western offshoots than Buddhism and Hinduism. There are no Muslim equivalents of Hare Krishna or Nichiren Shoshu on the streets of San Francisco or London. Muslim cults, on the whole, do not attract Westerners.

The rule of religious toleration applies particularly towards those outside the faith, provided they cause no threat. On the other hand, if a Muslim boy or girl is threatened morally — for instance by attempted conversion — the response is hardline. At the individual level, any young person who converts — whether to mainstream Christianity or to minorities like Rajneesh — is likely to be beaten, banished or locked at home by the family.

There are 900,000 Muslims in Britain.

Information from: The Muslim Association for the Promotion of Religious Tolerance, 20 Creffield Road, London W5 3RP.

SIKHISM

Sikhs believe in One God, the creator, and that His Name transcends barriers of race, caste and creed. He is experienced through the chanting of His Name which is done before sunrise every day. They follow the rule of the 'Five Ks'. All hair must be kept uncut (kesh) and tied on top of the head. It is kept tidy with a comb (kangha). Special underwear is worn (kachera) and a steel bracelet (kara) symbolising union with God; the dagger (kirpan) is the symbol of commitment to defend truth and those who cannot defend themselves. Health is important, natural foods and medicine are preferred and alcohol forbidden.

They were mainly centred on the Punjab, India but many sought new opportunities abroad.

The Healthy, Happy Holy Organisation is the education branch of the Sikh Dharma of the Western hemisphere, and was founded in 1971 by Harbhajan Singh Khalso Yogiji (Yogi Bhajan). This is reported to have over 5,000 Western followers in over 17 countries. Men and women wear turbans and practise Kundalini yoga and meditation (arousing vital energy). There are 250,000 Sikhs in Britain.

Information from: The Institute of Indian Culture (address as before).

THE CONVERSION OF EUROPE

There were about 3,000 years between the formation of Hinduism and Islam — that is far longer than between the birth of Jesus and today. These were years in which there was a slow shift towards a widespread belief in one God Almighty: years which saw the birth of some remarkable spiritual leaders, or prophets, of whom only Jesus is claimed (by Christians) to be the Messiah, the Son of God. From simple beginnings grew a variety of complex and competing interpretations on the same spiritual theme — the role of mankind and the way he should play it.

The next 1,400 years were to see Christianity spread, first throughout Europe, and as its strength increased so its role changed. The Church became, all too often, the aggressor, and its path red with blood. It developed huge riches and tremendous power, often at the expense of its people. Whenever there were rumblings of revolt, 'heretics' who threatened the Church's authority were crushed underfoot by the silken slippers of Rome, especially in the Middle Ages when the Popes ruled with a reign of terror, murdering, executing, torturing at will.

First of the scapegoats in the Middle Ages were the Jews, when most of Germany's Jewish population was accused of eating the flesh of children and exterminated.

Next were the Knights Templar and Knights of St John of Malta, who, as the first Christian warriors, gained enormous wealth during their Crusades against the Muslims (from the tenth century), but then became much envied by the Catholic Church. Their crime was said to be corruption by the East, that they had become obsessed by the occult and followed the Devil.

Of all the medieval persecutions the best known and most cruel were those of the witches. Over 3,000 of them were put to death, usually by burning.

In recent legal proceedings in America, evidence has frequently been produced by well-known psychologists, that cult members appear to be glassy-eyed and to move like mindless zombies. Medieval witches were accused similarly at their trials of being 'bleerie eyed', 'hunch backed' and 'afflicted with fowle odours'.

The Beghards and their female counterparts the Beguines, in the thirteenth and fourteenth centuries, belonged to no approved order and were organised in a half secular, half religious manner earning a living by taking alms and begging. They were often accused of covering immorality with excess piety.

The Brethren of the Free Spirit was a group which followed the writings of a Beguine, Marguerite Porete, and developed characteristics rather like those attributed to today's Family of Love (see p. 117). Many wandering Beguines were thought to be Free Spirits. Contemporary tales say they believed that if a man and woman had intercourse on an altar simultaneously with the consecration of the host, both acts were of the same worth.

THE NEW WORLD

The sixteenth and seventeenth centuries saw great waves of change break across Europe, leaving an uncountable number of spiritual pools isolated in their wake.

In 1517 Martin Luther, who said 'the faith of Jews, Turks and Papists is all one thing', lit the fire of Reformation. The new Protestant movement forced Catholicism to close ranks and revitalise itself. This led, in turn, to the formation of the reactionary Soldiers of Christ (the Jesuits) by Ignatius Loyola in 1530. The militant missionary activity of this time took Catholics to the New World, where they found, ironically, the polytheistic, cannibal Aztecs already worshipping a god born of a virgin and eating pastry images of him twice a year.

In sixteenth-century England, Henry VIII organised the birth of the Anglican Church, which itself eventually provoked opposition and the growth of a number of non-conformist groups who were greeted with suspicion and harassed, for what the orthodox considered to be anti-social activities.

By the seventeenth century in Europe, there were the Huguenots in France; the mystic Madame Guyon; The Quietists, whose Spanish leader, Miguel de Molinos, was yet another believer that the activities of the flesh did not taint the purity of the soul (every generation has one); and the Pietists, who tried to revive the excitement of the early Reformation.

Many protests were made by people trying to work within the reformed Protestant church — simple-living people with a strict morality, seeking a way to return to fundamental Christianity, although they differed over definitions of what that was.

The British Pilgrim Fathers took their Puritanism to America in 1620. The Reformation had given such small groups a chance to organise and, during the seventeenth and eighteenth centuries, some later became denominations in their own right.

The original vision of America was an ante-chamber to God's Kingdom. From the start the Protestant church in America was managed by laymen, which made it more accessible to ordinary folk.

So, in Pennsylvania the Moravians from Germany settled alongside the Amish, who to this day observe an eighteenth-century style of life and dress, and have become a tourist attraction. Roman Catholics congregated in Maryland, Episcopalians in New York. To Carolina went Dutch Calvinists, French Huguenots and Baptists, and to Georgia, Anglicans and Moravians. There were Quakers, Shakers, Ranters, Muggletonians, Separatists, Methodists, Seventh-Day Adventists, Plymouth Brethren, Pentecostalists and a host of others. All these and more from mainland Europe found their way across the Atlantic where they developed separate identities.

The Quakers, like the Salvation Army and the Mormons 200 years later, are typical of many new religious movements: at their start accused of every possible cult-like activity, they went on to become respected pillars of the community with influence world-wide out of all proportion to their numbers.

THE NEW WORLD'S TALE

THE QUAKERS OR THE SOCIETY OF FRIENDS, called 'toads and stinking rats' by their enemies, were never interested in gaining converts, only in quietly doing what they saw as God's work.

After more than 300 years, this tiny, solid community, founded by George Fox around 1652, still has only 180,000 members (140,000 in the Americas, 18,000 in Britain). Doctrinally, their beliefs were heresy, for they said the Bible was of secondary importance and that God is within us all . . . within each heart and not within the institution of the church. They ordained no ministers, nor observed sacraments. Very often they were provocative and offensive. Social boundaries were broken down. Friends wore plain clothes and addressed each other as 'thee' and 'thou'; members also refused to remove hats as a token of respect or take oaths — so Quakerism was not only theologically, but also politically, suspect.

Most heretical of all was the attitude of the majority towards Jesus, described in the introductory book of The Society of Friends in 1981. 'Jesus was a giant among prophets . . . a window into God . . . a man, born of human parents.'

By the time the first Quakers left England for America, their reputation had gone ahead. This was religion 'gone mad'. The Colony of Massachusetts passed a quick law to provide for the fining of anyone who sheltered a Quaker and the branding of Friends. Men's ears were to be lopped, women whipped. There were ten years of terrible persecution and three executions, but the spirit of Quakerism lived on, and by the time George Fox himself went to America, in 1672, the flow of religious emigrants from Britain, including Quakers, was continuous.

In the meantime in Britain, Admiral Penn sent his undergraduate son William off to Ireland to escape the clutches of the Quakers. Parental opposition did not work . . . William joined the Society of Friends and went on to found Pennsylvania. His influence on The Friends was leavening, for Penn sowed seeds of philanthropy and tolerance which were to become the hallmark of the movement. His was a practical philosophy which believed not in selling your soul but being a part of society and redeeming it. Quakers often went into trade and did well, caring for workers and servants alike: the names of Fry, Cadbury and Rowntree ring with respectability.

It is not surprising that today's Quakers are wary of using that word 'cult' as a description of any other belief . . . after all, there but for the grace of God go they. They see indoctrination by anyone, be they Moonie disciple or Quaker parent, as a form of violence — so theirs is a profound policy of *laissez-faire*. Leave the child free to find his own path. The limits of their toleration appear to be *in*tolerance, so the Quakers have as much concern about the activities of evangelical Christians because their approach is seen as aggressive and sometimes even dangerous.

Their answer to any such approach would be discussion and debate.

The end of the American War of Independence, in 1785, resulted in a Constitution which echoed the mood of tolerance which was already softening Europe. With no religion supreme or orthodox, every system of belief, in theory, became equal. The change was slow and the new democracy reluctant to abandon old ways, but gradually, as free-range religion found its feet in every State, every city spawned its local faith. America, which had so long been the dumping ground for European religion, great and small, turned the tables and began to export its home-grown movements, back across the Atlantic.

First of these was The Church of Jesus Christ of Latter-day Saints, the Mormons.

So, the *oldest* of the movements still branded today with the cult label is only 150 years old. The 'cult' of Christianity itself battled on for nearly 400 years before it was finally accepted as the religion of Rome.

But . . . it was not only The Saints who went marching in to nineteenth-century America.

The United States were born during the War of Independence, re-born during the Civil War, and by the end of the nineteenth century had become the show place of religious activity of all kinds.

From God's point of view 1893 was the vintage year.

The notoriously violent city of Chicago was host that year to the most extraordinary gathering of 3,000 holy men (no women). For the first time, Hindus, Muslims, Shinto priests, Confucians, Christians, and many others, assembled under one roof, for the World Parliament of Religions. It lasted 17 days. The euphoria and goodwill to all generated in those last throes of the century was, somehow, appropriate.

The Asian exclusion laws of the 1880s, which aimed to stop the flow of Chinese into America, effectively staunched the snow-balling interest in Buddhism and Eastern religion. But improved roads, communications, newspapers and education brought new awareness of a world beyond, and a taste for individualism.

The names of Emmanuel Swedenborg from Sweden, and the Austrian Friedrich Mesmer, had become familiar at the beginning of the nineteenth century; the writings of Freud and Jung launched new controversy at the end. The discovery of anaesthetic launched a crop of drug-related cults. Ologies became fashionable — especially psychology. There were those whose talents enabled them to contact the world beyond. The professional medium was in business.

An English lady — Ann Lee (1736–1784), known as 'Mother', was believed, by her followers, to be the first female manifestation of Christ. She arrived in America in 1774, teaching that procreation was unnecessary, since the Kingdom of God was at hand. Her movement, which practised a very simple communal way of life, flourished on the tide of millennialism (the belief in the second coming) throughout the nineteenth century — and was known as the Shakers.

William Miller (1782–1849), farmer and preacher in upstate New York, forecast the return of Christ and the end of the present world — for 20 October 1843. He based his judgement on the prophecies of Daniel in the Old Testament, and so much of America was caught up in the speculation that the *New York Herald Tribune* published an extra edition on 2 March, to refute his claims. Shops even closed, 'in honour of the King of Kings'. Seventh-Day Adventists (see p. 182), as his followers were called, gave up their jobs . . . but it was not to be. Undeterred by what they called 'the Great Disappointment', the Seventh-Day Adventist movement prospered:

Miller was succeeded by a visionary, Ellen White (1827–1915), who believed women should wear short dresses with pantaloons.

Even better known was the prolific and energetic Charles Taze Russell, whose zeal was fuelled by youthful fears of hellfire, which gave him a taste for writing graffiti on church walls. Tycoon owner of a chain of haberdashers stores, he developed his own brand of adventism, which said that Christ had, in fact, reappeared as an invisible force, in 1873.

Russell, who claimed to have written more books than Paul, John, Arius, Waldo, Wycliffe and Martin Luther put together, founded the Jehovah's Witnesses in 1881 (see p. 180). His was a tough message: We are awaiting the Battle of Armageddon against the Devil. Christ will then return and the dead will have a second chance.

In 1848, about the same time that Mrs Ellen White was seeing angels, the Mormons were creating their promised land and Europe was heaving with Revolution, two little girls in Wayne County, New York heard knocking on the wall of their home. It seemed to respond to their questioning.

Kate and Leah Fox claimed they were in touch with the spirit of one Charles B. Rosma, who had been murdered there, many years ago. Suddenly mediums emerged all over America, and Spiritualism was established, formally, as a profession.

A fall, on an icy pavement, in the winter of 1866, brought about the discovery of the controversial Christian Science (see p. 182). Mary Baker Eddy, who had for years flirted with the use of mental, rather than scientific, healing, came to the conclusion that sickness was all in the mind: there was no healing agent other than unity with God. The organisation she founded in 1876 was to become as condemned, for its refusal to accept medicine, as Jehovah's Witnesses had been for their refusal to use blood transfusions.

In 1875, a former circus girl, psychic and nineteenth-century 'hippy' went to a lecture on 'The Lost Canon of Proportion of the Egyptians'. She was the colourful Madame Helen Petrovna Blavatsky, daughter of a Ukrainian officer, and she decided to found a society to explore the occult. Madame Blavatsky moved to India, with her co-founder, Henry Alcott, in 1879 and together they developed a blend of spiritualism and eastern philosophy which became the Theosophical Society.

In Britain the movement was led by the formidable 'working-class heroine' and birth control pioneer, Annie Besant, who announced that Lord Maiteya, the spiritual master most closely associated with Jesus, would return in the body of a young Indian, Jiddu Krishnamurti. Krishnamurti was never very happy about this idea, and, although he accepted leadership of the organisation founded in his name, he disbanded it in 1929 and retired to California, to become a lecturer and freelance guru.

Theosophy itself led, later, to a wave of independent and, sometimes interlinked, mystical organisations such as the Rosicrucians (see p. 185), whose roots lay in Ancient Egypt, and the Anthroposophical Society. Founded by Rudolf Steiner, this is best known today for its schools, dedicated to the awakening of spiritual consciousness in children.

There were dozens of others, known and unknown, bubbling in the melting pot. Religions, ideologies, philosophies, cults and schisms.

The Holiness movement, which was concerned with self-improvement after salvation, and Pentecostalism which practised speaking in tongues, attracted large followings.

The Salvation Army (see p. 181) marched into America from Britain, Catholics and Jews came in large numbers from southern Europe, just as Protestants had done the century before. Atheistic Humanism flourished, and non-believing free-thinkers such as George Bernard Shaw in England were, for the first time, having a field day.

Some of the exciting seeds of ecumenism and curiosity about the East that were sown at this time, took root. Others lay fallow.

In America, between the two World Wars, prosperity brought advertising. Packaging became all important, and religion was not exempt. Quick off the mark, Herbert W. Armstrong founded The First Radio Church of God, and produced his give-away magazine, *Plain Truth* (see p. 72).

The Jehovah's Witnesses were streamlined into an efficient machine, by Russell's go-getting successor Judge Rutherford, who decreed 'active service, not ritual' should comprise their worship, and launched his 'new' hard-sell organisation on the world.

But not until the 1950s, in the despairing wilderness of the atomic aftermath and the disillusion of Korea, was there an explosion of a different kind. Where, indeed, did Mankind go from there?

Some went the way of the 'Beats' in America, beatniks in England. They simply dropped out. There was an international soul-searching revolt amongst the middle-class, well-educated young, against the values of their elders. But it was an intellectual revolt with no real impetus, and somehow it retreated to the university campus. There it was kicked back into the public arena by three young psychologists: Dr Timothy Leary, Dr Richard Alpert and Dr Ralph Metzner.

'The purpose of life is religious discovery', said Timothy Leary. His route to that discovery was through the use of psychedelic drugs, on which he and his colleagues had been conducting scientific studies. He was a charismatic character and a child of his time; what he said fired the imagination of an entire generation, and when he was sacked from Harvard they followed him.

You will not find Timothy Leary mentioned in books on religion. For during his early researches he convinced a group of ministers, monks and rabbis that, under psychedelic drugs, they had had 'the deepest spiritual experience of their lives'.

He also tried to have LSD legalised as a sacrament!

The Esalen Institute, where he worked, founded in 1962 and named after a local Indian tribe, is perched half-way along the Big Sur — that magnificent road spiralling above the Ocean between LA and San Francisco. A colourful setting, floating appropriately in and out of the Pacific mists, where glow worms and humming birds play. In the summer it is a centre for the exploration of human potential, often in the nude.

Here it was that Leary and his colleagues fertilised the drug culture. Of course, there had been others before them who had supported the use of drugs. The eighteenth-century poet Shelley wrote under the influence of opium. Mescaline was the nineteenth-century favourite of people like Aldous Huxley, Lewis Carroll and the fictional Sherlock Holmes.

The sixties were different because, for the first time, there was a huge market amongst the emancipated, well-off, but spiritually lost, youth of the day — led by their gurus and new idols, the music makers. They were carried away by the unimaginably exciting insights which psychedelic drugs could offer. Everyone began to 'turn on, tune in, drop out'. The Hippy Movement preached 'make love not war'.

Haight Ashbury is a street in San Francisco. Today it is a slightly seedy, sinister mix of burnt-out buildings, black magic shops, the occasional up-market café and a string of trendy second-hand clothes shops, supplying the youth of the city with the current fashionable cast-off clothes of the sixties. Guard dogs with spiked collars and muzzles are popular as pets. Once upon a time the Beatles were here. So were the Rolling Stones . . .

Haight Ashbury was one of the best known haunts of the swinging sixties: it was the nursery of flower power.

In 1965 President Lyndon Johnson repealed the immigration laws. Before 1960, 12,000 Indians had been admitted to America; by 1980, 380,000 were living there and with them came their teachers, their spiritual leaders. This time, America and the West was ready.

The words of Al Jolson had already pointed the way. 'California — here I come' . . .

Suddenly the sun had got his hat on and was coming out to play. Youth flocked west in huge numbers. Traditionally laid back, easy-going, over-the-top, California seemed a wonderful place to be; it was unlike anywhere else in the world, let alone in America. It still is.

Pick up the local free-sheet *Common Ground* today and you will find advertisements for well over 1,000 'alternative' groups, covering spiritual practices, psychic arts, healing, global change and intuitive science. There are probably as many tarot shops as bakers in San Francisco. Psychic Tea Rooms are the place to meet your friends.

The availability of Eastern religion, promised so long ago at the 1893 World Parliament, added an exotic new dimension to American life. Religion was, at last, for the young. Words like yin and yang were added to the vocabulary and far-away places like Kashmir and Tibet seemed alluringly accessible.

Those older alternative religions, such as Mormons and Jehovah's Witnesses which had kept their message alive, benefited from this growing interest in all things bright and spiritual. At the same time, there was a huge increase in the number of people attending evangelical and Pentecostal churches, whilst the Black Muslim movement gathered momentum. So, too, did an interest in the occult, witchcraft and Satanism.

By 1975, there were said to be at least 800 competitive denominations within Christianity in America, plus fast-growing, original, 'bespoke' self-improvement groups, tailor-made for *you*, and also the orientally inspired groups. Many, who were lumped together under one banner as 'Jesus People', began as a Christian antidote to Eastern threats. The great majority, though not all, began in California. One or two, such as the Moonies, which had been launched in remote corners of the East, found their market place in America.

There was, however, a price to pay for this freedom. It was feared that the activities of a few groups, Christian and otherwise, were at best anti-social and at worst possibly dangerous, especially as their ideas began to spread and be exported around the world by enthusiastic converts. Some had delusions of grandeur and dreamed of world power. Naturally there arose an orchestrated reaction, especially to recruitment methods and treatment of members. It came at first from within non-conformist Christianity — which was America's staple religion — and, independently, from anxious parents who felt their offspring being lured, not only into a style of life they could not understand, but also into real physical danger.

Yet more words were added to the language — 'brainwashing' and 'de-programming' — their origins in Vietnam implied, as was meant, that a state of war existed, and a whole new army of 'cult' specialists emerged to join in. There were psychologists, sociologists, lawyers, kidnappers and, by no means least, journalists and writers ready to jump on the bandwagon.

In 1972 a small group banded together and formed FREECOG - Free the Children of God. This was the first of many. The counter-cult movement had begun, and with it the twentieth-century Battle for God, leading on to an expensive, spiritual mud-slinging campaign.

THE MORMON TALE

The Church of Jesus Christ of Latter-day Saints –
FOUNDED 1830

HEADQUARTERS: *Britain: 751 Warwick Road, Solihull, West Midlands B91 3DQ*

USA: 50 East North Temple Street, Salt Lake City, Utah 84150

ORIGIN: *Christianity*

STATUS: *In Britain: Registered Charity 242451*

STAR SUPPORTERS: *The Osmonds; golfers Johnny Miller and Billy Caspar*

RESPONSE TO OUR APPROACHES: *Love-bombing at its best. Complete co-operation, an overload of information and hospitable welcome in Salt Lake*

A MORMON'S BELIEF

- I believe . . . that after the death of Jesus, Christianity lay fallow. The Catholic Church which developed in Rome was so far removed from His teachings, it was moribund from the beginning. Consequently all the Protestant or Orthodox movements which broke away are also severed from Truth. 'A twig from a dead tree cannot live,' they say. The Church of Jesus Christ of Latter-day Saints stands alone. Neither Catholic nor Protestant, it *is* the original church of Christ – restored.

- I believe . . . that mandate was given personally to the founder Joseph Smith by God in 1820. The gold tablets which were revealed to him and which he translated from Reformed Egyptian are known as The Book of Mormon and are Holy Scripture for the Western world as the Bible is for the East.

- I believe . . . God is not an impersonal force but is alive and can be seen and heard. 'As man now is, God once was; as God now is, man may become.'

- I believe . . . that as there is life after death, when families will be physically reunited, so there is life before birth. At the right time the spirit is sent by God the Father, to find its own way through the world, much like a child leaving home for school.

- I believe . . . the spirit is free to choose good or evil on its journey. There is a place for all in eternity but that place will be graded according to merit. The souls of ancestors who died before the possible benefits of Mormon baptism have that right too, and may be given the opportunity by proxy baptism.

- I believe . . . in the Trinity but that God, Christ and the Holy Ghost are separate and distinct personages, united in purpose.

- I believe . . . in personal revelation: that everyone is entitled to receive revelation for the area of his responsibility, an individual for his personal needs, a father for his family.

- I believe . . . in the literal gathering of Israel and in the restoration of the Ten Tribes; that Zion (the New Jerusalem) will be built upon the American Continent; that Christ will reign personally upon the Earth; and that the Earth will be renewed and receive its paradisaical glory.

- I believe . . . men will be punished for their own sins and not for Adam's transgression.

- I believe . . . in the privilege of worshipping Almighty God according to the dictates of my conscience, allowing all men the same privilege; let them worship how, where or what they may.

- I believe . . . in being subject to kings, presidents, rulers, magistrates in honouring and sustaining the law.

This is a brief summary of Mormon belief based on the 13 Articles of Faith set down by Joseph Smith, who concluded: 'We have endured many things and hope to be able to endure all things. If there is anything virtuous, lovely or of good report we seek after these things.'

Every three weeks the Mormon Church in Britain claims to open a new church; and at that rate is growing faster than the leading supermarket giant — certainly faster than any other Christian church. The Church now claims a total membership of 6,720,000 world-wide, with 36,000 full-time missionaries.

In their day, Mormon teachings were as revolutionary as those of the Quakers had been before — and Mormon followers were persecuted as dangerous pedlars of sedition. One hundred and sixty years later the all-embracing organisation, efficiency and honest-to-goodness commercial drive of The Saints remain a concern to most cult-monitoring groups. Films and books are still produced attacking, amongst other things, their beliefs as eccentric heretical arrogance, their missionary activity as an onslaught on family life, their secret Temple services as occult and their unique welfare schemes as a selfish attempt to ensure their own survival.

THE LONG MARCH OF THE SAINTS

The Mormons were founded in America in 1830. The overseas missions, for which they were to become famous and thoroughly disliked, began with England, in 1837, and the church in Preston, Lancs., remains the oldest continuous branch anywhere in the world.

With the pioneer's instinct, and their energetic encouragement of individual self-reliance and hard work, they survived, and over the last five years membership has increased, they say, by 25 per cent world-wide and is still rising. The main age for recruits is between 18 and 35 years of age and most recruiting is done by door-to-door missionaries.

In times of turbulent uncertainty today, The Saints go marching in, on a wave of confident, cheerful optimism. They have no place for consensus religion and, whilst they are happy to talk and work with other denominations, there can be no compromise on what they see as their unique relationship with God. They prefer to ignore, rather than sue, their critics, or to confound criticism with a flood of well-presented material, available free, for anyone with time to spare to read it.

With a smile, they relay a story told by their critics: 'St Peter is guiding visitors round Heaven. He whispers as they pass a large, shuttered building "quiet please. This is for the Mormons — they think they are the only ones here!"'

One spring morning in 1820, according to Mormon history, Joseph Smith, an uneducated 14-year-old farm hand, had gone to pray in the woods around his Palmyra home, in western New York. The boy wanted to be a Christian but was confused by the crop of sects that had sprung up since the Declaration of Independence. He returned home saying that he had received a vision and been told by God and Christ that he should join no church, but wait for further revelations.

Three years later, during the night of 21 September 1823, he had a second vision. This time the visitor was the angel Moroni. Moroni said he was the last Prophet descended directly from three Old Testament groups, who had sailed to America from Israel and founded certain of the ancient civilisations of Central America.

Moroni told Joseph that buried deep in a nearby hillside he would find a set of gold plates, inscribed in Reformed Egyptian. The plates were a complete record of these, hitherto unknown, migrations: the first 4,000 years ago by the Jaredites, the second in 600BC led by the prophet Lehi, from Jerusalem and the third, shortly after, led by Mulek, son of Zedekiah, King of Judah. For generations these peoples continued to practise the law of Moses, and their prophets taught of the coming of Christ. The gold plates told their story and of how, after Jesus was crucified and resurrected, He appeared in the Americas too, appointed disciples and gave them authority.

Some 200 years later, when these civilisations were fading, the historian-prophet, Mormon, gathered together all the writings of his people. They were buried in the hill of Cumorah, near Palmyra, by his son, Moroni, and forgotten until they were recovered by Joseph Smith.

It is these writings, known as The Book of Mormon: Another Testament of Jesus Christ, which are considered Holy Scripture equal to the Bible. They were translated by Joseph Smith with Divine help over a period of four years, written down by his friend Oliver Cowdery (and others) and finally printed in 1830 — attracting the first flood of Mormon converts. During that period eight other men saw the tablets and wrote a testimonial to the fact, which appears at the front of every copy.

In the meantime, Oliver and Joseph received the priesthood from a resurrected John the Baptist who, they said, had appeared to them on the banks of the Susquehanna River. Not long after his ordination Joseph Smith announced the establishment of the restored Church of Jesus Christ of Latter-day Saints (Saints meaning, simply, 'disciples'.) Since that time, the President of the Church has been regarded as a literal prophet of God, in the same sense as Moses, or Peter.

The first chapters of the Mormon epic were no romantic fairy tale and tell of very real persecution and suffering. Some of the early members were, undoubtedly, heavy-handed and arrogant. The records have been subject to all manner of changes. Many people did not — and do not — believe the story, especially since there was no evidence to prove Joseph Smith's account after the plates finally 'disappeared' with Moroni. To them it belongs to the realms of legend. To them the Mormons respond: 'OK. Show me Moses' tablets, or prove the parting of the Red Sea!'

In 1839 the movement was well-established and Joseph Smith decided to build a city on the swampy, disease-ridden banks of the Mississippi, to be called 'Nauvoo' — Hebrew for 'beautiful location'. It was described by Colonel Thomas L. Kane in 1846: 'half encircled by a bend in the river, a beautiful city lay glittering in the fresh morning sun, its bright new dwellings set in cool gardens . . .' By 1844 there were about 16,000 Mormons living in Nauvoo.

Polygamy became Joseph Smith's downfall and, although the practice was finally banned in 1903, its ghost has haunted Mormons ever since. On 12 July 1843 Joseph Smith had declared that the full restoration of the Gospel must include the restoration of polygamy, which was widely practised in both Old and New Testaments. It was not a popular decree, even amongst Mormons.

There are three possible explanations of Joseph Smith's action. The first two are not accepted by Mormons: that to early, energetic, pioneering men, one wife was simply not enough, or that so many men were being killed in the persecutions there was a surfeit of women. The Church's own account claims that polygamy was authorised by God and supported, not only by the Old Testament, but also by the sayings of Jesus.

Joseph Smith himself is reputed to have married up to 84 women. Such activities were intolerable to the puritanical people of America. In 1844 a group of ex-Mormons published the *Nauvoo Expositor*, which maligned the leaders of the city. According to the Mormon book, *Truth Restored*: 'Since the Illinois legislature, in the charter given Nauvoo, granted the city authority "to declare what shall be a nuisance and to prevent and remove the same", the city council met for some fourteen hours . . . took evidence, declared the publication a nuisance and ordered the mayor, who was Joseph Smith, to abate it.' Public anger at what was seen as suppression of the press burst into flame, and Joseph and his brother Hyram were arrested and murdered by a mob who broke into the gaol on 27 June 1844.

For 50 years, plural marriages brought more persecution to the Church than almost anything else. After Congress disenfranchised people living in polygamy, and a Mormon Congressman was barred from taking office, it was announced that polygamists would be excommunicated. There are still a few, small fundamentalist breakaway groups, based mostly in Mexico, but for the majority of the 'establishment' the subject is history and the Church today has no sympathy for them.

Joseph was succeeded as President by the former cabinet maker, Brigham Young, a 'modern Moses', who, because of persecution, organised the exodus from Nauvoo along the dreaded Oregon Trail towards the Rockies; 20,000 people in rickety wagons covered 100 miles a month. First came sleeting rain, icy winds and snow; children were born — and died.

One of the group, Eliza Snow, wrote: 'let it be remembered that the mothers of these wilderness-born babies were not savages . . . most of them were born and educated in the Eastern states . . . had lovely homes decorated with flowers . . . and to these homes, without lease or sale, they had to bid a final adieu and had started out desertward — for where?' In the spring followed the mud, so deep that three oxen were needed to haul a load of only 500 pounds. Everywhere they went, the brass band from Nauvoo played to cheer them and sometimes raise funds for food from frontier settlements.

In April 1847 a small pioneer group set off along the Platte River Valley, through Nebraska and Wyoming, towards the treeless basin of the Salt Lake. As Brigham Young rode out of the Canyon overlooking the undeveloped Mexican territory, now called Utah, he said: 'This is the right Place.' The river they named Jordan. The city — Salt Lake.

By the 1850s there were so many immigrants from Britain and Europe that there were not enough covered wagons, and families hauled their food and baggage on handcarts along trails previously taken by the ox carts. Two hundred people died on that terrible journey and are remembered now by a simple statue in Temple Square.

Under the leadership of Brigham Young, Mormons colonised over 350 townships, many with British names such as Leeds, Wales and Chester. In fact, agricultural colonisation of most inter-mountain States in those days was accomplished by Mormons. They founded the first English-speaking communities, in San Francisco, Colorado, Nevada and in Idaho. Because they believed that the Indians were descendants of the original settlers from Israel they were careful to be on good terms and many Indians were baptised. They started banks and opened America's first departmental store.

F.S. Dellenbaugh, historian of the West wrote, 'It must be acknowledged that the Mormons were wilderness breakers of high quality. They not only broke it but they kept it broken and instead of the gin mill and the gambling hall . . . they planted gardens, orchards, schoolhouses and peaceful homes.'

SALT LAKE CITY

Salt Lake City, American capital of the Church of LDS, and Disneyland, showplace of the Mickey Mouse empire, seem equally, at first sight, such stuff as Hollywood dreams are made of.

By night, the theatrically lit, fairy tale spires and turrets of the Mormon's Temple Square, in the Utah desert, rekindle a spirit of childlike wonder. By day, as the blistering summer sun beats visitors into the ice cream parlours (Utah has the highest rate of ice cream consumption in the world), there is a sense in which it seems there is no business like show business in the oasis city of Salt Lake. The stylish opulence, broad streets designed originally to accommodate a turning ox cart, the squeaky cleanness, multi-language tours, automated dioramas and dramatic architecture, brilliantly and beautifully landscaped amongst flowers and fountains do, indeed, resemble the attractions offered by their partners in tourism across the desert.

But whereas the Disneyland moguls know that their flock are day-tripping worshippers at the feet of Mammon, the Elders of the Church in Salt Lake City see every stone, every event, the words they speak, the clothes they wear, as an act of worship for God, which may touch the hearts and souls of their visitors for ever. To them each day 'is a challenging journey toward perfection, joy and eternal life'.

Annually, there are four million curious tourists to the spectacular 10-acre Temple Square complex, most of whom are not Mormon. In 1988 these included 30 Soviet Inspectors for the IMF Treaty, who gazed with the rest upon the huge white marble statue of Christ standing beneath a blue dome at the centre of the Universe.

They learn their Mormon history from a remarkable series of enormous murals, glowing with old-fashioned sentimentality, and from their free copy of the Book of Mormon. In Temple Square, in Salt Lake, and in the dramatic landscape of Utah, the everyday life and religion of twentieth-century 'saints' is on parade, with a huge team of some 1,400 immaculate volunteers, to give visitors a peep into any aspect that interests them — except the Temple.

The Temple

Dedicated in 1893, the soaring granite Temple, which took 40 years to complete, is, in a sense, a Mormon 'Mecca'. It is mysterious because, like the temples of ancient Israel, it is open only to believers of good standing, on the commendation of their local bishop. This is not a matter of secrecy but sanctity. 'They are expected to leave the world behind them and concentrate on things Divine.'

It is a 'compendium of LDS belief', with every feature, from the complex astrological designs around the walls, to the siting of the huge statue of Moroni on the east-centre spire, symbolising different aspects of their theology, telling the story of the vastness of God's creation.

There are now 37 such architectural songs of praise in the world, with a further ten under construction. Their role is unlike that of any other religious sanctuary because they are not used for regular worship and are shut on Sundays. There are many thousands of churches or meeting places to take care of these services. The Temples are used only for the sacred ordinances of marriage, baptism and the sealing of family relationships.

The interior of Salt Lake Temple is reminiscent of a Louis XIV palace; a fantasy in white and gold. The copper baptismal font rests on the back of twelve oxen each symbolising a tribe of Israel. The first floor is divided into rooms, one of which is the primeval world, one the Garden of Eden, the third our own imperfect world, and the fourth the Celestial Room.

The Temple function is unique. Those taking part are dressed from head to foot in white, sometimes with a green 'apron'.

Inside these ornate buildings couples are 'sealed for Eternity', after being married in church, and believe that they will be reunited, physically — bones and flesh — not only with their loved ones, but with their families after death. In the early part of the century, Mormons, living in countries where there was no Temple, were known to sell their homes, so anxious were they to make the journey to be sealed. After a divorce, or bereavement, men are permitted to be sealed again – and so be joined with more than one woman in Eternity. This privilege does not extend to a woman, who may only be married a second time for this life – and remains sealed to her first husband in the eyes of the Church.

Here too, in heated water, are performed the controversial proxy ceremonials of baptism (which were in fact mentioned by Paul in Corinthians 15), and confirmation of ancestors who died without the benefit of hearing the Mormon Gospel. They do *not*, contrary to popular belief, baptise bodies!

The Genealogical Library

William Shakespeare, Beethoven, probably Queen Victoria and all the American Presidents have been baptised by proxy, giving them the option of belonging, in Eternity, to the Mormon Church.

Mormon or not, there is a good chance that your ancestors' names *are* recorded here for posterity, along with many million others, in the tomb-like hush of the world's largest Genealogical Library.

Every day a team of some 200 photographers is busy around the globe collecting parish records and archive material, to add to the 1½ million catalogued reels of births, deaths, marriages, census records, wills and probates. Their optimistic aim is to locate as many as possible of the billions of people who, they believe, have walked the earth in the past 400 years. This is, primarily, so that Mormons may trace their own roots for at least four generations, and bring their family together in Eternity.

Over 2,000 visitors, daily, grow grey with fatigue as they search material gathered from 32 countries in the £2m library. Forty per cent of these are not Mormon. Only records in excess of 100 years old are photographed and copies are available to branch genealogical libraries the world over. Everything is duplicated and stored in an air-conditioned chamber deep within a granite mountain outside Salt Lake. Copies are given, too, to the parishes or organisations from which they came. What began as a self-perpetuating Mormon exercise, has become an invaluable service to archivists everywhere, although critics fear the possible abuse of privacy by the existence of such a comprehensive record of personal information.

The Tabernacle Choir

The spotlights beam a golden glow over the angel-blue dresses and dark suits of the 325 members of the Mormon Tabernacle Choir. Founded in 1847, as a means of keeping pioneer spirits high, it is one of the oldest vocal groups in the world and has toured 19 countries. Members travel from 100 miles away to rehearse.

The curious egg-shaped Tabernacle, which has been graced by a visit from every American President since Theodore Roosevelt, is made entirely of wood. The 'granite' pillars are pine, painted like marble; the seats are pine, painted like oak; the dome is carved pine – for pine was all that was available in 1863.

The Visitors' Centres
The visitors' centres offer a comprehensive starter-kit with no attempt at all at 'selling' membership.

THE MORMON WAY OF LIFE

Above all, comes the sanctity of family life. Large families are encouraged, 'in order to give all those souls waiting to be born an opportunity to be baptised Mormon'. Most programmes of the church are family orientated and explained in the 'Together Forever' room. Just as a father is considered the divinely appointed head of a household, so the Church itself is paternalistic, in its thorough-going care and control of its children.

The pattern of Mormon life is universal. Every Sunday the three hour services follow the same pattern in every country. Every Monday, whether in Tahiti or Stockholm, is Family Home Evening, with the children, or Sweetheart Night, when couples of all ages try to take special care of each other. Suggestions for a suitable format for these sessions are clearly laid down by the Governing Council and include prayers, fireside entertainment, group games, gospel discussion and social concerns. Single people have a programme designed for them, as part of the wider family of the church which also runs its own adoption agency to help childless couples.

Chastity is next to godliness. The body is sacred. There is to be no sex outside marriage. Divorce is recognised, but strongly discouraged. You will find no coffee or tea in a Mormon school canteen, no wine in the restaurant, and dress should always be respectful to God. In Mormon shops, in the welfare centres, even on the University campus, there are notices requiring 'shirts (buttoned) and shoes. No halter tops or tank tops, no shorts or cut offs . . .' A Mormon will always follow what are seen as the best standards of the country in which he works.

Alongside this restraint, there is tremendous emphasis on sporting activity, and a lively social life.

Self-reliance is a must. Responsibility for any individual's economic security rests, first with himself, secondly with the family and, if all else fails, with the Church, which cares well for its own. Mormons are encouraged to stockpile one year's food, clothing and, if possible, fuel, as a means of maintaining independence in hard times, such as job loss or illness.

The Brigham Young University
The Mormons run an impressively affluent University with its main campus at Provo, in Utah, and another in Hawaii. For them education is a duty. The Church operates elementary, secondary and post-secondary schemes in many parts of the world. These may be attached to the local school and offer supplementary religious instruction where none is provided, or they may be independent and self-sufficient.

But Brigham Young University — a town unto itself — is their pride. There are shops of all kinds, beauty salons, boutiques, a bowling alley, slot machines, cinema and an excellent canteen and non-licensed restaurants. The students, all 27,000 of them — observing the polite reminders on all the walls to dress with modesty — are well scrubbed and shining. Sixty-eight per cent of them come from outside Utah, and represent 50 states and 70 foreign countries.

The University is organised, like the rest of the community, into wards and stakes with Bishops and students automatically going on to serve their missionary time, before taking their place in the upwardly mobile streams of American life.

Welfare

Money can't buy you *anything*, in a bishop's storehouse! Everything with the Deseret (honeybee) brand label, from basic food to good secondhand furniture and clothing, is free to those who have their Bishop's approval. Bread is baked, and cheese made, on the premises. If possible recipients give labour in return for goods — the storehouses are all run by voluntary workers. Most of this operation is paid for by every Mormon fasting for two days a month. Money saved is given to the Fast Fund.

In many areas of the world the Mormons also run their own farms which supply food to the welfare schemes.

Tithing

Voluntary tithing and self-sacrifice have always been a part of Mormon tradition and most people, willingly, try to send ten per cent of their annual salaries to the Church. 'Tithing is the Lord's law of finance,' said President Gordon Hinkley, at a Priesthood Conference in 1985. Since many Mormons are successful in business, it is upon this money that the Church's enormous wealth is dependent, to pay for the building and missionary programmes. The Genealogical Library is supported by tithes, as is the vast production of books and free literature.

'There is no need,' say church leaders, 'for lucre to be filthy and it can, in fact, make a better world through its use in promulgating Christian ideals.'

The Saints are great achievers; two American Ambassadors, a US First Secretary of Education, two astronauts, several judges, a beauty queen and a host of media men and women have been practising Mormons. The Tabernacle Choir sang at the Inauguration of President Bush in 1989.

Forty per cent of Salt Lake City is Mormon, 80 per cent of Utah State — and yet within this stronghold many different denominations thrive. There has been a Jewish mayor and in 1988 the Catholic Mayor said, 'Salt Lake is not like Vatican City — the Mormons have no overall direct control. Individually they tend to be conservative and they are encouraged by the church to exert a good moral influence, but they never exert political pressure as an organisation.'

Today, the Church has a few real estate and business holdings, mostly in Salt Lake City, but neither owns nor controls any major national companies, nor does it invest in corporations with products inconsistent with its own moral standards.

There are no beer bottling firms, no convenience stores, no airline. Essentially, the Church's assets are a natural outgrowth from enterprises begun in the isolated pioneering days of the mid-nineteenth century. When they are no longer relevant they are abandoned.

It owns a newspaper — the *Deseret News* (first published in 1855), and now a number of television stations. It is involved with several agricultural enterprises and hotels, in which to cater for visitors, all of which pay taxes and fees required by law. It is from these commercial activities that the salaries of the General Authorities are paid.

ADMINISTRATION

The world leaders are known as General Authorities.

Church Government at every level is by councils and the supreme governing body of the Church is the First Presidency, comprising the President of the Church and two counsellors drawn from the General Authorities. The next most senior council is The Quorum of The Twelve patterned after the twelve apostles of the New Testament church.

In temporal matters the Presiding Bishopric of the Church have the key role whilst the Presidency of the Seventy supervise the work of the remaining General Authorities.

The Church has a system of Area Presidencies throughout the world in a move towards de-centralisation.

There is no paid ministry. All worthy males from the age of twelve are eligible to serve as ministers and each local unit of the Church, known as a ward, or branch, is presided over by a three-man bishopric drawn from amongst local membership. A Bishop is 'called' to serve and may hold that position for three to five years until his 'release'.

A similar pattern exists at regional level with groups of wards organised into stakes, and the stake presided over by a three-man presidency.

There are eight missions in Britain each presided over by a President assisted by his wife.

The men of the Church are divided into priesthood quorums and two representatives of these, known as home teachers, visit families on a monthly basis and report to the Bishop if anyone is in physical or moral need. A similar pattern exists with the women.

The Government of the Church is by Common Consent and each member (man, woman or child) has a right to vote on all administrative proposals and officers presented by local or general presiding authorities.

THE FLIP SIDE

The Mormon Church has been consistently attacked, not only for its curious beliefs, but also for its apparent monolithic and suffocating hold over members. It is seen as a monster from which there is no escape. Membership numbers are reputed to have been doctored, since many of the new churches are empty and it is alleged that membership statistics include many non-practising Mormons.

There are a number of movements specialising in anti-Mormon propaganda in the United States and in Britain; they are not large but they are vociferous.

In America, there is Ex-Mormons for Jesus, and Concerned Christians; in Britain, Christian Information Outreach lectures to churches and schools about the dangers of Mormonism.

They all claim that Joseph Smith was a Mason with a liking for the occult. They say the Book of Mormon is a fraud and the stories surrounding its discovery suspicious. Many people who are friendly to The Saints are also incredulous of their version of America's ancient history. Those who are against them see their beliefs as sacrilege.

It is not difficult to obtain literature explaining in detail the 'secret' ritual, despite the claim that ex-Mormons who speak out may be murdered. A former Temple worker, Chuck Sackett, has written a booklet, *What's Going on in There?* which follows, in suggestive detail, the ceremonial minute by minute. He describes the 'Garment of the Holy Priesthood' which is a white undergarment, to be worn next to the skin, day and night throughout life. 'A shield and protection from the power of the destroyer.' He also hints at sexual improprieties and eroticism, caused by the Temple workers anointing every part of the body, unclothed beneath a white tunic.

(Mormon leaders protest that this is preposterous since, as in the temple of old, there is strict segregation of sexes and men and women even sit separately.)

He claims that there is a direct link between Masonic and Mormon ritual, since the handclasps, the aprons, the beehive, the oaths of secrecy with penalties if broken, the star and sun symbols, all pre-date Joseph Smith and are closer to Isis and Osiris than to Christ. He is not apparently aware that Christianity itself adopted these symbols.

The literature from Christian Information Outreach states, for example, that to be a Mormon you must believe Jesus was married and had children. 'Not true,' says the LDS press office. 'Such ideas have, indeed, been discussed by individuals, in the past — just as the Bishop of Durham has queried the Virgin birth, and said he does not believe in the Devil. It is an interesting possibility — and, (with a smile) not so shocking if you believe in the sanctity of the family unit. But it is *not* a part of Mormon doctrine; the statement is rubbish.'

In recent years, there have been two full-frontal attacks on the Church: The first — a film, *The Godmakers*, which accused it of occult practices — and the second a book, *The Mormon Murders*, by Stephen Naifeh and Gregory White Smith (Weidenfeld and Nicholson 1988). Both film and book have been roundly denounced in America by a panel of some 70 members of the prestigious National Conference of Christians and Jews, which included Jews, Methodists,

Roman Catholics, Unitarians, Greek Orthodox, Baptist and seven Mormons.

The Godmakers was filmed by an independent producer, Patrick Matrisciana, in 1982 in Britain and the States, and was financed by an anti-Mormon group. The film states that ex-Mormons who reveal what they claim to be the secret ceremonies of the church are likely to be killed. It claims, amongst many other things, that Mormons 'take more barbiturate sedatives, tranquillisers, anti-depressants, stimulants, pep pills, heroin and cocaine than non-Mormons'.

The Mormon Murders is an onslaught on Mormon materialism, and their alleged plan to take over the world through the amassing of wealth and power. It tells a spine-chilling tale of forgery, murder, bomb plots and cover-ups. Somewhat charitably, it is on sale openly in the Deseret Book Shop in Salt Lake City!

THE MORMON MINUS

Peter and Jean have been 'stuck with three barrels of unused wheat' in their year's store cupboard — a legacy of their time in the Mormon Church!

Peter was his Bishop's President and had been a member for ten years; Jean, since she was eight years old.

'It was a real financial strain sometimes. You are encouraged to buy a house rather than rent, and it can be hard to pay a mortgage, keep your larder filled to bursting, contribute tithes and maintain the standard of dress expected. Men weren't even allowed to go bare chested when working on church building sites. It was exhausting too, we were all so busy at meetings, doing missionary work or social work that we had no idea what was going on outside. It was as though we were all holding hands, looking inwards.

'There was tremendous moral pressure and a lot of underlying guilt. The church is so well organised, there are "missionary of the month" incentives, and market ratings are analysed to see what is being achieved where. Many people get disillusioned, especially if they can't, after all, find a job when they come back from mission work. I guess there will be a lot of worn-out Mormons in Eternity.'

Peter and Jean were 'sealed' in a Temple ceremony.

'We used to spend a whole day sometimes, standing proxy at the Baptisms; there could be 300 in a day. I would pin a plastic card, bearing the name of the dead person, to my tie and go into the Celestial Room where there is a cloth division from the ceremonial area. The attendant knocks on the door, a hand appears — symbolic of God — and I would be introduced: 'Peter on behalf of . . .' and allowed in. Once the proxy baptism had been performed, that soul's name would be removed from the computerised list on the wall. Children love taking part in these ceremonies — it makes a day out for them.'

Peter and Jean left the church after a dispute, because they felt they were not being told the truth about the real teachings of Joseph Smith, and they had uncovered what they felt were inconsistent doctrines. They could no longer find the evidence that proved, beyond all doubt, that Mormonism *is* the restored Church of Christ.

'It isn't easy to leave, because when the church has such a hold on every part of your life you are scared and lonely. People were forbidden to speak to us and passed on the other side of the road,' says Peter. 'You are also asked to appear before an imposing panel of Church leaders to explain your reasons and many people are too intimidated to do this. We refused.'

Peter is now a Baptist and works with Christian Information Outreach. 'There were many things that were good about being a member,' he agrees. 'But once we started challenging the doctrinal claims, we realised God has changed his mind too many times in the Mormon Church.'

THE SCIENTOLOGISTS' TALE

The Church of Scientology –

FOUNDED 1954

HEADQUARTERS: *Britain: Saint Hill Manor, East Grinstead, West Sussex*	
USA: 6331 Hollywood Boulevard, Suite 1200, Los Angeles, CA 90028–6329	
ORIGIN: *Original, but embracing aspects of Christianity, Hinduism and Buddhism*	
STATUS: *In Britain: Non-profit making organisation*	
STAR SUPPORTERS: *Gloria Swanson; John Travolta; Priscilla Presley; Chick Corea*	
RESPONSE TO OUR APPROACH: *Letters and telephone calls were ignored for a year. We were then offered cooperation, provided we sign a solicitor's letter agreeing to submit the manuscript for approval. That letter never arrived. Even so, the manuscript was sent, in good faith, to Saint Hill and resulted in a total turnaround, cream tea and scones and a deluge of documentary material detailing the Scientologists' answer to their critics.*	

THE SCIENTOLOGY CREED

We of the Church believe:

- That all men of whatever race, colour or creed were created with equal rights.

- That all men have inalienable rights to their own religious practices and performance.

- That all men have inalienable rights to their own lives.

- That all men have inalienable rights to their sanity.

- That all men have inalienable rights to their own defence.

- That all men have inalienable rights to conceive, choose, assist and support their own organisation, churches and Governments.

- That all men have inalienable rights to think freely, talk freely and to write freely their own opinions and to counter or utter or write upon the opinions of others.

- All men have the inalienable right to the creation of their own kind.

- That the souls of men have the rights of men.

- That the study of the mind and the healing of mentally caused ills should not be alienated from religion.

- That no agency less than God has the power to suspend or set aside these rights, overtly or covertly.

We believe that:

- Man is basically good.
- He is seeking to survive.
- His survival depends upon himself and his fellows and his attainment of brotherhood with the Universe.

We of the Church believe that the laws of God forbid Man:

- To destroy his own kind.
- To destroy the sanity of another.
- To destroy or enslave another's soul.
- To destroy or reduce the survival of one's companions or one's group.

We of the church believe that the spirit can be saved and that the spirit alone may save or heal the body.

There is a sprawling blue building, in the orange tree-lined streets around Sunset Boulevard, Los Angeles, which was once the Cedars of Lebanon Hospital — the most glamorous infirmary in the world, where every film star of repute chose to be a patient, or to die.

Inside, hundreds of men and women, many in white 'naval' uniform, bustle, at the double. The spirit of their respected Commander, the late Lafayette Ron Hubbard, who died in 1986, is ever present on the television screen in the entrance hall, reminding them why they are there.

For the Cedars of Lebanon is now the international base of the Church of Scientology. Security cameras peer down from the rooftop, looking not for new members but for intruders and trouble makers.

The British headquarters, in the eighteenth-century Saint Hill Manor, East Grinstead, Sussex, were bought from the Maharaja of Jaipur in 1959. For eight years, the 30-roomed mansion and estate was the home of L. Ron, his third wife Mary Sue and their children, Diana, Quentin, Suzette and Arthur. The house remains today much as it was when they left and, although Mr Hubbard died in 1986, members of the family still stay there when they come to Britain.

In the 59-acre grounds, several hundred workmen (not all Scientologists) have built a unique medieval castle, with towers and ramparts which will, they hope, be used also by outsiders for concerts.

On a sunny summer day, by the open-air café, amongst the chalets and land-scaped gardens, the place has more the atmosphere of a French camp-site than of the hub of a huge international organisation.

Visitors are welcome every Saturday and Sunday afternoon for tea. Hundreds of people, including non-Scientologists, every year wander through the Monkey Room, where 500 monkeys representing famous people such as Sir Thomas Beecham were painted on a 100-foot mural by John Spencer Churchill. They can see the art deco, pink and yellow winter garden room, with its cocktail bar, and the study, where he wrote a number of his 600 books, published in 23 languages and 53 countries. His orderly desk, pens at the ready, is softened by simple presents from the children. There is a collection of organs and on the piano lies sheet music for Vera Lynn's classic 'We'll meet again'.

That is certainly the hope and belief of the 150 staff and 300 students at Saint Hill, where 'Ron's' birthday is still celebrated.

Since the beginning, Scientology, and its forerunner Dianetics, upon which the mighty empire of L.Ron Hubbard was founded, have been under almost constant attack. There has been court case after court case, in which the organisation has been, in turn, accuser and accused. Words like 'pathological liar', 'lust for power' and 'vindictiveness' have been used in America, and a High Court Judge, in a private custody case in London, said Scientology was 'immoral, socially obnoxious, corrupt, sinister and dangerous'. However, the Church of Scientology points out that it was not represented and had no opportunity to call or cross-examine witnesses, or to present evidence, and that the Court of Appeal in this case found that the judge's comments need not have been made in open court and that they were to form no precedent in any case of dispute involving the Church. Church leaders are indignant. 'If you were to place the awards and proclamations received by Mr Hubbard from government and civic leaders, compactly, end-to-end, they would stretch to 200 yards.'

There have been claims in the press that high pressure sales techniques and sometimes ruthless discipline have been responsible for suicides, breakdowns and financial ruin of members. These claims, says Scientology, are the work of the anti-cult movement, and in recent years have tended to be ignored by the press.

The activities of professional kidnappers have also been directed against the movement from time to time, when parents have attempted to extract offspring from its 'clutches'. The group sees such attempts as following in a tradition of similar cases, and points to the example of St Francis of Assissi, kidnapped by his parents who sought to remove him from the influence of the Roman Catholic Church.

Despite their protestations to the contrary, despite the unsolicited testimonials from those parents whose experience of the movement has been entirely positive, the spectre of Scientology *is* widely feared. The movement and in particular the leadership, which in order to work uninterrupted is located in an unknown headquarters, has created an aura of secrecy.

Their philosophy is seen as the supreme answer to personal and world problems and sets the Scientologist on a potentially higher plane than his or her fellows. Ambition, success, awareness of self-potential and spiritual immortality are among its goals.

Scientology was born in the fifties — a period which it calls 'The Age of Indecent Exposure'. In an internal book documenting those, undoubtedly witch-hunting, McCarthyite years, the Church claims that it was, along with many non-violent and non-criminal organisations in America, the victim of the FBI's Cointelpro (Counter Intelligence Programme). 'The Church became another target, a threat to the established order. This was not a position of its own choosing.'

It was 'launched into the teeth of the medical/psychiatric clique'. In 1951 Hubbard, they say, 'exposed' top secret CIA experiments with drugs and hypnosis on unsuspecting 'guinea-pigs'. They were desperate to find techniques which would match those being used by the Koreans on American soldiers. These tests were aimed to induce the patient to carry out acts contrary to his normal behaviour.

In 1988 *The Independent* in London (among other newspapers) ran a story 'A Shocking Secret Science', which told how nine Canadian victims of this period had been awarded £440,000 damages each. The US Government did not, even then, admit liability but agreed to settle.

Scientology leaders believe they have been paying the price of Hubbard's attack on the powerful vested interests of psychiatry and the CIA itself ever since. In particular, in America, they are locked in a continuing battle with Professors Jolyon West and Margaret Thaler Singer. They say that a politically orchestrated campaign has been consistently organised against their movement in America and in Britain. The evidence for this accusation was reproduced in the Scientology booklet entitled *With Malice Toward Some*.

This is why — they explain — the response to requests for information about the Church has been that of people under siege. The Church has rarely, they say, had an objective hearing in the Press.

So, find a tame Scientologist to talk to, and he mysteriously changes his mind. Phone calls are ignored, letters forgotten. On the other hand, there has been a determined attempt in recent years to persuade other churches and new movements, such as Krishna, to join them in an ecumenical alliance, presumably on the basis that 'united we stand, divided we fall'.

Because of the former litigation-happy reputation of the movement, especially in America, publishers are still wary of Scientology. There are few books which have been published independently. So far, there is no official biography of Mr Hubbard.

Yet there are probably about six million Scientologists (may be 100,000 in Britain, three million in America). Mostly they hold down jobs, run their own businesses and lead active everyday lives — unless they are on a course, which they very often are.

It must be assumed that large numbers of these are happy and contented with their lot. Contrasting views of what that lot is can be gleaned from ex-members, or from Scientology's own literature, available, at some expense, from their many centres. The bumper manual *What is Scientology?* costs £50!

SCIENTOLOGY AND DIANETICS

Scientology (Latin *scio*, to know; Greek *logos*, inward thought) is an applied religious philosophy, delivered by the Church of Scientology. It is the study and handling of the spirit, in relationship to itself, universes and other life and is used to increase spiritual freedom, intelligence and ability.

It has now been recognised as a religion by courts in the United States, Canada, Germany, Sweden, Austria, Australia, South Africa, France, Italy, Denmark and the United Kingdom, among others. But it still is not recognised by the Registrar General in Britain and so a Scientology wedding is not legal by itself.

Scientology evolved from the study of Dianetics (Greek — *dia* — through, *nous* — soul).

Hubbard claimed that his discovery of Dianetics reached deeper than man had ever gone in plumbing the mystery of life. His book, *Dianetics, the Modern Science of Mental Health*, had been published in 1950. He claimed it to be 'the greatest advance in mental therapy' — a workable technology for resolving the problems of the mind without drugs or hypnosis. Two months after publication, *Newsweek* reported that more than 55,000 copies had been sold, and 500 dianetics groups established throughout the USA.

Scientology marked a natural progression from the materialistic viewpoint to the spiritual. Ron Hubbard's title of 'founder' is applied to his development of the applied religious philosophy which led, in 1954, to the creation of The Church by a group of his followers.

Through its counselling techniques — known as auditing — Scientology aims to help an individual understand himself so that he can then understand the Supreme Being.

Scientology offers a method of unblocking the traumatic experiences of past lives.

The Church holds regular Sunday services, which are open to the public. These are described in a book subtitled 'Scientology is Here to Rescue You'. In this it is explained that the Church does not use prayers, attitudes of piety or threats of damnation. The book describes a Scientology christening (their word) in which the main purpose is to orientate the thetan (spirit) and introduce it to his or her new body. Weddings and funerals are based on the Christian formula but without reference to God.

Hubbard said: 'We find Scientology's earliest known ancestor in the Veda . . . we can look back across a certain span of time, across a great many minds and into a great many places where man has been able to sit still long enough to think . . . and find where it joins up with the present and to what we, in Scientology, are rightly indebted. If I had never been trained in an American University there could not have been enough understanding of the Western world to apply anything Eastern to, and we would simply have had the Eastern world again . . . So, we combine the collective wisdom of all those ages with sufficient impatience and urgency, and sufficiency of scientific methodology. If I have added anything to this at all, it has simply been the urgency necessary to arrive, which was fairly well lacking in the Eastern world.'

'Wisdom has no great tradition in the Western world. But if we are very industrious it will be up to us to make one.'

Scientologists claim that the knowledge they acquire is used to improve the quality of life in the communities in which they live. Their particular concerns are drug and alcohol abuse, family problems, crime and violence. They also conduct a wide-ranging programme in support of human rights and have fronted a number of international campaigning groups such as Organisation for Religious Freedom.

To help the novice grasp the religion of Scientology and its practical application, through the process of Dianetics, there is a specially written *Dictionary*. This explains the new language which Hubbard devised as the only way to describe an entirely new science.

Correspondence between members, internal instructions and noticeboards read like a television word game, and every magazine has explanatory footnotes. To the newcomer there appears to be as close a link to Ron's lifelong passion for science fiction as there is to ancient wisdom.

For instance.

The Thetan is the life force, the spirit, the soul — the individual, which is operating the body.

The Reactive Mind is that part of the mind which records and retains all moments of partial or full unconsciousness . . . so termed because it reacts unthinkingly and irrationally.

Bank is a colloquial word for the reactive mind.

A Clear is a being who no longer has his reactive mind and is so called because he has been cleared of wrong answers imposed on him by the reactive mind.

An Auditor is a counsellor who listens to and helps a member towards the state of Clear. Through auditing an individual progresses through stages of spiritual development to a state of total spiritual freedom.

Hubbard Guidance Centre is the location within the Church where auditing is given.

Somatics are uncomfortable physical perceptions.

Org. stands for organisation.

Fair Game was an expression that appeared in 1965. Though cancelled in 1968 this term is still used by critics as an example of the movement's aggressive attitude towards defaulters. Its literal meaning was that anyone expelled by the Church would no longer have its protection and was therefore vulnerable to outside ill wishers. It did not mean that Scientology would take the law into its own hands.

Raw Meat — new recruits.

Engram — a mental image of past experience containing pain and a real or fancied threat to survival.

The E-Meter — the electropsychometer is a device to measure spiritual changes in a person being audited. The first E-meter was built in 1950 and, according to Mr Hubbard, 'utterly dwarfs the invention of the microscope'.

It registers emotional reaction through tiny electrical impulses generated by thought. It assists the counsellors towards the areas in the subject's life which should be addressed by Scientology religious counselling. It provides a way for Man to rise to social and constructive levels of which he has never dreamed. It is *not*, they say (supported by an affidavit from an independent Professor of Chemistry at California Institute of Technology), a lie detector. Its effectiveness is hotly disputed.

The History of Man written by L. Ron Hubbard, is ranked by Scientologists in the same league as Darwin's *On the Origin of Species* and Bronowski's *The Ascent of Man*. The introduction hails it as 'a cold blooded account of your last 60 trillion years'.

Survival is understood to be the basic single thrust of life, through time and space, energy and matter. Man does not survive for self alone, nor for sex, nor yet for the species of Man. He apparently survives along eight separate channels — called dynamics — which represent the fundamental urges and drives motivating life.

The eight dynamics are: (1) The urge towards existence as one's self; (2) the urge towards existence as a sexual activity; (3) the urge towards existence in groups of individuals; (4) the urge towards existence as Mankind; (5) the urge towards existence of the animal kingdom; (6) the urge towards existence as the physical universe; (7) the urge towards existence as spirits; (8) the urge towards existence as infinity, or supreme being.

The Reactive Mind, which carries unconscious, destructive images of pain, prevents the true self (Thetan) from realising its full potential and ultimate goal — survival.

Thetans were, originally, spiritual beings who entered the Material-Energy-Space-Time realm of Earth, evolving upwards to become human with no memory of the previous existence.

Dianetics is all about getting rid of that 'vicious Reactive Mind', rediscovering the Thetan within and so reaching a state of Clear. 'I count it as my greatest pleasure in life to see a person free himself of the shadows which darken his days,' said L. Ron.

> 'Only the Clear has the natural mental sharpness, the quick intelligence, the calm confidence, not only to survive, but to grow, prosper and succeed. You too can be Clear.'

The ultimate aim is to restore the Thetan's original capabilities, so that he can become O-T (Operating Thetan) — a state which has not yet been reached. 'Neither Lord Buddha nor Jesus Christ were O-Ts. They were just a shade above Clear', said Hubbard in an interview just before he died.

> 'Through the religion of Scientology and the Science of Dianetics the blind again see, the lame walk, the insane become sane and the sane saner.'

Unfortunately, to the outsider, the situation is often far from clear.

THE COST

The way into the Church is usually via one of Ron's books, published by the New Era Publications and available in most popular bookshops, or via door-to-door leaflets or by a standard personality test — 200 questions handed to passers-by, on the streets of any town.

The questions range from 'when passing a beautiful child do you avoid showing interest rather than looking and smiling?' to 'do you often sing or whistle for the fun of it?', or 'are you disturbed by the noise of wind or a house settling down?'

Your responses will, almost certainly, show you could do with a Communications Course.

And herein lies the rub. For this is the first step on a journey, through course after course, to reach the ultimate levels within the organisation ... at a cost which could run to many thousands of pounds ... without books or equipment.

There have been stories from the anti-cult movement about families floundering in debt after being sucked into the remorseless whirlpool of expense. The *East Grinstead Courier* reported the bankruptcy of a local member as a possible result of his over-spending in the Church. Scientology leaders say that the costs are tailored to the means of the individual and are clearly discussed. 'Spiritual gain cannot be measured in financial terms.' What is the cost of 'total freedom'? Critics say that once a pupil has embarked on a course they become afraid to opt out and so destroy their hope of 'total freedom'. The Church says that many leave after taking only a part of the course, with no problem.

Start on the road to Clear and you have the choice; a weekend Dianetics Seminar is £40 ... a de-toxification process called Purification can cost up to £2,000 ... books (all by L. Ron himself) range from £7.50 to £162 ... the essential E-Meter can cost from £1170–£2,750, though these are sold only to those who have completed enough courses and have a personal experience of its spiritual gains. Anyone proposing to take an Auditing Course is offered a professional reduction 'to the able who can and will help in getting our job done.'

That job is well under way — despite the death of the leader.

L. RON HUBBARD AND THE HISTORY OF SCIENTOLOGY

L. Ron Hubbard was, by any standards, an extraordinary man — a flame-haired charlatan, a liar and schizophrenic madman to his detractors. But his official, biographical booklet, issued by the Church, says he was an explorer, philosopher, educator, artist, author — whose fiction sales have reached 27 million, humanitarian and friend to millions.

In the Church's latest glossy publication called, simply, *Ron* the photographs used to support the 'legend' are scarcely those of a self-effacing philanthropist.

We see a nonchalant young Ron gazing skywards in double-breasted twenties suit and trilby hat. There is Ron the dashing radio announcer. Ron the deep-sea diver, Ron the glider pilot and Ron, legs astride and arms akimbo, the daring test pilot. Many of the facts about his life, his academic record and naval experiences have been contested in the press.

He was born in Tilden, Nebraska, on 13 March 1911, and brought up in Montana. His father was US Naval Commander Harry Ross Hubbard. By the time he was 19 he had travelled more than a quarter of a million sea miles.

In the pre-war years he became the 'Barbara Cartland' of adventure stories and science fiction, turning out dozens of new titles such as *Gun Boss of Tumbleweed, Hell's Legionnaire* and *Man Killers of the Air.* Royalties from his stories financed his research into the human mind.

His early studies took him into the area of atomic physics, if you accept the 'authorised' story, or into the purchase of a phoney PhD if you believe his obituary in *The Times* (though an affadavit from Sequoia University confirming the degree does exist).

In 1987 *The Sunday Times* ran a series of articles based on Russell Miller's biography of Hubbard, *The Bare Faced Messiah. The True Story of L. Ron Hubbard* (Michael Joseph 1987). (A case was brought by the Church against the publishers to remove paragraphs relating to personal documents of Mr Hubbard's.) Some of the allegations and counter-allegations are interesting witnesses to the elusive nature of the truth. For almost every step in the 'authorised' life of this controversial figure there is a different version, as is shown by the following examples.

Says the *ST*: Mr Hubbard's war wounds were imaginary.

Say the Church: Mr Hubbard's naval discharge papers clearly show injury.

Says the *ST* in an article throwing doubt on Hubbard's war record: 'In the war Hubbard did his best to avoid seeing action.'

Says the Church, quoting Col. L. Fletcher Prouty (rtd) former Chief of Operations for the US Joint Chiefs of Staff and not a Scientologist: 'Hubbard has been awarded a unit Citation. This award is most important ... made only by the President of the United States to those combat units performing particularly meritorious service.'

In the *ST* of 8 November 1987 it stated: 'L. Ron Hubbard has often said: "if a man really wanted to make a million dollars the best way to do it would be to start a religion".'

The Church points out that this statement was originally made by George Orwell (to be found in his *Collected Letters*) and not by Hubbard.

After the founding of the Church, executives began wearing dog collars, auditing sessions became confessionals and the first religious services were held. The religion was open to all faiths — Jew, Christian or Buddhist.

This was a sound decision. The Church and all its allied organisations flourished. Persistent rumours over the years that by the end of the decade Mr Hubbard's income amounted to more than the President of America's salary are strongly denied by Church leaders and sworn by their lawyers in court.

'Mr Hubbard did not at any time receive money from the Church. He did, like any author, receive royalties from his books and since about 80 million of these are in print they provided ample means to pursue his research and other work. Even in the thirties Mr Hubbard financed himself out of his own writings.'

The events of these years have been given a slightly different colouring in Russell Miller's biography. He claims that Hubbard decided to convert Scientology into a Church, in a shrewd attempt to jump on to the crest of the religious tidal wave sweeping America. Besides, there were tax concessions for churches.

Much of the material in Miller's book has been discredited by the Church on the grounds that he used evidence from an ex-member who had confessed to forging documents. This was the period in America in which Scientology and the State became locked in a running battle. File number 156409 was opened by the CIA on the organisation, to try and untangle the network of medical and scientific businesses and organisations now operating under many names there.

Hubbard alleged that Scientologists were being persecuted by the FBI and possibly even being driven insane by the use of LSD ('the insanity producing drug so favoured by the American Psychological Association'). He conducted an indefatigable correspondence with the authorities.

In the 1970s a series of congressional hearings into the activities of the CIA proved that they had been engaged in mind-control research involving American and Canadian citizens. The recent case in Canada, in which substantial damages were awarded to victims, has, not surprisingly, given the organisation a morale boost.

Hubbard once wrote that the only way to defend anything was to attack, and his organisation has always been quick on the draw.

He started the Guardians Office, which became the strong arm of the Church — a powerful, protectionist force. When the Hubbard family moved to Saint Hill in 1959, the event was marked with some awe by the local *East Grinstead Courier*, which described him as a man whose 'work for humanity is known throughout the world'.

News of events in America had, clearly, not reached the quiet English countryside and the newspapers were more interested in L. Ron's agricultural theories (he promised to revolutionise the growing of seeds by treating them with radioactive rays).

In 1961 a special briefing course, under Mr Hubbard's personal supervision, was announced. This consisted of taped lectures which were constantly updated, as new knowledge was revealed. The questionnaire, given to newcomers, asked for information such as 'have you ever had intercourse with a member of your family?' 'Have you murdered anyone?' It was later alleged, though not proved, that this information was used to control members, who were punished if they broke the rules.

Local folk in East Grinstead were first amused and then irritated by their intense new neighbours, who wore badges which declared 'don't talk to me I'm being processed'. Gradually, as Saint Hill filled to overflowing, there was growing unease at the way local shops and businesses all seemed to be run by Scientologists — even if they did join in community activity and help at the local fête.

There was an air of secrecy developing around the mysterious mansion in the Sussex countryside.

In 1963 Commodore L. Ron, wearing a peaked yachting cap, embarked on another imaginative venture. He resigned his managerial positions, bought a former schooner, the *Enchanter* and, in 1967, took to sea with his freshly formed Sea-Organisation, all smartly turned out in braided naval gear. In time, several other ships were added to the fleet which moved from port to port.

Sea Org. is a fraternal body consisting of the *crème de la crème* — dedicated Scientologists who take a vow of eternal service. It is not a corporate organisation and members are bound only by their own agreement. The concept is akin, they say, to taking Holy Orders and pledging to serve God for ever — now and in future lives. Russell Miller alleges that it was a ruse to get rid of bureaucracy and enable L. Ron to continue with the propagation of Scientology behind 'a screen' of business management courses.

The sea was used as a base because it makes an excellent training environment and Mr Hubbard was concerned with the training of sufficient competent executives to take over the administration of the ever expanding Church.

To attend to his needs on board, Hubbard started a children's group known as the Commodore's Messenger Organisation, made up of the offspring of members. There was no school aboard, so to belong to the Messengers was popular distraction, and provided experience of responsibility.

The Messengers today are one of the senior management bodies within the Church.

In 1989 (three years after Hubbard's death), the Sea Org. was given a fresh boost, with the launching of a luxury cruise ship, *Freewinds*, claimed as the first completely Thetan environment.

Freewinds Relay Office and land base is in Clearwater, Florida. The Freewinds brochure, offering 'your route to infinity', is described as a religious retreat, with exclusive courses.

All through the sixties, alongside the unending battle over tax frauds, there were dozens of well-publicised civil cases, brought by ex-members and their parents all over the world. Nearly all of these failed, whilst Scientology also managed to secure the withdrawal of a number of allegedly libellous books, exposing their alleged iniquities. The flow of best-selling books by L. Ron himself continued unabated but mud stuck to his Church.

In 1968, after a debate in the House of Commons in which the Minister of Health, Kenneth Robinson (Labour), said 'its methods can be a serious danger to the health of those who submit to them', a ban was imposed on Scientologists coming to study in Britain.

In 1970 Richard Crossman, who succeeded Kenneth Robinson, ordered an enquiry which recommended that the ban be lifted. This was not done for a further nine years.

In his diaries Richard Crossman has recorded: 'I find it almost incredible that a minister and his civil servants should be so reckless as to publish a White Paper (on Scientology) . . . on insufficient evidence.'

Scientologists believe that the lifting of the ban was delayed by pressure from psychiatrists acting as advisors to the DHSS in particular. In 1989 at the request of one of his Scientology constituents, Tim Renton, Minister of State at the Home Office, confirmed in writing that Mr Hubbard and foreign Scientologists were indeed free to enter Britain from that time, subject to normal immigration rules.

In the meantime the Snow White programme was designed and orchestrated from Saint Hill, to 'legally expunge' some of the allegedly false reports known to exist on FBI files.

Hubbard was, so *The Guardian* newspaper reported later, also convinced that 'the UK was a central part of a mysterious agency, intent on destroying his church, and that two, British based, mental health organisations were involved'.

But he did not, they insist, direct the operation. He left it in the hands of the Guardians Office and, after the United States Government refused access to Scientology files, some members, including Mary Sue Hubbard, took the law into their own hands. In 1977 they broke into Government offices and photocopied the relevant documents. The result was a massive raid on Scientology offices and the subsequent arrest and imprisonment of the law breakers.

In Britain, too, major re-structuring of the movement became necessary. Twelve senior members of the Guardians Office had allowed the thrill of the chase to go to their heads, and there was a period in which libel actions were launched against British newspapers, Scotland Yard and the Department of Health and Social Security. They were excommunicated by the Church for misuse of funds in 1983, after the then external affairs director, Mrs Edith Buchele, uncovered what she described as 'a complete mess'. The Guardians Office was closed down, some members were moved to America and a newly declared policy of openness resulted in an invitation for *The Times* to visit Saint Hill.

The last years of L. Ron Hubbard's life were as mysterious as its beginning. He became a virtual recluse, gave no press interviews and did not appear in public after 1980. Rumours abounded, first that he was drifting around the world aboard his boat, then that he was dead. His wife, released from prison after a year, had no idea where he was. His eldest son, Ron Jun., filed a lawsuit in 1982 claiming that his father was either dead or mentally incompetent — but the judge ruled he was still alive. Certainly his apartments at Saint Hill were kept ready and welcoming for the leader who never returned.

In 1983 he broke silence in an extensive interview with the *Rocky Mountain News*, which throws some light on the man and his attitudes at that time.

'**Q.** What was your reaction when you first heard what some of Scientology's organisations were up to, which led to the court cases?'

'**A.** I learned about it like everyone else — after the fact, and I could only shake my head in dismay. Since I had not set foot in a church and since I had resigned my positions in 1966 and turned the direction of the organisations over to various organisations and bodies, they had to learn on their own how to handle the growth . . . Whatever they did, if they did it, was a violation of any policy I ever wrote while Executive Director years ago.

'**Q.** Why have you not set foot in a church since the mid-sixties. Why don't you appear at Scientology Congresses?'

'**A.** When I turned the direction of the Church over to others in 1966 I decided to step back, research and write . . . the fact that Dianetics and Scientology have continued to prosper is proof of their viability.'

Still the recruits poured in.

Asked to answer the question, 'why?', one German Jewish member said: 'I am sick to death of being labelled a member of a cult when in fact Scientology is the only religious philosophy I know which states no precept other than man is a spiritual being and basically good, not evil . . . in Scientology one finds one's own way out of the mess the world, and obviously man, is in.'

On 24 January 1986 Ron Hubbard died at his ranch near San Luis Obispo, 120 miles north of Los Angeles. He was 74. The official announcement was made on Monday, 27 January, and said that 'L. Ron Hubbard discarded the body he had used in his lifetime for seventy four years ten months and eleven days. The body he had used to facilitate his existence in this universe had ceased to be useful and had, in fact, become an impediment to the work he must now do outside its confines. The being we knew as L. Ron Hubbard still exists.'

He was buried at sea, and having provided for Mary Sue and three of his four children, left the remainder of his fortune to the Church.

His last books, written during those last reclusive years were a ten-volume series entitled *Mission Earth*.

DEREK THE SCIENTOLOGIST

Derek Field is a Fellow Member of the Institute of Chartered Accountants, practising since 1962. He is also a Scientologist.

'In June 1955 I had been in hospital with pleurisy. I was doing my articles as a chartered accountant in Birmingham at the time and my boss, who was a very conservative elderly accountant, saw I was not on par. He urged me see a Dr George Gilford. "I'm not sending you to him as a medical doctor — he's got something," he said.

'When I saw him he told me he was a Scientologist. I said, "how does it work?" He said, "I ask you questions which are designed to help you find out something about yourself." I was Church of England at the time but not strong. I'd been looking for something. George gave me 50 hours of processing and I got something out of it.

'Thereafter I studied the books and got a great deal and I started doing better from that point. Then I learned that two years earlier Gilford himself had been dying in the sanatorium in Birmingham. Hubbard was lecturing there and agreed to see him. He sat on the edge of the bed and gave him a series of mental exercises so that when, a few hours later George's wife went in to see him, he was sitting up angry and aggressive with the world. That was the end of his TB. George went to London and did the professional auditing course and got himself in very good shape. My boss saw him after this.

'At first I used to attend a couple of local groups and we'd do group processing. Then in 1958 I came first to London and then eventually to East Grinstead, saved, and did the training course myself.

'Between 1966–76 I was on the staff, and they were the happiest years of my life. I was accountant for the Church dealing with all tax matters in the UK and supervising finances across the world. I haven't audited for years because I started my own practice and am too busy. I act as accountant to a number of Scientologists but I have many clients who have nothing whatever to do with Scientology. Only two of my staff belong to the Church. Even my secretary is not a member. Clients know me — they know I am straight, and so far as they are concerned this means Scientology is straight. I have never had any problems.

'It *is* quite expensive, though if you are a staff member you don't have to pay for courses. But if you see how many people are involved in one hour's therapy and the size of Saint Hill, you appreciate the enormous overheads there are. It must be viable.

'What I have gained is priceless. If I look on my life, the things I value, the spiritual values are all down to Scientology. I have a far greater pleasure from life, a better ability to communicate and assist people so it has made a happier life for me and I hope for others. Behind that is a lot of technology. Using the knowledge in *The Science of Survival*, for instance, there is a complete analysis of a person, so that you can assess behaviour level and get a great understanding of each and every individual. Scientology gives you the tools to sustain good relations with every one.

'If you interviewed 900 Scientologists you would find 99 per cent of them would feel as I do.

'My wife belongs to the Church and my daughter, Elva, works at Saint Hill. I would have preferred her to go to University — she is a brilliant scholar and got eleven O-levels at 15 but she said "I want to work in Scientology". It was her choice and she is very happy. She has just taken over as head of the London Foundation.

'Church policy is that if a parent is concerned they should be brought down to Saint Hill to see exactly what their son or daughter is doing. It is rubbish that parents can't have access. Saint Hill is open.'

THE WORLDWIDERS' TALE

The Worldwide Church of God –

FOUNDED 1952

HEADQUARTERS: *Britain: Elstree House, Boreham Wood, Herts. WD6 1LU*

USA: West Green Street, Pasadena, Los Angeles, California

ORIGIN: *Christianity*

STATUS: *In Britain: Non-profit making corporation*

STAR SUPPORTERS: *None Known*

RESPONSE TO OUR APPROACHES: *Immediately friendly. Generous with time and literature*

WE BELIEVE . . .

- In God, the Creator and in Christ's Divinity but not in the Trinity. The Holy Spirit is seen as an expression of God's power and not a physical being.

- Jesus is everyone's personal Saviour but salvation is a gift of God. It cannot be earned.

- The Bible – both Old and New Testaments – are the word of God. As a result, only Bible-based religious traditions, holidays and practices such as Pentecost, the Day of Atonement and Passover are observed. Christmas and Easter are not. The Church does not prohibit individual observance of national holidays such as Thanksgiving or the Queen's Silver Jubilee.

- The weekly Sabbath is Saturday, a time of rest and spiritual reflection.

- Dietary laws are also Biblical. No pork, no shellfish but wine, in moderation, is permitted.

- Britain, America and the white English-speaking nations of the world are the true descendants of the lost tribes of Israel and Mennasah and so are the rightful inheritors of the birthright promised by God to Abraham, although not seen in the terms of recovering any 'home-land'.

- The Church supports the present goals of European Unity but warns that such political union could provide a framework for future 'unsavoury acts' as foretold in the Bible.

- We believe in the literal Garden of Eden and the fall of Man for rejecting God's offer.

- God gave Man 6,000 years to prove his ability to govern himself.

- We are at the end of that time. Armageddon is near. Man is poised to destroy himself and Christ will intervene.

- The chosen people will escape to a safe haven in the Middle East.

- Those who reject God will not be tormented, they will simply disappear.

- In the Kingdom of Heaven on Earth, when the world will be transformed and deserts will bloom, Christ will rule with the Saints and, together with Man, will rebuild civilisation. People, who are created as spirits, will retain their own identity but will possess many of the attributes of God.

In the golden Fall of September 1933, American listeners heard the first wireless broadcast by evangelist, Herbert W. Armstrong. It was incorporated later as 'The Radio Church of God' in 120 countries.

By 1992, its descendant, the Worldwide Church of God, reckons that Britain will have 40 television channels and hopes 'to be on as many as possible'. Already the Church, who also ran the first religious programme on cable television, is watched by 15 million viewers in Europe on a Sunday afternoon.

Herbert W. Armstrong was born in 1892 in America, to Quaker parents, though his family came originally from King's Lynn in Norfolk. He was baptised in 1927 and became involved with the Church of God, which was a branch of the Seventh-Day Church of God and cousin to the Adventists. In 1933 he began his independent ministry.

A flamboyant former advertising agent, he was a brilliant mega-media man from the start. Not only did he use the air waves to put over his message but also in 1934, three years after his ordination, published a free mimeographed magazine called *The Plain Truth*.

Herbert Armstrong managed to present Jesus as God's PRO, the Bible as His handout and the Worldwide Church in a subsidiary supporting role.

His programme was popular but progress was unremarkable until, in 1941, it was broadcast from Hollywood and the focus as a radio worship service was dropped. Instead, concentration was to be on the application of Biblical principles to twentieth-century society. The title was changed to 'The World Tomorrow'.

In 1947, Mr Armstrong moved to Los Angeles and opened a college to train ministers and other personnel for his now expanding church.

His broadcasts continued from the tiny studio on Orange Grove Boulevard in elegant Pasadena. His wife always sat opposite him at the microphone because he hated talking into space. She was his constant companion, and there are many who believe it was her death which later threw him temporarily off-course. In 1952, the first five ministers were ordained and by 1953 The Radio Church of God was transmitting on Radio Luxembourg in Europe. Mr Armstrong's son, Garner Ted, joined him and together they swept the organisation along on a spectacular 20-year wave of success. In 1959 they launched in Britain.

Today, the monthly magazine — which is still free — is a professional glossy, colour production with a circulation of 6.5 million and a readership of some 20 million people. Its articles focus mainly on Biblical approaches to contemporary problems.

The radio programme, 'The World Tomorrow', has spun into space and is now not only watched on television all over America but is telecast throughout Europe, Australasia and the Far East. The message was, and is, presented much like network news, by men in smart suits. World events, controversial topics and family matters are aired and discussed with no heavy religious overlay. There is none of the 'blabbing and flaffing', which tele-evangelist Jimmy Swaggart admits characterised his programmes.

The organisation which sponsors both magazine and broadcasts was renamed 'The Worldwide Church of God' in 1968. It survived ten years of scandal after scandal in the seventies, and now has an audited income of some $200 million and 94,000 baptised members in 120 countries. There are 42 congregations and about 3,000 members in Great Britain. Despite the fact that weekly services are two hours long and tend to be light on entertainment, heavy on intellect, the Church has grown 17 per cent since 1986.

Tithing at a basic 10 per cent of each member's gross income is one of the cornerstones of the Church and the primary reason for its wealth. There is a second tithe which is saved personally like a piggy bank and is for use at Church festival times. The third, voluntary tithe is contributed every seven years in America to be used for needy members. In Britain, where there is a Welfare State, this is not considered necessary and it is rarely used. From the beginning there has been no fundraising from outsiders. Yet still the money rolls in: £10,000 cheques every month, $1m from one letter. Nor is there any missionary activity or proselytising. Accusations of 'soft sell' tactics are rejected.

'We firmly believe that Christ and God add members, as and when they can. Of course, if God chose to call vast numbers of people we should be supremely happy. For instance, we have an average weekly audience of 1.19 million on television in America — and only 90,000 baptised. If you want to look at it that way we aren't very successful; if it *is* a covert missionary operation it is highly flawed!'

Herbert Armstrong died in 1986, at the age of 93, and was succeeded by the present leader Joseph K. Tkach, who is believed to be less of a charismatic showman and more of an administrating businessman. Mr Tkach exchanged the company plane for a cheaper, British, DC111.

Even so, there are no plans for increased targeting in Britain, or Europe.

'We just take advantage of things as they happen. Our feature programmes on AIDS, ecology or ethics appear on satellite television and we get some very thought-provoking letters from the British. Viewers like us because there is no waving of hands or emotion. We don't consider ourselves an American religion, anyway, since one-third of membership is outside the United States.'

Because the Church owns few buildings and has a policy of no *local* advertising, it has an unobtrusive low profile amongst the communities in which it operates.

But the international headquarters, on a 33-acre site in the former millionaire suburbs of Pasadena, are about as high profile as it is possible to be.

They are home to the Church's Ambassador College and also one of the finest concert halls in the United States. Great international artistes, such as the Vienna Phil-harmonic Orchestra and the late Artur Rubinstein, perform here regularly — a lift was specially installed for Pavarotti.

The opulence is staggering: black granite from Angola, green granite from Brazil, the Shah of Iran's two 650lb Baccarat candelabra containing 802 crystals apiece, a 37-foot fountain designed by British sculptor, Sir David Wynne, and one of the largest installations of Turkish rose onyx in the world.

The explanation for such extravagance? 'We believe God is a God of quality — whatever you do is presenting God and so you don't do a half-baked job.'

In the cool, palatial entrance hall of the main building are glass cases contain-ing gifts from world leaders to Herbert Armstrong and also to Joseph Tkach as Chairman of the Ambassador Foundation. The Foundation, which is sponsored by The Worldwide Church of God, supports educational and cultural projects in areas as far apart as Sri Lanka, Thailand, Syria and Israel, with a view to fostering cultural and ethnic co-operation. The Royal Opera House, London and the John F. Kennedy Center for Performing Arts in Washington, have each benefited from its funding, as have many archaeological and humanitarian projects.

So there are photographs of both Mr Armstrong and Mr Tkach on their near-Royal travellings, side by side with Indira Gandhi, Queen Sirikit of Thailand, King Hussein of Jordan, Prince Charles. In 1988 Mr Tkach was on board *Britannia* with Prince Andrew and Fergie.

ORGANISATION

The 1,400 ordained ministers are appointed by the international office, and work in the Church Administrators' Department. The College campuses are admin-istered separately. Cultural activities are directed by the Ambassador Foundation.

Each country is administered by a national director — responsible in turn to Pasadena.

The Church publishes details of costs and contributions and donors receive regular accounts of expenditure.

Accountants are internationally respected Arthur Andersen and Co.

AMBASSADOR COLLEGE

The Worldwide Church of God has its Colleges in the United States, too. The largest, in California, the original Ambassador College amongst the close cut diacondra lawns and fountains of Pasadena, California, was opened in October 1947 and now stretches over a 15-acre landscaped campus.

Six hundred and fifty students — some non-Church members — come here from all over the world, and are on a theologically based curriculum which focuses on the liberal arts, including economics, mass communication, psy-chology, journalistic skills and speech. Students are encouraged to spend a part of their time in practical social and aid work abroad.

They aim to leave with a BA degree and between 30 and 40 per cent of each graduating class become employees or ministers of the Church. The rest return to take up professional posts in their home region.

Ambassador College is not accredited but is pursuing the lengthy process of accreditation and expects to be accepted shortly.

On the 40th anniversary celebrations in 1987 the Governor of California wrote a congratulatory letter referring to 'your exemplary record of service ... you should take great pride in your fine reputation which will continue to enhance California's educational community for years to come'.

THE FLIP SIDE

It is now nearly 16 years since the first scandal rocked the Church. Although there have been many reforms and changes of doctrine and policy, former members accuse it of hypocrisy and double talk and are still rattling skeletons in the gilt-lined cupboards of Ambassador College.

For years, for instance, it was alleged that Worldwiders were not permitted medical treatment and insurance, but this practice was stopped in 1969 and it is known that when Mr Armstrong was dying he himself was cared for by professional nurses. Today, the Church is 'not in the business' of approving, or disapproving, medical treatment.

1972 was the year the Church published *1972 in Prophecy* — a study in possibilities — rather like *1984*. It was repeated as a forecast of fact and has they say been misinterpreted. There was disillusion that the disaster and the beginning of God's Kingdom, when His chosen people would leave for safe hiding in Petra in the Middle East, did not happen. Instead there was an exodus of 50 Church leaders in 1974.

In 1974 Garner Ted was charged on a number of sexual offences, sent into exile and finally banished from the Church. There was also internal upheaval over the marriage of divorced members and changing the date of Pentecost.

Leaders who left set up a hard hitting opposition watchdog 'Ambassador Report' — which began to publish a regular bulletin exposing the alleged iniquities of the Church.

These attacks have several themes: (a) personalities; (b) doctrine; and (c) practice.

First under the spotlight was Herbert W. himself, usually portrayed as an autocratic, extravagant, power-hungry dictator, indulging in sexual perversion and incest with his daughter. These were not proved, and denied by her.

The present leader, Jo Tkach, is claimed by some to be a tough bully whose high school record and naval career are questionable.

Ambassador Report accuses the Church of keeping its converts through the fear of disenfranchisement, and loss of salvation ostracising those family and friends remaining in the Church.

Those who do leave say that former friends are told not to speak with them, and will walk by on the opposite side of the street.

It is also critical of Church leaders' 'pay and pray' treatment of the faithful — demanding money to breaking point from the poor as well as the rich, a burden many cannot support. The third tithe, to provide funds for the deprived, has, it is claimed, been spent on material acquisitions with too little concern shown for social programmes.

It also alleges that, despite outward appearances, computers are still used to pry into the personal life of members and check whether they are paying tithes. If not, it says, they are accused of robbing God and subjected to a flow of heavy, threatening letters.

A few years ago, in an exposé in the Ambassador Report, it was stated: 'We would like to go on record condemning the WWCG's unethical, gestapo-like practice of prying into members' donation records, whilst publicly giving the impression that a person's name and any other facts gathered will be kept strictly confidential. We detest the practice of using a person's donation record to determine which employees to lay off . . .'

CHARLES'S STORY

American, Charles Hunting, was in a very high position in the Church for 22 years. He left eleven years ago, after the death of his wife, a much loved and respected member who did refuse orthodox medical treatment. He said in a broadcast in 1988:

'You begin to think in an unusual way, especially as you benefit yourself. I had a large home in England, was driving around in a Jaguar, had an unlimited account, furnished at Harrods, had a tennis court and could hire the Boeing 747 at any time. I felt because of my obedience to God I was being prospered by him.

'On one occasion I went with Herbert W. to Harrods. In 15 minutes he spent $45,000, including solid gold dinner ware. Wherever we went we took the best suite in the best hotels. "Let us enjoy what we are doing in the service of God," he would say.

'Anyone can live as an oil sheikh in Arabia, if their expenses are paid. He had no need of a large salary.

'He bought his way in to the international social circle. We gave $15,000 to the Lebanese President's wife's pet charity. The meeting with Golda Meyer, cost $250,000 to the Arab–Jewish fund for the young. Prince Charles was trapped into being photographed because Armstrong supported the opera house he was interested in. President Begin walked out of his office and was surprised into a picture but he never knew the man. Franz Josef Strauss was treated to a trip to the Grand Canyon. God was never mentioned. Only the British Royal Family have steadfastly refused contact.

'I got out. Once you question you are separated immediately from the Church and from people who have been your friends for years. You have theological AIDS.'

The Church strongly refutes these statements as gross exaggeration and as untrue.

IRENE'S WORLD

'Twenty-five years ago when I was 19, my fiancé showed me some copies of *Plain Truth*; we were both very impressed. We read the doctrines and we just couldn't fault them. After we were married it took three years for us to make up our minds to join, after lots of discussions with elders. Bill is a thinking man, not the over emotional type and slow to act, so our final commitment was very much a balanced, intellectual decision.

'At the time I remember being surprised how little pressure to join was put on us by the Church. In fact, I said, "I don't think they want us." Now I realise that this is because they want to be sure you are someone who is really serious.

'We both came from very set, Church of Scotland families and our parents were very shocked at first. But they saw we were happy and as we made a whole new circle of friends within the Church, they were included so that it added a new dimension to their lives.

'Our two sons are 21 and 19 years old. It's funny, you are not encouraged to indoctrinate children — it is important that they work life out for themselves. So when Stephen was 15 I thought "here we go" and expected the rebel stage. He had lots of friends in and outside the Church but at no time did he refuse to go. When eventually he decided to have counselling for baptism he went to his grandfather — outside the Church circle — for advice and grandfather said "go for it". Our youngest son is not yet baptised; when he is ready we will talk it all through but it is up to him.

'Of course over the years I have heard all the criticisms of the Church, especially in the seventies. My first reaction was then that Herbert Armstrong should have disproved it all and taken action. We had checked it all out ourselves and we did not believe what was said — after all, Christ himself was constantly berated.'

THE MOONIES' TALE

*The Holy Spirit Association for the Unification of World
Christianity – the Unification Church (Moonies) –*

FOUNDED 1954

HEADQUARTERS: *Britain: 44 Lancaster Gate, London W2 3NA*

USA: 4 West 43rd Street, New York, NY 10036

ORIGIN: *Christianity*

STATUS: *In Britain: Registered Charity 256598*

STAR SUPPORTERS: *None Known*

RESPONSE TO OUR APPROACHES: *Guarded at first. Co-operative on meeting. Willing to give time and hospitality, both arranged and impromptu, in Britain and at the ranch in California*

MOONIE BELIEF

We believe . . .

- In one living, eternal true God, beyond space and time, who possesses perfect intellect, emotion and will, whose deepest nature is heart and love.

- The first man and woman were tempted into illicit love by Lucifer who usurped the role of mankind's true father (Adam) so that, thereafter, all people are born in sin.

- God's first wish for Jesus was that he should take a physical bride, so that they would become True Parents. But Jesus was rejected.

- Christianity's world mission is to prepare the world for Christ at the time of the second coming.

- God's ideal desire for men and women is threefold: to be one with Him, bodies and minds united in harmony, centred on His love; to be united by God as man and wife and so give birth to sinless children, establishing a sinless family and ultimately a sinless world; to become lords of the created world.

- God's will that all people be restored to Him is predestined. He has called certain people and groups to help him.

- Jesus, active in his spiritual body, will commission a person, still in his Earthly body, to complete the task of bringing the Kingdom of Heaven to Earth. This must be a man of extraordinary spiritual stature. He will implant Jesus deeply in all hearts and enable everyone to live the life of

Jesus. He will establish, through marriage, the ideal family which God desires and he and his bride will become True Parents, on whom all fallen mankind can be grafted.

• It is the privilege and responsibility of all Christians to search for and recognise the Messiah.

MOONSTRUCK

The Rev. Sun Myung Moon — the man whom his followers believe to be the Messiah — earned for himself a place in the *Guinness Book of Records* when he conducted the biggest mass wedding in the world: 6,516 couples in 1988.

Weddings, which are probably the best known public face of the Moonies, are absolutely central to Unification Church theology. Every enterprise it conducts has as its *raison d'être* the idea of a 'true family' and global harmony, symbolised by marriage.

The power that persuades 3,000 girls, side by side in identical Moonieform dresses, to be linked forever to bridegrooms, often not from their own countries, by a Korean evangelist who speaks little English, seems on the face of it shockingly close to hypnotic mindlessness. The Moonie sees it differently.

To the Moonies, marriage is a mission. Happiness and holiness, says Rev. Moon, can only be achieved spiritually through the vocation of marriage and the creation of sinless children in a God-centred family. This was God's plan for Adam and Eve, thwarted by Satan. It was His plan for Jesus, thwarted, due to His rejection by the people. It is now His plan for members of the Unification Church, with the Rev. Moon this time acting as His agent. By 'Father', as he is known, and his wife 'Mother', adopting all the members of their Moonie family on Earth they can, with effort and dedication, be united to God as part of His True Family.

Most members over 25 have been personally matched and married by the Rev. Moon. This process is seen as one in which God guides the choice of partner according to the best fulfilment of His will and for the benefit of mankind.

The primary motivation and sustenance of marriage is spiritual. It is not of the flesh. 'We love God more than we love each other,' they say. So, there is no sex before marriage.

Young Moonies — especially those in the West brought up on a tradition of romantic love — understand that the preparation for such a union must be long. So there is no pressure to hurry, no fear of being left on the shelf, for anyone who would like to be married will be found a partner when they are ready. The trust in Rev. Moon is complete and so his failure rate is low: though divorce is known, against all odds, it is rare.

Couples who are already married when they join usually go through a voluntary period of sexual abstinence before being blessed by Rev. Moon.

The children of any marriage consummated outside the Church are considered to bear the burden of original sin. This could, surely, present problems if a couple, with children, become Moonies and then go on to produce 'sinless' babies — that is, free of original sin. But no. There are many Moonie families with children born either side of the divine fence. The explanation given is that sinless children will simply have a greater potential to respond to God and therefore stand a better chance in life.

Before the betrothal ceremony a great deal of research is undertaken by Rev. Moon and he may well spend time interviewing couples before they are introduced. Candidates, too, have been through a lengthy period of preparation in order 'to be ready to receive God's guidance', through Father.

When the time has come to be betrothed, couples mingle in a vast hall. Names are called out one by one — Americans who have chosen French partners raise their hands, the Chinese who chose a Swiss, the white English who looked for a black African, and so on. The mixing of races and nationalities is a part of the divine plan for world unity. Rev. Moon them moves around the hall, pairing anxious and excited men and women by a touch on the shoulder.

At this stage, there is the option of a second chance. If the chosen partner is immediately repugnant a couple may agree not to pursue the idea and return to the circuit.

Matched couples share a glass of holy wine, as in communion, symbolically establishing a new, spiritual lineage and wiping out sin. Marriage is so spiritual that consummation is not permitted for at least 40 days. Very often they are separated immediately and sent abroad on missions, before being allowed to settle down to the serious physical role of becoming True Parents themselves.

Usually women adopt the homeland of their partner and though all are encouraged to — and mostly do — keep in touch with their relatives back home, the system effectively means that they are now a part of Rev. Moon's family. There is no longer any attempt to deny the inevitable loneliness and homesickness that can follow for some people. But the problems of uprooting are seen as a challenge to be overcome, by endeavour for God, and a natural part of the process of spiritual growth. Those who participate do so willingly.

George Robertson is a former Buddhist who writes children's stories for the BBC in Scotland. He married his pretty bride Annie in 1982 and is on excellent terms with his Austrian in-laws who aren't Moonies but who are, so he says, happy at their daughter's happiness.

'I sensed at that moment something far greater than any of us was present. There was sanctity and a feeling of grace.'

The administration in each country tries to find friends of the same nationality for foreign newlyweds but an amazing 80 per cent of Moonies speak more than one language long before marriage. Their belief in one universal church encourages the study of language as a means to an end.

The Jesuit sociologist, Joseph H. Fichter, of New Orleans has said: 'When Catholics talked about "having a vocation" they almost always meant the life that required permanent celibacy. This was the perfect spiritual path. The Moon people have turned this around. If you really want to do God's will you marry and have children.'

However, marriage is by no means all there is to being a Moonie. It involves total commitment to an ideology which becomes the supporting mesh for every aspect of life.

The new Moonie is offered a religion which focuses on the here and now. It shows a clear way, with well-defined boundaries to change the world for the better and create Heaven on Earth. It is aiming for a world in which all men and women enjoy the living relationship with God.

It is a practical, not mystical, ideology: its emphasis is on living for the good of the whole, rather than on introspective self-improvement and the insistence that this good can only be achieved by obedience to God through his sanctioned representatives. Individual conscience is not suppressed but the restoration of God's Kingdom will only be achieved through team effort.

Unification Church theology is explained in the *Divine Principle*. This is a complex and comprehensive work, interpreting the relationship between world cosmology, history, science and God and based on the insights of Rev. Moon over a period of 14 years. He claims it was 'worked out' with much personal struggle as a result of revelations to him from God 'and was not just handed to him on a plate.' The *Divine Principle* offers fresh interpretations of the Bible and additional doctrine.

All creation, it says, is formed of male and female, positive or negative elements, rather like the Chinese understanding of yin and yang. These interact continuously, in a give and take chain of being, leading to union with God. In other words, 'I exist for my family, my family exists for society, society exists for the nation, our nation exists for the world. All the world exists for God.'

The process by which mankind achieves this union is called religion. The Unification Church is, therefore, on an open collision course with Communism, which it sees as a Godless ideology. It is intent on solving the confusion resulting from the spread of such atheistic materialism.

Once this unity is achieved there will no longer be any need for religion, or prayer, or a saviour. Absolute truth will be understood. The UC was formed to be that catalyst and, so, to save the world.

To his 'family', the Rev. Moon *is* the promised Messiah. To his opponents he is the anti-Christ.

There are no half measures about the Rev. Moon. From his home in New York, he heads a Church, and the Unification Movement, with an unexpectedly small membership and a contrastingly large network of wide-ranging businesses and organisations. The Unification Church is 'involved in relating to all major religious traditions and all fields of human endeavour', which means active interest in international religious affairs, science, the arts, politics, welfare, commerce, industry and communications.

The 1988 Unification Church publication *New Vision for World Peace*, lists and introduces the best known of these involvements. The Moonies have, for instance, been responsible for setting up or supporting bodies as diverse as: the International Relief Friendship Foundation, a non-profit making organisation creating and sponsoring agricultural and rural development programmes and emergency relief; the International Highway Project for the building of a pan-continental high speed artery; the *Washington Times* (President Reagan's favourite newspaper); and The Little Angels of Korea Folk Ballet Troupe, who performed before HM the Queen in 1972.

Since the industrial world is 'the foundation upon which God's kingdom will be built', the Rev. Moon is regarded with reverence by his supporters, as an industrialist with heart. At International Ocean Enterprises, a fish processing plant, they are producing 'Shark Jerky' — a resource-conscious rival to the all-American 'Beef Jerky', which looks like boot leather, was originally chewed by Indians, then by cowboys and now by gum-bored kids. His Il Hwa pharmaceutical company in Korea is aiming to knock Coca-Cola off its pedestal with a rather sweet barley-based look-alike, McCol. The New York City Symphony Orchestra, the Universal Ballet Company and the Ocean Church, which offers participants an opportunity to learn marine farming by developing their own seamanship skills, each owes its being to the Rev. Moon.

The profit making commercial organisations, staffed mainly by non-Moonies, all donate to the church and support its charitable projects. Although the Rev. Moon acts as an adviser and watches over their spiritual and ethical ethos, he is no longer involved on a daily basis and draws no salaries. The Church does not, however, donate to any political party. Individual members are encouraged to support those of any party the Church thinks are right and opposes 'all evils'.

More controversial is CARP (The Collegiate Association for Research Principles) and CAUSA (The National Council for the Church and Social Action) the thinly disguised anti-Communist section of the movement. CARP is an international student movement, which maintains chapters in many universities and has been regularly accused of deceptive recruitment and of hiding its allegiance to the Church. It has been banned from some campuses — a decision which the Church finds unjustified in view of the 'extraordinary array' of extreme political movements that *are* allowed. CAUSA conducts international seminars and works 'to defend human rights and fight all forms of totalitarianism'.

The Rev. Moon's personal success at winning friends in high places has survived an almost consistently bad press. The conferences and rallies are usually attended by high-ranking and independent observers from all walks of life. The regular offering of freebie trips to Korea for American Christian clergy, by the Moonie-sponsored ICC (Interdenominational Conferences for Clergy), has raised more than an eyebrow or two in conventional circles. Those who fear there is no such thing as a free lunch say that non-Moonie support of such conferences lends respectability to the organisation, which is quietly organising a world take-over. But human nature being human, well over 7,000 Americans have already accepted the Rev. Moon's invitations. The ICC began approaching British clergy in 1989.

The United Methodist World Mission in Korea issues warnings to clergy, tempted by the idea, and says that the Church is better known for its commercial products than religious activity in Korea.

Dr George Chryssides, Senior Lecturer in Philosophy at Plymouth Polytechnic, who was a visitor to the Assembly of World Religions in New Jersey in 1985, does not agree. The conference, organised by the Moonies under the banner of the International Religious Foundation, was an 'ambitious attempt to bring together the leading representatives of the historic religions of the world'. Dr Chryssides observed afterwards: 'If a religious movement which has been criticised for allegedly discreditable activities, can manage to mount conferences and events of a high calibre, then the movement equally deserves the credit it has earned . . . if the Moonies wish to incorporate other faiths they are certainly not the first religion to have done so. If such theological method is not permissible, mainstream Jewish and Christian theologians must think again!'

THE REV. SUN MYUNG MOON

Sun Myung Moon was the fifth of eight children, born in 1920 in north-western Korea. His parents converted to Christianity when he was ten and at the age of 15, he says, Jesus appeared to him and repeatedly asked his help in fulfilling God's mission of building the Kingdom on Earth. Over the next few years, during a period of spiritual searching, he completed his education and studied electrical engineering at Waseda University, Japan. He established his first ministry, in Communist North Korea, in 1946, which led to imprisonment and torture.

After liberation by United Nations troops in 1952, he fled to Pusan in South Korea where he wrote the first draft of the *Divine Principle*, which was published in 1957. In the meantime, he had gathered supporters about him and founded the Holy Spirit Association for the Unification of World Christianity, which sent its first missionary to Japan in 1958. In 1960 he married Hak Ja Han and set about completing the unfinished business of Christ's mission — children. Mrs Moon produced 13 babies over the next 20 years.

The movement was very successful first in Korea, and then after a long slow start in Japan, where the 'family' concept grafted well on to Shinto foundations. The United Methodist World Mission Korea has imposed sanctions on clergy who participate and says that the Moonie influence in Korea is 'minuscule'. Established churches 'shun him like the plague.'

Even so, various denominations do co-operate. Wherever he went, the charismatic character of 'Father', as a truly holy man, divinely sanctioned controller of the freeway to Heaven, seemed to overcome any problems his followers may have had with understanding the detail of his complex message.

That message reached Oregon University in 1959 when Dr Young Oon Kim (who became better known as Miss Kim) enrolled as a student. Miss Kim had been a professor of New Testament and Comparative Religions at Hwa University, Seoul, but was converted to the Unification Church in 1954, at the age of 39, and, as a result, was dismissed. She was followed to America over the next few years by a number of missionaries whose names were to become both familiar and shadowy. They included Col. Bo Hi Pak, who became assistant military attaché at the Republic of Korea Embassy in Washington, David Kim (no relation) a United Nations Scholar, and Yun Soo Lim who married Dr Mose Durst, first President of the Church in America. Doris Walder, one of the first Western converts, married the Englishman Dennis Orme in 1969 and, with him, went on to run the British 'Family' for the next decade.

These people, and their first recruits, had very different personalities and styles of leadership, which was to result in very different operational methods for each group. The Far Eastern Moonie and the Western Moonie are very different animals. They were, though, mostly Korean or Japanese with little knowledge of Western psychology, and whilst some were very spiritually based, others were more aggressive and dynamic. Anyone joining the Oakland family in the California Bay area was likely to experience a way of life quite unlike that of any family in Britain. But by 1963 there were still only about 21 converts, mostly white, lower middle class Protestant. There was a hard road ahead.

The original, rather ineffective, group autonomy was superseded in 1965 when Sang Ik Choi arrived from Japan, with a package of new organisational practices and a fervent vision of a material Heaven on Earth. The Japanese miracle, in which 'the apple became as large as the water melon', had come to America.

He developed a much more systematic and uniform training programme, which provoked rumours that the Moonies resorted to Korean prison camp methods of brainwashing and mind control. There was a historical bitterness between Korea and Japan, which led Unification Church leaders at that stage to gloss over its national origins. This was how, in the sixties, visitors could sit through an entire weekend course without hearing the name of Rev. Moon. In the same way, Californian street missionaries were encouraged to be vague about their Messiah, and the practice of 'Heavenly Deception' (the end justifies the means), as preached by St Paul, became notorious. Today, the use of heavenly deception is frowned on.

Communal living as 'families', with members called 'brother and sister' became regular practice, and this, too, led to hair-raising speculation about the ghetto-like nature of the organisation. Conditions were often primitive, and demands on members tough.

Stories circulated that people were being enticed off the streets and campuses to be offered a life of slave labour selling candles and flowers, in order to raise money for a man who held them in Svengali-style control, by sinister techniques.

Sociologist Dr Eileen Barker spent many months down among the Moonies. She interviewed dozens of members, attended workshops, cooked in their kitchens, sang at their seminars and, to the relief of her own husband and children, emerged on excellent terms but unconverted. 'I found them eminently resistable.' The fact is that most people who are subjected to the Moonies' attempts to recruit them are perfectly capable of refusing to join. Her book, *The Making of a Moonie*, is generally accepted to be a unique, objective study of a new religion, but caused a complete break with the outraged anti-cult movement.

Nevertheless, Japanese drive and business methods seemed to work and each year membership doubled until, in 1971, the California group had a budget of $250,000.

Under Mr Choi the original family was growing up and becoming a fully fledged organisation. During this period, too, the Church's political attitudes became better known, with the formation of the Freedom Leadership Foundation to spearhead the attack on Communism.

The Rev. Moon made his third world tour at the end of 1971. His first public speeches in the West launched a three-year period of intense evangelisation, during which he was to be heard at massive rallies and achieve international fame. This drive for new recruits was matched by an equally hard-hitting drive for funds. Until then money had been raised largely by tithing Moonie businesses, or from individual donation. Large sums were sent from Japan, where 120 sales teams worked all round the clock, and it was from this source that the capital was raised to begin purchasing property in the States.

In 1972 the Maryland community began a candle business and soon factories were set up in a number of centres, with 'express candle vans' bussing supplies from place to place. There were still only about 30 members involved in this work, but by 1973 they were each averaging individual sales of about $1,000 weekly. Doorstep sales of candles, dried flowers and peanuts became an exhausting way of life for new recruits. The roller coaster was on its way.

The Rev. Moon preached that the Advent would take place in America — upon whom he began to place joint responsibility for world salvation with Korea. On New Year's Day 1972, he announced that God had directed him to make America his home. That year the Church purchased East Garden in Tarrytown, New York State for $625,000. This is where he lives today (he has a home in Korea too).

In October 1973 he spoke through an interpreter, at the Lisner Auditorium, Washington, DC.

America's existence was according to God's Providence, he said. God needed to build one powerful Christian nation on earth for his future work. After all, America belonged to God first and only after that to the Indians. This is the only interpretation that can justify the position of the Pilgrim settlers . . .

'During the Independence battles of 1776 I am sure George Washington prayed like this: "God, it is you who led your people out of Europe . . . you don't want us to repeat the dull gray history of Europe . . . I will build one nation under God" . . .

'The time has come for the American people to be awakened . . . God is leaving America . . . God is leaving America's homes. God is leaving your churches, God is leaving your schools. Unless this nation lives up to the mission ordained by God many troubles will plague you . . .

'The future of the entire world hinges on America. God has a very great stake in America. Somebody must come to America and stop God from leaving.

'I know that God sent me here to America. I do not come for the luxurious life. My followers in Korea bade me farewell in tears. But working only in Korea would delay world salvation. America must be God's champion. Even under persecution somebody must begin. Someone must bring God back home. The fate of the entire world hinges on America. God has a very great stake in America.'

In 1978 the One World Crusade (which Moon had launched in 1973 to create the True Family of Man) brought 800 missionaries to Britain and community houses were set up all over the country.

LIFE AMONG THE MOONIES

Who is seduced by the Unification Church? It is predominantly a middle-class movement, whose message appears to attract young, articulate people, mostly men, between the ages of 18 and 28, to become full-time members. Home church (residential) members are somewhat older, and include more women and ready-made families.

The possible new recruit's first encounter with the Moonies begins, usually, with an invitation to an informal 'family' meal and conversation in one of the centres, which range from the sparse and tatty to the positively palatial. For some people this is as far as it goes. They may return, study the *Divine Principle* for themselves and make up their own minds about whether to join or not. A great many do not. The voluntary defection rate is very high. Eileen Barker says: 'From a usually very reliable source I heard that about 30,000 people had joined and left the Unification Church in America during the seventies.' She believes that UK membership has probably never been more than 600.

Many first-time visitors are families — some of whom may be won over, others not. Parents have been brought in by the enthusiasm of their offspring and vice versa.

There is, however, much pressure to go on a weekend workshop (cost £16, a seven-day workshop costs £40; a 21-day seminar is £120) as this, they believe, ensures it is no longer possible for the movement to be accused of winning recruits under false pretences. A new Moonie will have been thoroughly coached in his religion before joining, even though he may not be fully aware of every ramification of his Church's world-wide activities.

Originally, in Korea, all members remained at home with their own families, and the habit was carried across from Japan to America and then to Britain. Today, members are able to choose whichever option they prefer. In Britain fewer will remain in a 'Family' community; the tendency now is for members to carry on living and working where they are.

RETREATS

Some of the Moonie residential properties where retreats are held are interesting houses, in beautiful settings.

Livingstone House, built for David Livingstone of African jungle fame, is set in the wooded commuterland of Chislehurst, Kent. Its Gothic individuality and spacious accommodation make it an ideal retreat. Pictures of Moonie heroes are hung above the stairs: Wordsworth, Field Marshal Viscount Montgomery, Earl Mountbatten, Bede and St Cuthbert are there with Rev. Moon. There is a talking parrot in the dining room. The dormitories are spotless, the food cooked with care, on a rota basis, by existing members. Moonies are non-vegetarian and do not forbid drink, with discretion.

For those whose school days are well behind, or who are unused to intensive study, the introductory course alone is a blockbuster. Long lectures, and even longer films, lead to brainache, rather than brainwashing. There is time for recreation, croquet on the lawn, music, but bedtime is late. Members themselves rise for a devotional service at 5 a.m. Always, there is someone ready and willing to talk, to discuss and answer questions. It is all very friendly. The weekend workshop is followed by an in-depth week's seminar, leading to a three-week course, by which time recruits are actively participating in housework and play. At the end of it all, a high proportion still drop out.

Camp Aetna, USA

The unbelievably evil smell of skunk marks the wildly beautiful goldrush road from San Francisco. The Moonie bus deposits its passengers in the undulating Wild Horse Valley, somewhere in Napa County. The log cabin complex is a peaceful bolt hole for members of all ages and all colours. The Church's surrounding golf course (the oldest west of Mississippi) is a popular venue for hundreds of outsiders, who mingle with Moonies in the bar and bask in the natural hot springs. Ronald Reagan came here for an Inauguration celebration.

Camp Aetna, rather like the more infamous 'Camp K', was the centre of seventies' controversies. In the heady, love-bombing superficiality of California much friendly pressure was brought to bear on bewildered recruits. Many had come from abroad, leaving distraught families with no idea where they were. Inaccessible, extremely quiet, it must, sometimes, have felt like a prison from which escape was difficult.

Members themselves agree: California was like nowhere else in Moonieland, with much more emphasis on the community itself than on the Bible or the message. But the 'gung-ho' days of heavy recruitment are mostly over, and life in the 300 or so houses of the Bay area is less frenetic, more involved with the outside world. There are 200 Moonie children there today, some of whom attend the nursery school. Witnessing is rarer. Converts, they hope, will be attracted more by example and so they have moved into an era of fairly successful co-operation with any scientists, politicians, clergy, welfare workers, cultural organisations and so on, who are unafraid of being seen side by side with a Moonie.

ADMINISTRATION

The World Unification Church *is* the Rev. Moon. It is a pyramid structure, over which he has almost complete authority. His second tier is a Board of Trustees, who are mostly Korean, living in the United States. Each country has its own President. Beneath them is the vast network of departments which carries out the day-to-day work of the Church. Three men mastermind the organisations and projects, created to infuse the world with Moonie ideals.

The question of succession has not yet been resolved, or even discussed, though it is assumed by many members that one of 'Father's' children will follow him.

KAYE THE MOONIE

Kaye was 27 and a promising young lawyer in New Zealand: 'In fact, I was the first female attorney in the country. But I was thoroughly fed up with all the divorces. So I took a holiday and went off to California and there I met the Moonies. I went to the notorious Camp K for a weekend and I was impressed. I moved on to Canada but something made me want to go back and this time I decided to stay.

'My parents really were dreadfully upset, they hadn't even thought I was religious. I was one of eight children and it was a disgrace to the entire family that I was throwing away my career. I felt my commitment to God was far more important. Mum and Dad came out to see me and they knew I was really happy but it was hard for them.

'Next time I met my brother and sister they were actually scared of me; they had read all kinds of things about the food we eat, and thought that if they looked at me directly I would bring them under my spell. I gave them material to read and they were better able to understand. Although they would far rather I was living at home they see I am trying to live a certain standard of life, committed to certain moral principles and that my friends are good, sincere members of the community.

'If I had stayed in New Zealand I doubt if I would have ever married, I was far too career orientated. Now I have a husband and children. We are happy and although we are very different, we are learning from each other. There is just as much chance of success in working on a marriage that has been arranged, as there is with one that is relying on physical attraction.

'We feel it is our responsibility to work at the partnership, blessed by Father. Physical, emotional love may follow, but it is a distraction in the establishing of world harmony and the greater good. We all think of the long-term future of the world and this partnership is our contribution to that.'

THE MOONIE GRANNY

Sometimes the enthusiasm of the children of the cults attracts their parents' curiosity. So it was with Ruth, from San Francisco, who is now a dedicated Moonie in her sixties. Her daughter, Isabel, was well on the way to being an atheist and, as a good Presbyterian herself, Ruth had been praying for her return to the fold.

'Then I heard that she was getting up to pray at 5 a.m. and was quitting University. I thought "oh my God"; life had been quite serene and then suddenly this bombshell. I joined Isabel on a Moonie, two-day workshop, to see what it was all about, and when I read the *Divine Principle* I couldn't challenge it. This was Truth for me and it has been one of the best things in my life.

'My husband and I were already in the throes of parting and so we split up, and I joined the church. Isabel was married to a member from Anchorage, Alaska in 1982 and they have two children, I am living with my son in San Francisco. He isn't a Moonie, he is a lawyer and it just didn't hit him, but we get on well and there is no problem that our religion is different.'

THE FLIP SIDE

The portfolio expounding the case against the Unification Church is many inches thick. On a personal level there have been several spectacular kidnapping charges brought to court in the United States, and a number of books written by former Moonies who have 'escaped'. It is not hard to find examples of ordeal by Moonie: the mother who sat weeping whilst she tried to find her daughter's face in a photograph of 600 brides; a brother whose twin deserted him; parents who were left with a Moon grand-daughter whilst her parents went abroad on a mission; the family whose ancestral home was sold to raise money for the Church.

There were visa problems for the many Church members who went to America in the seventies. This was the time when, not surprisingly, the parents of such illegal immigrants often had problems finding their children. Kaye Allen admits: 'In those days there was at least one kidnapping *from* the Moonies a week . . . over 300 in a year, and so members felt justified in hiding their friends in this way. Sometimes they changed their names.'

In 1977, after an FBI investigation, the US Department of Justice had found 'no information' warranting legal action or further action, into charges of brainwashing, involuntary servitude or kidnapping by the Unification Church. On the other hand, in Britain Moonies lost their famous six-month libel battle with the *Daily Mail* in 1981. It was, at that time, the longest, costliest libel action in British legal history. The High Court decided to uphold allegations in the newspaper that the Church broke up families and brainwashed young people and awarded damages of £750,000 plus costs.

In the USA there have been investigations into political corruption, tax evasion and fraud. There have also been regular appeals to Governments and to the European Parliament to be more watchful of alleged Moonie abuse of civil and religious liberties. There have been frequent articles in the press about what is believed to be a dangerous undercurrent: the possible Japanese hold on the Moonies because of their financial input.

The anti-Communist underbelly of the Church had been given a new lease of life by Miss Kim, when she formed the Freedom Leadership Foundation in 1969 to strengthen links with Korea and Japan. This led to a telegram of support from President Nixon, with whom the Rev. Moon had previously had breakfast. It also led to investigations by a Committee of the United States House of Representatives and publication of the mammoth Fraser Report.

This alleged that the Rev. Moon intended to make Korean President Park dependent on him. To this end, it was claimed large sums of Government money had been brought into America, illegally, from Korea and Japan to help the political lobbying against Communism and on behalf of President Nixon. Rev. Moon, it said, was deeply involved in preventing Nixon's impeachment. Unification Church members were at this time (1974) said to be infiltrating Congress. There certainly was a great deal of political action.

The Fraser Committee, however, retracted its main allegations later and admitted: 'despite its previous assertions to the contrary, the sub-committee had to concede that the Unification Church is not an agent of influence in the Korean Government.'

Rumours also flourished that the Moonies were involved in the sinister manufacture of arms. It is true that Rev. Moon owed the Tongil Manufacturing Company in Korea. It is true they made gun parts. It is also true, but rarely stated, that the Korean Government had insisted that all industrial concerns should turn over a small proportion of their output to the increasing national need for guns. But mud sticks, and these stories have never entirely gone away, despite the retraction of the Fraser Report.

An article in the *Washington Times'* rival — the *Washington Post* — led to some further claims in the 1987 autumn issue of the *Japan Asia Quarterly Review*. The writer, Narusawa Munco, quotes the *Post* and says: 'The Japanese branch of the Rev. Moon Sun Myung's Unification Church has transferred, at least, eight hundred million dollars, over the past nine years, to finance the Church's political activities and business operations . . .' He also described an investigation by the Japan Federation of Bar Associations into what is known as the 'Spiritual Sell' scheme.

Unification Church members are alleged to visit unsuspecting families and persuade them to protect themselves and their ancestors with the purchase of holy paraphernalia. These goods, such as model pagodas and vases costing anything up to several million yen, are made at a stoneworks enterprise owned by the Church in Korea. They are imported by Happy World in Tokyo which is run by Church officials. '90 per cent of the capital of the US Unification Church and 80 per cent of the Korean Church, its true headquarters, comes from Japan,' he quotes. The charge is that some of this money is used to support the Nicaraguan Contras.

On 22 February 1988, after a four year investigation, the British Attorney General made his controversial decision not to proceed with his case to strip the Unification Church of charitable status.

He had alleged, amongst other things, that: (1) It is political since its doctrines say it should fight and overcome Communism; (2) It contains secret teachings; (3) There is a deceptive, fraudulent claim to Christian nature; (4) The doctrines lead those who accept them to a belief that it is desirable to amass wealth for the UC.

In Parliament, MP for Bolton West, Tom Sackville, said: 'It's time we stopped giving charitable status to such vile organisations.'

The decision was celebrated by the leaders of many mainstream Churches and the Rev. Clinton Bennett, of the British Council of Churches, spoke at a cele-bration in Lancaster Gate, London: 'If a case had existed, with four years to prepare, the Attorney General with all of his resources would not have hesitated to proceed to trial. He didn't. No case to answer.'

MOONIE MAN

Robert is a lecturer in academic psychology at a London college. He is also a craft baker and for seven years was an active, happy member of the Unification Church. 'Spiritually, the beliefs never burned inside me, but I suppose I was look-ing for God through the manifestation of those beliefs in other people. And I met some really nice people.

'I was studying medicine at Cardiff University when I met a girl from the Moonies. I went to stay for a week on their farm near Reading and hundreds of people had also arrived from Europe because the Rev. Moon was coming. I was bowled over by the incredible atmosphere and Mrs Moon's Buddha-like serenity more than by Father himself.'

Robert left University because he wanted to be in on the excitement and trying to study at the same time was too much. 'I was falling asleep.' He went on board the Moonies' converted bus, known as 'Sampson', and with 13 other young men toured the country selling flowers, pot plants and preaching. 'We could make £100 a day.'

'We would set ourselves a "condition" in order to keep up the pace. It's a system of self-denial — if you are about to tackle a difficult task, such as fund-raising or even meeting your parents, you swing the spiritual balance to your side by undertaking an appropriate "condition" which means, perhaps, taking a cold shower every day for a week. It gives you an amazing spiritual boost.

'My parents did the best possible thing. After their initial shock they agreed "not to make life difficult" — and so, when eventually I did leave, it was easy to stay with them. I doubt if I would have had the courage to leave the security of the Church at all if I had only had a bed-sit to go to.

'I had a period in America and then came back to help in the accounts depart-ment at Lancaster Gate. The British leader then was a bully. This created a hier-archy of bullies. Since God works through Rev. Moon, he also works through Father's appointed leaders and if they scream and shout, they say they are expressing the wrath of God.

'There was a lot of politicking within the organisation. I tried to economise but was told God's representatives deserve the best. It was getting me down. We all make mistakes but when the people you believe represent God made mistakes it is very difficult!

'I was put in charge of a bakery in Sheffield and began my City and Guilds but my work was undermined by the boss. I went to Burnley and the same things happened. I knew what I was doing — both bakeries could have been successful but I wasn't allowed to use my skills. I tried to seek help from London but all I got was a rollicking. I thought "s-d this". I packed my bags, asked them to drive me to the station and I left. It was as simple as that.'

THE TRANSCENDENTAL MEDITATORS' TALE

The World Government of the Age of Enlightenment –
FOUNDED 1959

HEADQUARTERS: *Britain: Mentmore Towers, Mentmore, Leighton Buzzard, Bucks.*	

USA: 5000 14th Street, NW Washington, DC 20011

International: Seelisberg, Switzerland

ORIGIN: *Yoga/Vedanta*

STATUS: *In Britain: Registered Charity 270157*

STAR SUPPORTERS: *Clint Eastwood; Cher*

RESPONSE TO OUR APPROACHES: *Extremely unhappy at the prospect of being included at all. Complete rejection of the labels of religion, or 'cult'. Reluctant co-operation in the hope of counteracting misunderstanding. Appalled at the 'vicious' and unfounded attacks of evangelical Christianity.*

Transcendental Meditation is a science and has no religious creed. So, what are the truths which the Maharishi and his followers believe can turn the Age of Science into the Age of Enlightenment and create for mankind an ideal society?

WE BELIEVE

- The purpose of the Science of Creative Intelligence is to provide the theoretical and practical knowledge necessary to assist human consciousness to enjoy its full potential.

- Creative Intelligence is the impelling, non-changing, eternal life force which expresses itself in the evolutionary process, creating and ordering all forms and relationships in the universe.

- Its source is in the Unified Field, identified by physics and recognised by many scientists – the deepest level from which all laws of nature and matter are continuously promoted.

- The Unified Field is itself an integrated, harmonious state of perfect order and all possibilities.

- The human brain is so sophisticated that it is possible, through TM, for our consciousness to identify directly with this field.

- The power of the Unified Field is nourishing. Those who are trained in Sidhi techniques can stimulate its effectiveness in their own consciousness and, in groups, enliven its self-interacting dynamics.

- Human beings do not have to remain in ignorance.

- With the discovery of the Unified Field of all the laws of nature and the development of its technology, there is nothing that cannot be accomplished. Every nation now has the chance to create Heaven on Earth.

WHAT IS TM?

The red brick former mill town of Skelmersdale, Lancashire, had around 7,500 unemployed until, in 1987, a strange other worldly, saucer-shaped dome appeared, in the muddy wastelands outside the town. The Transcendental Meditators had arrived — not from outer space, but from all over Britain. They said they had come to build the Ideal Village, though exactly who they were and what they were really doing in their dome was, at first, a puzzle to local folk.

Transcendental Meditation is claimed to be the most natural, direct route towards physical health and spiritual well-being.

It was brought to America in 1959 by Maharishi Mahesh Yogi. From simple beginnings it proved to be the springboard for an international movement, which today administers an all-embracing network of academic, scientific and philosophical institutions based on a belief in the urgent need for a revived awareness of ancient Vedic knowledge. The first Centre in Russia has recently been opened in Moscow. Two major British companies are training their executives in TM as a management aid.

The sign at the magnificent entrance to Mentmore Towers, the British headquarters in the former Rothschild mansion, reads 'The World Government of the Age of Enlightenment'.

This is defined as a 'non-political, non-religious, global organisation, with the participation of the people of over 120 countries.'

The teachers of TM, world-wide, would like to be seen as wearing the acceptable white coat of a medical profession, rather than the mystical aura of Eastern religion. They are *not* preaching a religion, though their goal is spiritual. They are therapists and, they believe, like doctors, deserve recognition within society. What they teach is a technique, so natural you are hardly aware of what you are doing; nor do you need to understand the fundamental physics or the psychology, with which many non-TM scientists agree. Rather like sitting down to a meal, it is not necessary to know about proteins, vitamins and calories, to realise that you enjoy it and that it is doing you good.

The Maharishi's wisdom, which they would like to share, is beneficial to everyone — Jew, Catholic, Mormon, Moonie and atheist alike. It does not require conversion. Nor, say the advertisements in the national papers, do you need to be clever, or rich.

Advertisement is the only method of recruitment and none of the other 'cultic qualities' defined by the cultwatchers can fairly be attributed to TM.

Suspicion seems largely based on a Christian fear that Transcendentalists are a front for creeping Hinduism.

About 150,000 people practise TM in Britain and some four million world-wide. Captains of industry, judges, cabinet ministers are known to meditate. You can, it is true, take TM at this level and stop there, continuing in the privacy of your own home and weaving what you have learned into the handling of daily life. There is no obligation to spend more than the initial £145. However, you can go on, as many do, to dig deeper and to make it a way of life. In this case, it probably does help to be reasonably well-off and intelligently alert, for courses are not cheap and are intellectually stimulating and demanding.

Since TM offers the direct line of communication between mankind and awareness of the eternal peace and harmony at the source of all being, there is no aspect of life which is not embraced and will not benefit.

Western science, so they say, is objective but is only a part of all knowledge. Vedic science is subjective and objective and is the totality of the process of gaining knowledge. It begins with experience; to gain knowledge you must develop consciousness.

You may progress to learn of the Maharishi's Science of Creative Intelligence, the most advanced level of which is the TM-Sidhi Programme. (Sidhi is an adaptation of the Sanskrit word 'sihdi', meaning supernatural.) You may, so they say, learn to fly.

And so it came to pass . . . that about 300 professional people, of all religions and all ages, sold their homes all over Britain and moved, with 100 children, to Skelmersdale. They came, fired with enthusiasm to play their part, collectively, in the Maharishi's breathtakingly optimistic plan for the creation of Heaven on Earth. Each financially independent, but pooling their expertise and donating a great deal of their time, they worked under the benevolent umbrella of the Ideal Village Association, run by an elected committee.

Spacious, up-market houses were built and landscaped. A picturesque but run-down period farmhouse was converted into a school for their meditating children. The nearby empty Courtauld's factory was purchased and then leased to some 40 compatible, small businesses, employing a mix of local and TM labour. Unemployment dropped.

At the centre of their community they constructed the wood-lined Golden Dome, in which to meditate together for half an hour, every day, before work and again in the evening. 'We have rediscovered the profound value of silence within our own consciousness, and from this deep level of rest our lives have become more vital, dynamic and focused.'

A queer lot to be jostling shoulders with the gritty, no nonsense northern neighbours! Besides, rumour had it that these smart executive types were, literally, flying by night.

Yogic flying is, in fact, fundamental to the advanced stage of the TM-Sidhi Programme, which had brought the villagers to Lancashire. Bouncing, ball-like, from the base of the spine in a cross-legged sitting position, looks impossible. Peter Pan and Wendy certainly made flying easier! But experts can apparently rise several feet in the air and the moment of levitation is said to be the moment of maximum mind-body co-ordination and spiritual awareness.

The imagination and scepticism of the national press had already had a field day in 1986 at the first National Yogic Flying Championships in London, with such headlines as 'Bouncing Back to Happiness', 'Uplifting' and 'World Peace gets off to a Flying Start'.

Even so, when the Ideal Village Golden Dome was finally inaugurated in 1988, the ceremony was attended not only by 1,000 visitors from all over the world but also by many feet-on-the-ground, local dignitaries, and the then MP for South Lancashire and the Chairman of West Lancashire County Council. Their new neighbours' energetic combination of economic acumen and ideological enthusiasm was much admired and their friendly input to local life greatly appreciated.

The County Council Chairman spoke with sincerity of 'the great quality of contribution your movement is making, and will continue to make, to the quality of life, here in West Lancashire'.

If all goes well, as it has so far — there is a waiting list for houses in the Ideal Village — its residents are confident that that contribution will not be confined to Skelmersdale.

They believe that once the square root of 1 per cent of any population is practising the TM-Sidhi Programme in a group, its accumulative benign influence will ripple outwards and affect the whole. It takes 100 to reach a million. So, once Skelmersdale has attracted 3,000 meditators, they will be able to improve positivism and happiness throughout Europe. Crime, accidents and sickness will decrease.

This is known as the Maharishi Effect and has, they say, already been proved to work, in the parts of the world where the TM-Sidhi Programme has been tried, or where other Ideal Villages have been built.

At the Global Inauguration of the Maharishi's Programme to Create World Peace in 1987 it was claimed:

- 'Between 1972-3, eleven United States Cities with more than 1% of the population practising TM, were compared with 11 control cities, matched for size and geographic region. An 8.2% drop in crime was found in the TM cities, and an 8.3% increase in the controls.'

- 'In 1984 three researchers analysed the effects of TM in the Lebanese community of Baskinta, where more than 1% of the population were meditating. They examined the amount of shelling and damage in Baskinta and neighbouring communities between October-June 1972 and a control period. There were decreases of violence and damage in Baskinta. When the meditating group in Jerusalem was large enough, war deaths in Lebanon dropped by 75%.'

- 'TM-sidhas also led the United States economic recovery in 1982-3. 80% of the increase in the bull market occurred in the week following a marked rise in the number of TM-sidhas in the Maharishi University Golden Domes.'

The Maharishi's goal, of a permanent group of 7,000 meditators in India is enough, he says, to ensure perpetual world peace.

The Maharishi's TM-Ayurveda health programme is practised in health centres in

many parts of the world. The emphasis is on the prevention of illness and maintaining the body's natural balance. It is entirely in tune with the West's growing
awareness of the sense of a gentler, holistic approach to health. Treatment
programmes include rejuvenation therapies, herbal foods, diet and, of course,
meditation.

The programme has been tested in many objective medical establishments
and by many countries.

The Swedish Government recorded a far lower proportion of TM practitioners
entering mental hospitals – one out of 350 compared with one in 20 of the
general population.

After a five-year study, using data from 600,000 clients of a major American
insurance company, for example, a group of 2,000 TM practitioners had:

44% fewer visits to hospital

53% fewer admissions to hospitals

70% fewer days in hospital

55% lower incidence of tumours

87% lower incidence of heart disease

30% lower incidence of infectious disease

87% lower incidence of nervous disease

In Holland, the largest health insurance company (Het Zilveren Krus) with
750,000 members, offers a 30 per cent premium reduction to anyone practising
TM, the largest reduction to any other group being 15 per cent. In Japan,
similarly, the health insurance union of Sumitomo Heavy Industries (50,000
employees) sponsors TM in seven of its nine divisions.

WHERE DID IT ALL BEGIN?

When an Indian becomes a monk it is the custom to forget his past – so the
leaders of TM prefer not to labour on the early life of their founder.

Maharishi Mahesh Yogi was born Mehesh Prasad Varma in about 1911 in
Jabalpur, Madyar Pradesh, India. Little is known about his early years. He gradu-
ated from Allahabad University with a degree in Physics in 1940, but renounced a
scientific career to study with Guru Dev at Joytir Monastery and remained there
until the Guru's death in 1953.

In 1958 Maharishi announced his intention to take Guru Dev's teachings on
meditation to the world and to launch a spiritual regeneration movement. He
founded the International Meditation Society, journeyed to the United States and
to London and then returned to India, where he concentrated on training
teachers.

At about the same time that Bhagwan Shree Rajneesh was conducting his own form of Tantric meditation camps, Maharishi was touring and lecturing at Universities around the world. There was an increasing but fairly low key interest in what this tiny bearded guru, with a flower always in hand, had to say.

And then came the Beatles. 'The Beatles will always be with us' they say with resignation today. In fact, when Paul McCartney asked not long ago if he could help in any way, Maharishi advised him to help by not helping!

In January 1968 the Beatles, together with Mia Farrow the actress, made a pilgrimage to the Maharishi's centre in Rishikikesh and TM became headline news. The Rolling Stones followed and flower-power, which was already disillusioned and wilting, found a new purpose. TM was reputed to be the antidote to drugs.

It has been alleged that the fees which were paid to Maharishi by his fabulously wealthy young followers were sufficient to launch his crusade in style. 'The Beatles did not give us any money,' say today's leaders.

By the end of the decade, about one million people had enrolled on Maharishi's basic course. His face became familiar in newspapers and on television the world over. His chuckle earned him the title The Giggling Guru.

HOMES OF PURE KNOWLEDGE

Mentmore Towers is a palace of monumental grandeur, set in 80 acres.

Built in 1855 for Baron Meyer Amschel de Rothschild, it is the only remaining example of the domestic architectural genius of Sir Joseph Paxton (of Crystal Palace fame). The ghosts of Disraeli, Gladstone, Napoleon III, Czar Nicholas and Winston Churchill are but a few whose memory lingers in the Sicilian marble halls and along the pink alabaster balconies. The black marble fireplace in the glass-roofed Grand Hall is by Rubens, the gilded boiseries, lining the dining room, were brought from the Hôtel de Villars in Paris. The two ton plate glass doors were brought on a horse and cart from France. It contains the first lift in England and the first hot water and central heating system — all still working.

The entire crumbling pile was wanted by no one, certainly not by the Labour Government of the day, and was auctioned at Sotheby's spectacular Sale of the Century, in 1978, for just £230,000. The contents were sold, to the public, for an additional £6.8 million. The new owners — with dreams as grand as the building that is now their British headquarters — were The World Government of the Age of Enlightenment.

From time to time, some of the former splendour is recreated, when statesmen, scientists, scholars and academics from all over the world gather for conférences and banquets. They come to hear of progress being made by researchers at the University of Natural Law, established at Mentmore in 1982. Its laboratories contain sophisticated equipment for the study of neurophysiology, psychology and biochemistry.

This extraordinary house, which once required 100 servants to maintain its lavish, extravagant life style, is now the home of Pure Knowledge, cared for by some 30 young sidhas, in retreat. They are full-time students of TM at its most advanced, who are there to develop consciousness, without distractions. It is monastic, in an academic rather than a religious sense, and they are not paid by the organisation.

TM students come here, as they do to other residential centres, for weekend courses or longer. They are taught to think at a subtler, deeper level, to relax, to get rid of deep rooted fatigue and gradually they experience a slowing of the metabolic rate.

Mentmore Towers is open to the public — there are guided tours, slide shows, a gift shop and tea rooms — and tickets are also available, when appropriate, for the banquets.

Though Mentmore Towers is unique in Britain it is only one part of the TM empire which has acquired an impressive variety of buildings from which to orchestrate its programmes, such as the European headquarters in a beautiful former hotel in Seelisberg, Switzerland and the Maharishi International University at Fairfield, Iowa set in 40 acres.

THE GLOBAL UNDERTAKING

The World Plan Executive Council operates from Seelisberg.

World headquarters is at Maharishi Nagar, in India.

The International Meditation Society has the task of introducing TM to the general public.

The Spiritual Regeneration Movement concentrates on the over-thirties. The Student International Meditation Society works within the campus, and the Foundation for the Science of Creative Intelligence is in charge of promoting TM within the business community.

There are some 360 World Plan Centres: 300 in the United States and 60 in Britain.

The World Government of the Age of Enlightenment invites 'the whole world to enjoy the perpetual sunshine of the Age of Enlightenment'.

Head of the World Government is Maharishi himself, who insists that his role is not to overthrow, or supersede, the work of others but to act as an adviser.

There is a Supreme Chief Minister in charge of ten ministries, each with its own Chief Minister. These are: the Ministry for the Development of Conscious-ness; the Ministry of Natural Law and Order; the Ministry of Cultural Integrity; the Ministry of Education and Enlightenment; the Ministry of Celebrations and Fulfil-ment; the Ministry of Prosperity and Progress; the Ministry of Information and Inspiration; the Ministry of All Possibilities; the Ministry for the Capitals of the Age of Enlightenment; the Ministry of Health and Immortality. This structure applies to each of the countries where the Government has been established.

The ministers are not paid.

The Constitution of the Government is based on the unfolding of knowledge in the Rig Veda, ancient Hindu scriptures.

Transcendental Meditation is one of those philosophies which has become successful enough to support the Foundation of a University — also in Fairfield, Iowa. Its courses are a natural progression from those taught in the Maharishi schools.

'There are two sides to knowledge . . . that which we seek to know, and the knower. When the knower is ignorant about himself the whole structure of knowledge is as if baseless.

'Unified Field based education enlivens the common basis of the knower and the known . . . students grow in awareness that all streams of knowledge are but modes of their own intelligence. They come to feel at home with everyone and everything. Their creative genius blossoms with increasing confidence and self-sufficiency. They cease to violate natural law and enjoy the fruit of all knowledge — the ability to accomplish anything and, spontaneously, to think and act, free from mistakes.'

THE IDEAL VILLAGE CHILDREN

The 100 or so children from the Ideal Village, Skelmersdale, go to school, daily, in a pretty converted farmhouse and barn. It is a calm and orderly place. Parents have been moving to Lancashire from all over Britain to give their offspring the opportunity of a Maharishi-based education.

The British school is based on the American School of the Age of Enlightenment, in Fairfield, Iowa. This was founded in 1973 and has been granted the rare accolade of college status, because of its high academic standards.

The Maharishi-based system provides an underlying framework to life, in which all subjects are referred back, with relevance, to the individual and are integrated with each other so that they have a visible meaning. The children become aware that all subjects are an expression of their own experience. They learn that life is in layers and that the whole is the sum of its parts. Beginning with birth, for instance, pupils learn about growth — the first principle. How they grow . . . how their hair grows . . . how nature grows . . . always in harmony.

This is the Maharishi's Principle of Unified Field Education. Every day begins with meditation, which the children learn to do without effort — no closed eyes — or artificial postures. The aim is 'restful alertness'. On to this foundation is grafted a high-achieving, academic curriculum.

In three years, the Skelmersdale school has grown from 18 to 100 or so children. There are three departments, ranging from nursery to sixth form, and all staff are fully qualified, as well as being trained in Maharishi's Technology. The school has been recognised by the Ministry of Education and is a registered educational charity and a company limited by guarantee.

Fees are £200 a term in the lower school, £400 in the upper school, and the necessary income is found through fundraising and by covenants, some from local businesses.

The Maharishi's school is a community project, with an unusually active level of parental involvement.

There is a Council, elected by members of the Ideal Village Community, but which also contains key outsiders from the locality, with which there is a good relationship.

Parents, who are, of course, converted to the concept of the Unified Field, seem delighted with the enthusiastic, orderly and creative changes in their off-spring since starting at the school. Teachers say that they are a joy to teach. 'It's like being a midwife . . . you see them blossom before your eyes.'

THE FLIP SIDE

The controversy around TM has centred on its medical claims. Critics say that it is no more effective than many other forms of meditation. They are cynical too about what is seen as Maharishi's opportunistic change of label for TM from a religion to a science. This is a front, they say, for a Hindu-based religion, which is steeped in secret ritual, and a commercial enterprise with grandiose plans to take over the world. They say that TM provides the Maharishi with a self-gratifying ego-trip.

To prove the point several of the anti-cult organisations have reproduced copies of the TM instructor's initiation ceremony, or puja. This is a three stage ceremonial. The first stage consists of a recitation of the names of those beings in legend and history who are believed to represent the line of apostolic succession through which the holy knowledge of TM mantras has been passed; the second stage concerns the offering of flowers and fruit; the third is a hymn of praise to Guru Dev who is identified with the three major Hindu deities — Brahma, Vishnu and Shiva. When the ceremony is complete the initiate is then able to receive his mantra and is allowed to meditate.

(The organisation denies that this ceremonial involves any religious belief, or any belief at all. Nor, they say, is the TM practitioner involved; he is merely a witness. Its sole purpose is to create a suitable frame of mind for an important event.)

There is scepticism, too, about TM's sweeping scientific and health claims and some anger that the techniques are used in so many state educational establishments.

LYN'S MEDITATION

'My first experience of TM was very good. I had suffered from depression and had been having counselling to help me. My counsellor practised TM and she suggested that I should try it, too. She was very calm and understanding and I was impressed so I thought I had nothing to lose. I went along for a preliminary interview and filled in a questionnaire before going for a training session. I committed myself to several nights and at first it was as if all my worries and cares were lifted. I felt lighter, expanded and was seeing deeper into myself.

'But then I began to experience the sensation of tunnelling — being pulled backward very fast — and unfortunately I was interrupted, bang, in the middle. This left me with a dreadful headache. Next day I was really agitated and didn't know what to do with myself. I couldn't keep still and I wanted to climb up the walls. It was really awful. But even so I went along to the class again. I didn't say anything, though it was obvious there was something wrong. Afterwards my tutor talked to me and suggested I cut the meditation period to five minutes, instead of twenty. I did this and I began to feel wonderful again and gradually built up the time. But ten minutes was the maximum I could do without getting a head-ache.

'These headaches were caused by all the stuff coming up from my sub-conscious — it was like a black force pressing on my head. Then my teacher left; I needed his support to see me through so I stopped going. I think that perhaps I just wasn't ready and that the ground needs to be thoroughly prepared before anyone in a weak psychological state embarks on TM.'

BARBARA'S MEDITATION

Barbara was a nurse, a single parent with two lively sons aged eleven and twelve, when she first heard of TM on the radio.

'I was tired, anxious, uptight and spiritually starved,' she recalls, 'despite all attempts at going to Church and trying alternative religions.

'I really took it up as an alternative to tranquillisers. My health improved almost immediately and over the next few months I became less irritable, calmer and more peaceful, more in tune with nature. It was like water in an oasis.

'I began to investigate the proven scientific research and was very impressed with the results.

'Being a nurse I was passionate about the suffering of some of my patients and was also watching my colleagues bending under the strain of their job.

'I made a nuisance of myself telling them about TM — I stuck it under their coffee cups. Quite a lot did take it up and at one time there were nine of us in our practice meditating. My sons started too and so did my mother — she had angina, yet today she is 95 and very fit.

'Right through those years, in retrospect, I was developing a deeper sense of peace within myself and being spiritually enriched. It grew so subtly that one couldn't jump up and down with delight — there was just a slow development of stability within myself and a closeness with nature.

'I became more and more sure that medical intervention was not the path to health. My goal was always prevention so I brought up TM when appropriate and found that it helped. I was specialising in cancer care at this time and a lot of my patients took it up — they knew it could not provide a cure but it eased the pain and brought peace of mind.'

THE HARE KRISHNA TALE

The International Society for Krishna Consciousness –
FOUNDED 1965

HEADQUARTERS: *Britain: Bhaktivedanta Manor, Letchmore Heath, Herts. WD2 8EP*

USA: 1030 Grand Avenue, Pacific Beach, San Diego, CA 92109

ORIGIN: *Hinduism*

STATUS: *In Britain: Registered Charity 259649*

STAR SUPPORTERS: *Hayley Mills; George Harrison*

RESPONSE TO OUR APPROACHES: *Open, anxious to hear criticisms and demonstrate adaptability. Organisationally and individually hospitable.*

KRISHNA BELIEF

We believe:

- Krishna is the eternal, all powerful, all knowing, all attractive, seed-giving father of all living things and He is the sustaining energy of the entire cosmic creation.

- From time to time He manifests Himself in an understandable form, such as Buddha. Chaitanya Mahaprabhu (1486-1534), learned teacher and saint, was the most recent incarnation of Krishna.

- He was the founder of the Hindu line of tradition, or sampradaya, known as Krishna Consciousness, which seeks to reawaken the relationship of the individual soul to a personal god, Krishna, through the chanting of his name.

- Krishna Consciousness is a monotheistic religion which is not exclusive; others such as Christianity are on the same course. There are details, due to climate, culture and people which are different, but the principle is the same – God, or His representatives, come to reclaim conditioned souls. Krishna Consciousness is a part of Hinduism with reflecting aspects of all religions.

- The Absolute Truth is contained in all the world's great scriptures. But that which provides the key to the process of consciousness is the most ancient of all, the Vedic Hindu literature of 3000BC, especially the book of knowledge, the Bhagavad Gita, which is the literal record of Krishna's words.

- Vedic knowledge should be learned from a spiritual master whose motives are pure and whose mind is concentrated on Krishna.

- The way we choose to live this life will determine our fate in the next.

- Reincarnation. Our real self is the soul which inhabits the body and gives it life. This soul is eternal, a fragment of Krishna and after life will transmigrate, experiencing life again and again until it returns to join Him in the spiritual realm.

- To think of the body as the true self is 'maya' or illusion. It is just a vehicle for the soul. It is neither good, nor bad, it is how we use it that is important.

- That devotional service must be a part of everyday life. Every act should be performed with Krishna in mind – chanting, offering up food, worship, gardening, sex.

- By cultivating a bona fide spirituality, we can be free from anxiety and come to a state of pure, unending blissful consciousness, in this lifetime.

King Birendra of Nepal has more than a passing interest in the pretty village of Letch-more Heath, Hertfordshire. His Majesty has never driven along the twisty English lanes approaching the village but, as the world's only Hindu monarch, he is sympathetic with the problems facing its most unlikely residents. Just past the health food shop, through the huge iron gates, the smell of wood smoke blends with the unfamiliar scent of incense, for the re-named Bhaktivedanta Manor is the British headquarters of the International Society for Krishna Consciousness — ISKCON, known better as the Hare Krishna movement.

Hertsmere Council says it has 'nothing against' the movement. But, at weekends, when the local Church congregation is wandering home for Sunday lunch, or calling in for a pint at the pub, some thousand or more vegetarian, Hindu visitors are arriving at the temple for alcohol-free Sunday devotions. On festival days that number is nearer 25,000. So the authorities have been persuaded that Hare Krishna must go. Since 1986, the tussle between ISKCON and the local authority has even reached Downing Street for, in a letter to Mrs Thatcher, the President of the National Council of Hindu Temples described Bhaktivedanta Manor as 'the most important Hindu shrine in Europe'.

Krishna Consciousness is generally respected by most Western Hindus as a legitimate, if austere, branch of their religion.

The worship of Krishna as the supreme godhead goes back several thousand years and is elaborately presented in the Vedic literature of ancient India. Hinduism is the modern term for a range of faiths which have their roots in Vedism. One of these is Vaisnavism (the worship of Vishnu Krishna and His incarnations.) There are, again, many forms of Vaisnavism and one of these is that established by Sri Chaitanya (1486–1534), who challenged the caste system, inspired the Bhakti (devotion) movement and brought the religion to the people by organising sankirtan (public congregational chanting of God's holy names). Vaisnavism is open to all; there is no distinction between an adherent by birth, or one by commitment.

The success of the post-war ISKCON has provided the Hindu population of many countries with additional temples, where worship is conducted to a very high standard, and much-loved festivals. In return, they have supported ISKCON financially since its beginnings in the sixties and respond to attacks as a threat to Hinduism.

Of all new movements, Hare Krishna is the most visible and up front.

To the passing public, in the streets of London, Bombay, New York or even way-out Amsterdam, the bright orange robes, the smiling, painted faces and shaven heads of the Hare Krishnas are, at first, a source of slight embarrassment. The haunting chant of 'Hare Krishna Hare Krishna Krishna Krishna Hare Hare Hare Rama Hare Rama Rama Rama Hare Hare' has a curiously anaesthetic effect, which devotees claim 'tames the wild horses of the mind'.

Critics are convinced that 'taming' is a euphemism for brainwashing, and that the sinister and repetitive power of the chant is a well-known Eastern technique for paralysing free will.

Yet, probably half Krishna converts are attracted by this first encounter and their restaurants around the world. These have become inexpensive, gastronomic havens, where lunch time lectures, with free food, entice students, office workers and travellers of all ages.

Of these, about 200,000 men and women have taken the dramatic decision to become devotees and so submit themselves to a physical life style, which is monastic in its self-denial and discipline, and an intellectual regime, which many find hard to understand. ISKCON has centres in at least 40 countries. There are probably about 5,000 community members living within the British temples; 10,000 belong to the broader congregation living outside. In America the number is about 30,000. There are even 10,000 devotees in Russia, where the religion has been recognised in Leningrad and Moscow and the first temple is being built.

There are some 400 temples world-wide. In Britain these are centres of priestly training. It is often different in the USA, since entrepreneurs have made some temples dependent on orthodox ways of making money. This has, undoubtedly, helped the movement's bank balance, but in Britain the public can't reconcile the making of money with religion and devotees themselves frown on such materialism. The British devotee is as different in personality from the average American devotee as Christian tele-evangelist Jimmy Swaggart is from the Archbishop of Canterbury.

Politically, ISKCON is committed to the Green Movement, to conservation and to the ideals of Mahatma Gandhi, including a programme of poor relief, 'Food for Life', which operates throughout the Third World.

Future plans are for progressive reform, but many social questions have not yet been tackled because devotees have been 'too busy surviving'!

In its devotion to a personally austere, frugal life style, its intellectual demands and its insistence on a spiritual dimension to daily life, ISKCON's relationship to ortho-dox Hinduism is somewhat akin to the relationship between Jesuits and the Roman Catholic Church. It is certainly not considered phoney.

The problem is that Westerners cannot easily accept that a white person can be a Hindu. For the random traveller on the underground or bus, anyone who needs to dress up in the gear of an alien culture must be a little odd to say the least! Indians, on the other hand, entrust even their most sacred rites of passage such as weddings and funerals to a white priest. Western Krishnas see the dhoti (robes), the sikha (pony tail) and the tilaka (painted faces) as an honest attempt to stand up and be counted.

These material trappings link devotees world-wide to a cultural tradition of great antiquity and spirituality. No undercover proselytising for them.

The Krishna way of life involves eating no meat, fish or eggs, drinking no alcohol, tea or coffee, taking no drugs, no gambling, having intercourse only for procreation. In addition devotees must chant 16 rounds on the japa beads daily, read for an hour from the many works of Prabhupada, their founder and, most important, practise devotional service.

There must be a period of at least a year before a devotee may be initiated and given a devotional name.

This is the first stage of full-time commitment and is a rite of passage which involves a serious bond between the initiate and his spiritual master. It cannot easily be broken. Celibate male devotees wear saffron, married men wear white; all women wear saris. Most of the married devotees live and work outside the temples, have mortgages and go to work in ordinary jobs. Celibate members tend to remain within the community.

It is not until several years later that men or women, celibate or married, can be considered for 'Brahmin' initiation to become priests. Only those who have undergone further training and shown themselves competent and dedicated are accepted and, after this stage, it is much more difficult to withdraw from the movement, just as the decision to renounce her convent would be traumatic for a nun.

The next stage, usually when families are grown up, is for some men to take sannyasi, a rite of renunciation, which means leaving wife and children. Only three British devotees have ever gone so far. In America, where life tends to be a little more volatile, there have been many more.

The standard Hindu perception of the psychology of a woman is that she needs protection by a man. If she is not protected her nature is such that negative qualities come through. On the whole she is happier in a subordinate position. However, men and women are equal spirits in different bodies.

There is a great deal of external pressure and internal debate about the need to re-examine the position of women within Hinduism and within Krishna. 'We shall have to adapt and change — to deal with the society we are in, which may need different perceptions. There are other ways in which we are quite progressive — there is no problem about a woman being a priest or a spiritual leader for instance.'

THE KRISHNA SCHOOL

The day before the end of term is a noisy time for any school and the Krishna Gurukula School at Bhaktivedanta Manor is no exception. The 40 boys and girls, between the ages of 5 and 15, may start their day at 4.30 a.m., six days a week. They may be growing up within a demanding moral and religious code, closely linked to a rigorous academic programme, but there is no shortage of laughing and chatter. The floors and desks are littered with colourful materials being skilfully used to make deities and models to celebrate Lord Krishna's birthday. Books are everywhere: *The Wind in the Willows*, classics, Krishna folk tales. They steer clear of too much fantasy and fairy tales. 'The basis of the religion is trying to think of Krishna and serve him 24 hours a day. If we divert their minds they can't really distinguish between what's real and what's not,' the teachers explain.

There is an increasing number of Krishna schools around the world, some more austere than others. In the early experimental days, children were sent abroad to the only school available in India but this caused great distress and the practice has been stopped.

At Bhaktivedanta, in their pink or blue check dresses, or saris, the girls are taught by five full-time staff, alongside the boys. Some board, others come in from home. The school is run by a Board of Education, with a steering committee which includes parents democratically guiding policy. It is recognised by the Ministry of Education.

They now have a programme leading to GCSE and also tackle typing and computer work as well as arts and crafts. Two-thirds of the fees are subsidised by ISKCON since most Krishna parents are not well off.

The aim of the school is to prepare children to work outside the community and to give them the confidence that they can tackle any job — Temple President or cab driver. There's a warm easy-going relationship between pupils and staff — plenty of reassurance and hugs when needed — though unmarried adults do not make physical contact with the opposite sex, even by shaking hands.

Some of the truths children are taught are: mercy, kindness to all, magnanimity, truthfulness, equality, charity, cleanliness, benevolence, poetry, humility, friendliness, competence, restraint (no unnecessary speaking or over indulgence), respect.

Those who attend the Gurukula School do feel a bit 'different'. They are never required to wear their saris or Indian dress when playing outside in the community, travelling on buses or at the shops. Even so, they lead a life style far removed from those of other children in their neighbourhood. As teenagers, they are as likely as any state school pupil to rebel against parental ideas and, like them, they tend to return later to the 'fold'.

ORGANISATION

The International Governing Body Commission set up by Prabhupada in 1972 meets annually in West Bengal. There are 29 members of the GBC to decide policies and standards. Twelve of these are initiating Gurus and are in charge of the spiritual work of the religion, each responsible for a different part of the world. The chairman and secretary are changed each year, by rota. Each member is responsible for a geographical area or a global concern such as agriculture. The centres all answer to their GBC member but each is autonomous and not financially dependent on any other.

This means that there is no world leader, or even a central voice — and so, no dangerous finger on the button, but it also means that individual zones are developing their own maverick character and what happens in one may not happen in another. There are women on the Temple Governing body in Ireland, and women have been given equal status there for some time.

The greater part of the movement's income is from covenants and donations, largely through the Hindu community; there seems to be no greater pressure to donate than there is in any Church where the organ needs restoration or the kneelers must be renewed. Initiation and its preparation are in themselves free.

HOW ISKCON BEGAN

After Chaitanya's death in 1534, Krishna Consciousness declined but was not forgotten. Over 400 years later, in Allahabad, a 69-year-old pharmaceutical sales-man retired. His name was Abhay Charan De, and after a lifetime's service to the Gaudiya Vaishnava Mission, where he had been initiated in Krishna Conscious-ness, he felt inspired to spread Chaitanya's message world-wide.

In the Hindu tradition, he was ready to move away from material things and concentrate on spiritual development, so he became a sannyasin. He was given the name of Caranavinda Bhaktivedanta Swami Prabhupada and in 1965 left his wife and home for New York with 40 rupees and a caseload of his published works.

In sophisticated New York, Prabhupada's appearance was odd, to say the least. His golden complexion and forehead decorated with the white clay stripe, cotton dhoti, pointed rubber shoes and chanting beads were fine for an Indian Vaishnava (Krishna follower) in Bombay but hardly the gear for Fifth Avenue. It was not until he melted into the more cosmopolitan Bowery District that he began to attract the attention of some serious young soul-searchers, many of whom had already been on the hippy trail to India. They felt a sense of nostalgic security with this elderly guru.

In July 1966, Prabhupada set up ISKCON and in September initiated his first disciples. Within a very short time, ISKCON was established in centres across the United States — but its greatest following was, at first, not surprisingly, amongst the open-minded young of the West Coast. To finance the new temple Prabhupada laid on a concert at which many famous rock stars played. A publish-ing company was set up and Prabhupada himself was, with phenomenal energy, translating and writing sacred Hindu works. He produced over 70 books in 12 years and was acclaimed India's 'greatest spiritual and physical ambassador'.

In 1968, three married American couples, Mukunda and Janaki, Syamasundara and Malati, Gurudasa and Yamuna arrived in Herne Hill, London to bring ISKCON to Britain. After a great deal of lobbying, they met George Harrison at the Apple Studios and were invited to lunch with the Beatles. Theirs was a fruitful friendship, as it had been for Maharishi.

A year later the devotees appeared, in all their Eastern glory, on 'Top of the Pops' in George Harrison's version of the Hare Krishna chant. On the first day that record sold 70,000 copies and reached the Top Twenty. George Harrison told Mukunda later: 'The idea was to spiritually infiltrate society . . . one of the greatest thrills of my life was to see you on "Top of the Pops". It's pretty hard to get on that programme. It was like a breath of fresh air.'

For the first seven years the movement grew fast. They developed a following of ordinary people who became their greatest asset, even though they were not 'paid up' members.

The Friends of Lord Krishna (Nama Hatta) were established to forge links between devotees and people of any religion interested in, but not necessarily members of, ISKCON. There are about 1,000 of these in Britain alone and a network of non-member support groups is being set up all around the country.

Bhaktivedanta Manor is the most important Hindu centre in Britain and is the only Hindu Theological College training priests in the Vedic tradition. Training is free, devotees are required instead to work their passage in the temple. Bhaktivedanta is a rambling, mock Jacobean house in 17 acres of well-loved and tended grounds; the cows in the meadow provide milk for the Indian sweets, offered to all guests, vegetables are grown for residents and the gardens and greenhouses keep the house and the temple self-sufficient in colour and perfume, all year round.

The Manor was given to the devotees, by George Harrison, in the heady days of 'My Sweet Lord'. With money largely donated by the Hindu community, a massive gilt altar was constructed in India and flown to Britain. Its size and sheer grandeur are reminiscent of Spanish cathedrals but the colourful gods, Their Lordships Shri Shri Radha-Gokulanada and Shri Shri Sita-Rama Laxman Hanuman, look considerably happier and less oppressive than many of Christianity's effigies. At one end sits the flower-bedecked, life-sized representation of His Divine Grace.

There is a lot of noise in the Temple . . . the rhythmic chanting of mantras, the Indian music, bells, babies, visitors from the local council chatting. Outside, children wheel on bikes and, on a Sunday, families picnic everywhere; inside the Manor, in the airy, high ceilinged rooms, peace for meditation and reading.

There are daily services at 4.30 a.m. after which the deities are stripped of their night clothes, bathed, re-dressed in their daytime glory and offered food, water, light, incense and flowers.

After the early devotions there is a study period and then the main meal of the day, eaten together, before devotees go to work, maybe teaching, gardening, distributing books, cooking or working within the administration of the organisation.

Families living outside the community follow much the same routine in their own homes, but obviously adapted to the needs of everyday life and jobs.

Amongst the crowds on festival days waft a fair sprinkling of disturbed, lost souls, some high on forbidden drugs, the inevitable flotsam and jetsam of youth, for whom the well-tended grass of Krishna contentment at first looks so green. The movement has an extremely good record for helping young people with a drug problem and a great many, long-standing devotees came to ISKCON through that particular route. There are those who float in, and finding the spiritual discipline too tough to take, float out again. There are those who can't cope with the outside world and remain, and who may, understandably, provide witch-hunters with fuel for the fire. Sometimes, the most intelligent — Westerners, African and Indian alike — who are attracted initially by the simple spirituality of ISKCON, may not cope with the strange hypnotic chanting, the emphasis on meditation and the long hours which derive from a totally alien culture — so they crack.

This is when the rumours fly — and rumours there are in plenty.

THE FLIP SIDE

In America, the 'king-like' role assumed by Kirtananda, President of the New Vrindavan Temple complex in West Virginia, has caused an internal split, which has rebounded on the movement as a whole. New Vrindavan, with its exotic gilt architecture and statues of Mary and Jesus alongside those of Krishna, has been a hugely successful tourist attraction since it was completed in 1979 at a cost of £271,000 ($500,000). It has been the centre of a number of scandals and is considered by the majority of orthodox Krishna devotees to be a travesty of the true teachings of Prabhupada.

The Governing Body expelled Kirtananda in 1987 after all attempts to control developments had failed. However, he continued to thrive — as a cult breakaway — and his name was constantly confused with mainstream Hare Krishna.

A dramatic letter was sent, from headquarters, personally to all members in January 1989. It said:

'Kirtananda has changed NV into a Christian millenarian sect . . . Vedic teaching, with history moving in endless cycles is far from millenarium . . . but I have heard NV's spokesman explain how the demonic, materialistic civilisation will be brought down by nuclear wars, social chaos . . . Aids . . .

'Kirtananda's fantasy of the Walled City of God is modelled on the New Jerusalem. In my judgement Kirtananda's adoption of Christian dress, liturgy and paraphernalia is not a matter of preaching strategy or ecumenism.

'I think we ought to consider it a strong possibility that if Kirtananda feels his back against the wall, he may well seek final justification and vindication in martyrdom, for example by provoking a suicidal shoot-out with the police [guns were being stored at NV]. On our part we should make a concerted effort to enlist all devotees who still have friends in NV, to persuade them to leave, if only for their own safety. We should see whatever else we might do to forestall some final cataclysmic shedding of blood. Not only may people be killed or injured but no matter how far away from Iskcon Kirtananda deviates, if there is some climactic shoot out, it will always be remembered as The Hare Krishna shoot out.'

There are those who sincerely believe ISKCON to be 'the most evil of them all', who speak of seeing huddled groups of people whose 'minds have blown' around Krishna Temples. They even claim that members are taught that it is better to die than leave the movement ; that the body itself is of no value in the reincarnation scheme of things, and so how, most effectively, to cut their wrists. Much of what is said may well have once been true — or almost true — certainly in America.

Even so, no one has ever taken ISKCON to court on any major account in Britain. There has been only one reported case here of a devotee whose parents hired professional kidnappers to rescue him, and since the families of lapsed members tend to build a protective wall around their offspring they are reluctant to speak. So it is very hard to establish first-hand evidence of brainwashing or ill-treatment.

The pain of parents is real but appears so often to be based on emotion and a misunderstanding of Indian culture rather than on proven malintent by the devotees. Most Krishnas are not Pied Pipers, luring followers into a trap: their chanting, for instance, is a devotional device with sixteenth-century origins in Bengal and not a brainwashing technique, even though it may well have that effect on people who are already under stress before joining the movement.

As a safeguard, ISKCON now says it works with qualified psychiatrists to help those coming to the movement with behavioural and psychological problems.

The distribution of books, in return for contributions, has angered many people. Originally, the issue was fudged by devotees, who said they were giving, not selling, and therefore not flouting the law. Inexperienced members, faced with hostility, sometimes took the line of least resistance and did not explain for whom they were collecting. There is a rather more dignified approach today — guidelines have been laid down by the leadership and there is a real effort to keep within the law relating to obstruction and street trading.

This has resulted in a better relationship with the police and, in fact, Hendon Police Training School students now visit Bhaktivedanta Manor as part of their initial training.

In America, the growth of Krishna Consciousness has been very different and more openly confrontational towards parents and State. The message is the same as elsewhere, but the methods are not. The hard sell, the image-polishing wigs and the truth-shy patter were never quite 'British'.

At one time, O'Hare Airport, Chicago swarmed with enthusiastic missionaries seven days a week and complaints of ruthless 'hustling' were justified.

Many times in America Krishnas have been taken to court on charges of abduction and brainwashing.

Best known of these was the case of Robin and Marcia George in 1983. The plaintiffs alleged that they had been psychologically imprisoned by religious conversion within the Krishna movement. ISKCON was fined a crippling $300,000 but, on appeal, a formidable array of sociologists and psychologists, from Britain and the United States, spoke out in defence of the movement. The final result is still pending.

ONE MAN'S KRISHNA

Ranchor, born Richard Prime, in 1950, was one of the first pony-tailed devotees in London. With short cropped hair, he now lives with his Swedish wife, Lilashakti, and two children, Rupanuga and Anasuya, in a comfortable flat off London's Tottenham Court Road. Rupanuga is at the Hare Krishna school, as a weekly boarder, though many Krishna children attend State schools.

Ranchor works as a consultant for Icorec (The International Consultancy on Religious Education and Culture), a Christian-inspired group, part-funded by the Gulbenkian Foundation, which aims to promote greater understanding of world faiths. He was co-organiser of the multi-faith pilgrimage to Canterbury, attended by the Archbishop of York and the Archbishop of Canterbury in 1989.

Ranchor makes no attempt to deny the movement's growing pains, or the heartache many parents have suffered through mutual lack of communication.

'In my early days, as a Hare Krishna devotee I was largely to blame for the rift with my parents. I was so utterly absorbed in my life that I didn't have time to think what they were going through — it wasn't important to me. I was just 20 when I first met the devotees one Saturday afternoon, in Portobello Road street market in London. I thought they were great, though I couldn't understand what they were about. I was steeped in religion as I had been brought up a Catholic in a Catholic boys' boarding school. When I left, I turned my back on it all and did all the things I hadn't been allowed to do. I'd decided to be an architect and got a place in art school but I needed a religious meaning to life. The first time I visited the Hare Krishna temple I recognised a depth of spirituality which I realised I was looking for.

'My mother was a passive parent but my father was the opposite — and there was an emotional rift which never really healed before he died.'

'If religious experience is strong, at that age, whatever the religion, it has the effect that you are discovering possibilities you never dreamed of. If my parents had shown a positive interest it would have been different, but they didn't and I didn't have time to worry. We were sitting on something like a nuclear explosion; it was so powerful and we were going to change the whole world in five years! We were all kids, living in a world of youth.

'We still have a lot to learn because as a movement we are young and growing. We are trying to understand the criticisms, to move away from the fanatical religious zeal of the early days and to be more open.'

PAUL OF THE KRISHNAS

Paul used to leave his robes behind in the Krishna Temple in Dublin each morning, and went off to work wearing a business suit. He was the boss of a hugely successful management training centre.

'I slept in a sleeping bag on the floor, led the spiritual life of a devotee and then became an executive by day.' Paul had started the business as a means of providing an income for the Temple, which would enable new members to spend less time fundraising and more on the devotional life, for which they had joined. But his success brought conflict with the movement's leaders.

Paul left ISKCON in 1988, after eight years, and is still in charge of his snowballing enterprise.

'Most people who take to spiritual life are not really looking for truth. There are the distressed, those desirous for material improvement, the curious, and then there are those in search of absolute truth. I think most of those I saw were distressed. My own distress was completely alleviated by joining ISKCON — in its purest form it is wholly positive. But there are hiccups in the way it is run, and the way people are dealt with.

'I was at the University of East Anglia, studying English and American literature and philosophy, and I had become disillusioned with academic life.

'I was in turmoil after a broken love affair. I knew if I didn't sort out whether there is a God and whether I was a spiritual being, I could spend my life barking up the wrong tree.

'I had just read the Bhaghavad Gita and there were details of the Hare Krishna Temples in the back. So I went along to the Sunday lunch they organise for visitors. The atmosphere was magical, and a succession of people spoke to me — genuinely friendly, well-informed people, leading an admirably strict life.

'The Temple President called me in to his room and we talked about who I was, and what I was doing. He asked me to stay and check it out. It all made perfect sense, so I shaved my head and that was it. I stayed for eight years.

'It seems, from the other side of the fence, like a huge decision but in reality it isn't. It can be retracted. The only real pressure I have ever seen, on those wanting to leave, was benevolent — on the level of compassion, rather than as a means of recruitment. Being cruel to be kind.

'Krishna has a good track record with drug dependents because any genuine, strict spiritual practice will help. Dependency of any kind arises because there is something essentially painful or unsatisfactory in a person's life. I was so satisfied for a long time by my life within Krishna I did not need anything else. It is quite remarkable.

'I invited my parents to come to Ireland for a visit which was quite upsetting for them because I was defensive and far from a loving son. I was really immature and of course I had a shaved head. Father is liberal and laissez-faire and mother reacted as she always did — "my son is my son". But she found it difficult to explain to friends. She was embarrassed. When they saw that I was OK and happy they didn't mind. My father even admitted that if it were not for my mother he would not mind doing something like I had done. It was the only approach they could have had.

'I began to wobble myself, first as a result of having married and feeling it was a fairly seriously wrong decision from the outset.

'It all seemed like a nightmare after a while. There had been no one standing over me to force me to marry but there was a lot of peer pressure and I did not take the commitment seriously enough. This all made me unhappy as a person and was the single most important factor in my eventually leaving the movement.

'Meanwhile I gradually began to realise I was not going to be the great saintly person I had thought.

'I felt it would be nice to start a business that was sufficiently profitable to enable newcomers to practice the spiritual life in a conventional way, rather than doing something for which they were not cut out and did not join the movement.

'My motivation was pure, but the fact that I had gone into business was not really approved, so gradually I became a black sheep. It was assumed that I had no spiritual interest and I felt ostracised. This really depressed me.

'About September 1987 I decided I had to leave. My wife and I had become more estranged. In the meantime two children had arrived — we hoped they would bring us together, but it got to the stage when I knew I could not ruin the rest of all our lives and I would have to go.

'There was a great deal that was very good during my time in The Temple but the movement is tremendously naïve and badly managed. It urgently needs devotional counsellors nationally who will not try to preach or interpret in philosophical terms. There is a fear of expressing fears and emotions and a pretence they do not exist, at all levels. Sometimes new devotees feel an obligation to keep their reactions philosophical and not emotional and this can build up internal pressures. There are not many leaders within the movement prepared to open up. They have not learned how to talk about experiences or bare their souls and there is an element encouraging the stiff upper lip which can be hard to cope with.

'I don't feel resentful or hold anyone responsible. You could not point any fingers . . . it just happened.'

THE KRISHNA GIRL

Jenny was sixteen and squatting in London without a job.

'One day, in the underground a woman came along collecting money, and I was embarrassed because I only had 50p. She gave me a card inviting me to a free meal. I thought "that can't be bad", so I went along, and was annoyed I had to sit through three sermons first, although what they said made a lot of sense.

'I was brought up in children's homes and so I was tempted by this ready-made family. When they invited me to stay for the weekend, I didn't realise it would mean getting up at 3.30 a.m. You get used to it, but the first few weeks, of five hours a night, are awful.

'I thought they were a load of very pleasant cranks. I went on the minibus to their farm in the country and oddly enough the bus broke down! So, I stayed another week-end and ended up being there for six weeks. At the end of the time I'd made friends.

'I can't say I joined for ideological reasons though I did come to believe it all. I was a disillusioned Roman Catholic. I'd only ever seen hypocrisy and the one thing cults have is sincerity in their religion. There is something attractive about that.

'I wanted people to love me and a secure place to live.

'I could have ended much worse. I learned trades whilst I was there and I came out more articulate.

'I was secure and happy, rather like a cow being fattened. Women are at a disadvantage. Prabhupada stated that women have a brain half the size of a man's. They treated us like total morons. Part of it is the Hindu culture.

'You don't sleep with anyone, even when married, except for once a month. I wasn't looking for a boyfriend but I couldn't understand why we could not have men as friends. I had always been a tomboy and I missed male friends; it wasn't sexual. I remember being taken into a little room and told that all the problems arise over women, all wars are fought over them, lust and sex are at the root of all trouble.

'I ran into trouble because I criticised and questioned; I remember one bad winter, when we were collecting money 18 hours a day one of us had a period. The bloke in charge was very unpleasant, demanding proof. It was humiliating, too, that the women's ashram didn't have its own money and we even had to ask for sanitary towels. When we needed a bra we had to ask one of the men devotees. It is dehumanising.

'If you are ill it is because you have been evil in your past life. If you are so ill that you can't work, they throw you out. They don't keep anyone who can't work. What happens when you get too old to work?

'In fact I collapsed, from exhaustion, on the street and spent a week in hospital. At the end of a week a procession of devotees came to take me back and I carried on, with an 18-hour day. I was so bad, I was just sitting crying my eyes out and one of the girls (she also left because of what happened) took me to the hospital and the social worker put me in touch with the anti-cult group Deo Gloria. This time the devotees didn't visit and told me not to come back till I could work. By the end of the first week I was enjoying Dallas and EastEnders. I'd never been allowed to read whilst I was in there; nowadays I have a house lined with books.

'I'm 23 now and I don't think there is a special age at which you are responsible for your actions. I didn't decide to leave as such; I agreed to go somewhere for a rest, but not to leave. Nobody de-programmed me. I just had the opportunity to think, to question . . . in four and a half years, I hadn't had a chance to question. I was never totally brainwashed.

'Intelligent people like to be a big fish in a small pool and it panders to the egotistical nature of kids, who want to be important.

'I can't say that I am sorry about the time in Krishna. They gave me a home and a family when I needed it. It's just that I have grown up.'

THE FAMILY OF LOVE'S TALE

(née The Children of God) –

FOUNDED 1969

HEADQUARTERS: *Unknown. Contact points: BM Box 7191, London WC1N 3XX; PF 241 8021 Zurich, Switzerland*

ORIGIN: *Christianity*

STATUS: *In Britain: Not Known*

STAR SUPPORTER: *Pop star Jeremy Spencer, Founder and lead guitarist of Fleetwood Mac.*

RESPONSE TO OUR APPROACHES: *None. But our unannounced arrival at the door of one of The Family homes, produced unexpected coffee and prayers and an eager wish to co-operate, in return for fair play. This was not easy — since an official interview never happened, and the only further contact was a long written response.*

THE FAMILY OF LOVE BELIEF

- The world is evil, confirming the Bible prophecies that we are in the End Time.
- Moses David is God's Prophet for the End Time.
- He has declared war on the wicked ways of the world.
- He is in communication with the spirit world and his revelations, though independent of the Bible, are from God.
- Moses David's followers are the harbingers of God's New World.

When 100 or so well-dressed men, women and children from Mission South used to gather on a Sunday afternoon in the Sports and Social Club of the Charing Cross Hospital, Hammersmith, in 1988 they were usually welcomed by the Club Secretary. With their bibles and their guitars, he assumed they were just another Christian group. He was wrong. And when their true identity was discovered they 'disappeared'.

Mission South is only one name for the Children of God, now known as the Family of Love, fundamental Christians who believe explicitly in the word of the Bible, and are campaigning vigorously again in Britain. The book, which the secretary believed to be a Bible, is a compilation of the illustrated letters of the founder, Moses David, to his flock. These Mo-letters, as they are called, have been circulating regularly amongst members world-wide, since the early 1970s.

They cover an enormous range of topics. But it is the correlation of sex with Christianity and the interpretation of the Old and New Testaments which are so controversial that David Berg (alias Moses David) himself is nowhere to be found.

His followers have been forced 'underground' and now operate under pseudonyms, distributing posters and 'music ministry' cassettes in universities and even amongst Church congregations. The landlords in whose houses they live are mostly unaware of who they are. They remain incognito, for fear of harassment or persecution of their children by neighbours; they have no central address and regularly change their name.

WHAT'S IT ALL ABOUT?

The comic strip drawings in every Mo-letter are explicit illustrations of Moses David's teaching; the headings speak for themselves and for all there is an official answer.

'You *are* the Love of God' is illustrated by a nude crucified through her private parts. Caption explanation: 'This is illustrating something you would probably not understand or believe. If you notice there is also a picture of Jesus on the Cross beside her. When one of our women is willing to make love with someone, as a last resort, to try to prove God's love to them and win them to Jesus, it is like a crucifixion, a great sacrifice, in which she, like Jesus, is laying down her life nailed to a cross of self-sacrifice in order to bring God's love to a lost soul.'

'God's Whores.' Illustrated by a woman lying on top of a man in bed. Explanation: 'I love shocking titles that wake people up. The Lord showed me how he, literally, shares his wife, the Church, with the world to prove his love. Now that's the truth isn't it? He is doing it all the time, in whatever way you want to say. Why not the bed? What's the difference? The only Bible those boys are likely to read is that gorgeous gal with her bosoms hanging out. That's the kind of love they can understand, that's the kind of love they can see and feel, before they can ever understand the spiritual love of God.'

'Jesus and Sex'. Illustrated by a woman squatting over a man holding his penis. Explanation: 'Receiving Jesus is like sexually going all the way . . . but finally rejecting Jesus is like in love making we get to the last step and you refuse to ---- me.'

David Berg himself is often drawn indulging in sex; 'If you look at Bible history you'll make the shocking discovery that most of God's greats had oodles of wives, women, mistresses, harlots and what have you,' he explains.

Now read on . . . in their own words . . .

'The Children of God are a Bible-based movement dedicated to following Jesus Christ. Every one of us is personally committed to obeying Jesus' command to bring The Good News of God's love to our fellow men.

'Of course we promote sex. And so does God. He created it! He Himself made those organs and nerves to feel so good.

'God's first command to Adam and Eve was be fruitful and multiply. Which of course means they had to have sex! God commanded it.

'Our beliefs regarding sex only form a very minor part of our doctrines and practices. But because sex is viewed by many sanctimonious leaders today as absolutely forbidden, the fact that we are open about it, and enjoy it, causes them to condemn us as a free sex cult. Thank God we *are* free!

'Like any religious organisation we have rules of behaviour our members are expected to follow. Granted, our rigorous schedule of Bible study, scripture memorisation, prayer, witnessing and telling others about The Lord may seem extreme . . . but what's the difference between what we and our members do, and the average novitiate monk or nun? Can you imagine how silly it would be if a nun grew weary of monastic life and then complained the vow of poverty wasn't fair, because it had caused her to miss her favourite television programme.'

The letters of Father David (alias Moses David alias David Berg alias Mo) have provided the general training and instruction needed in order to serve the Lord and preach the Gospel, and they have helped explain the Bible in such a way we can practically apply it to our lives.

Father David has said: 'We are waging a world-wide war. Not on the side of the left, not on the side of the right . . . but on the side of the only One who is really right — God.

'We are the last people of God, the last Children of God, the last Family of Love, the last Church like the early Church, the best Church.

'It's taken 2,000 years to get to the point where God can, finally, in the last desperate hour of the World's history, get a group of people to do what he said. Because of the failure of the Churches, God has had to raise us up, a New Church, a beautiful, sexy, fanatical, radical Bride, that will do the job the Old Church has refused to do.'

MOSES DAVID

According to his daughter, Deborah, David Berg was descended from a long line of notable Christian pastors and evangelists. In 1745, three Jewish Christians left Germany having been declared 'dead' by their orthodox family. They became Mennonite farmers.

One of their descendants, David Berg's grandfather, became millionaire President of Virginia College and built some 50 churches. His mother claimed she had been miraculously cured after five years' paralysis and consequently founded the Alliance Tabernacle Church in 1925. David was born into this overtly devout evangelistic tradition on 18 February 1919. But Deborah is convinced that this was a veneer. He was spoilt but never taught to accept guilt or ask forgiveness, which led to obsessive paranoia.

By the time he married secretary, Jane Miller, in 1944 the entire family was active in the new revival movement.

David Berg built his first church, in Arizona in 1949, with his own hands. In her autobiography, *The Children of God*, Deborah recalls riding on top of old adobe blocks as they were transported on an old flatbed trailer from some nearby ruins.

He left in 1953, having been thrown out because the whites didn't like his policy of integration and giving their wealth to the poor. There were also the first whisperings of sexual misconduct, from which grew his contempt of the established Church. Over the next few years, he continued evangelising and teaching, until, in 1967, he joined his elderly mother, Virginia, on Huntington Beach, California, where she was preaching and distributing free peanut butter sandwiches by electric cart to the long-haired, free-loving hippy counter-culture. He was 49, jobless and, says Deborah, unbeknown to Virginia, following a life style closer to that of his 'flock' than she might have wished.

There was a new word in the air at the time — 'teenagers'. The Berg family jumped on the bandwagon and called themselves 'Teens for Christ', with more peanut butter sandwiches and lots of live music. David grew his hair and the youth came flocking in. When Virginia Berg died, in 1968, the brakes were off.

David Berg was in the right place at the right time. He preached revolution and the kids loved it. 'The parents want them to follow in their footsteps, in a selfish, dog eat dog economy, in which they not only murder one another but conduct massive slaughter of whole nations. The young people are fed up with . . . a pagan, cruel, whore-mongering false Christianity. They're trying to return to the peace-loving religions of old.'

In April 1969 Teens for Christ left Huntington Beach and established a community in Vienna, Virginia. He assumed the name of Moses David, had more 'direct revelations from God', and preached doom and gloom for America unless she returned to the ways of God and the Bible.

For the first time his adultery was acknowledged — and justified as 'The Lord's doing' with scriptural backing. However, his honesty with his flock about his sexual practices apparently eliminated the tears and throbbing emotion which were to be exhibited many years later when the television evangelist Jimmy Swaggart slipped on the bananaskin of sexual morality. The confessions made no difference to the success of the ministry. He promoted the idea that sexual freedoms between consenting adults, when practised in love and hurting no-one are allowed by the new 'Law of Love' of the New Testament.

Deborah Berg has described as follows: 'David Berg, in blatant violation of God's laws, claimed that God had blessed his sin and made it pure. Each disciple, in direct violation of his or her conscience, participated in a collective, unified violation of conscience. We all partook of his sin.'

Her story is strongly contested by the movement today on the grounds that she is seeking revenge for her own expulsion.

The Children of God which America saw at that time were a free-ranging, rebellious organisation which constantly ran foul of the authorities for their open preaching and witnessing. A television documentary underwrote their credibility and attracted even more recruits. By 1971 there were some 2,000 members. Until 1971 the morality of members was strict: no dating, no hand holding.

Moses David completed a nine month tour of Europe and Israel, preparing the way for a CoG campaign, and on his return began to re-shape his message. 'If you had perfect love, as the Bible speaks of,' he told Deborah, 'you would understand that with other members of the "body", who also live within this perfect love, we can share freely with each other and there are no boundaries, not even sexual. All things are lawful — all things.'

The bad publicity was growing. Ted Patrick was making his name as a professional kidnapper. As 'Black Lightning', he was in head-on confrontation with the dozens of new religious groups. Then his own son joined CoG. As a result FREECOG was formed — the very first parents' group against 'cults' and was soon acting noisily in opposition to David Berg. Even so the CoG swept on under the national umbrella of the Jesus People movement of which they were the avant-garde and it was with this cover that David Berg arrived in England in 1972. Billy Graham . . . Cliff Richard . . . the Jesus People . . . to the public it was much the same, though the CoG message was different and they didn't hide it.

He never returned to the United States.

A quiet, middle-class suburban street was the unlikely centre of the Children of God's international launching.

They were the first of the tide to sweep across the Atlantic and their sincerity impressed a wealthy, Christian property developer. His name was Leslie Frampton. He had founded the Deo Gloria Trust some seven years before.

Two of his five sons joined the CoG, and Leslie Frampton soon realised he had made a mistake. David Berg moved abroad. But before the quiet American left, his missionaries had already been sent to Latin America, Australia and New Zealand. By the end of 1973 there were 200 colonies established in about 50 countries.

This expansion was supported by Mo's decision to publish his letters — which, until then, had been only for internal consumption. 'Litnessing', as it was called — the giving of literature and asking for donations — was added to their regular 'witnessing'. Publishing houses were set up and, by 1976, 68 million pieces of literature had been distributed. The movement that had previously been poor, living off money given by a few disciples and well wishers, had found a way to become more self-supporting.

Mo began to use the letters as a means of stimulating what he began to call 'misconceived Christian morality'. They were collected and published, like a cross between Mao's little Red Book of thoughts and the Bible. Under such headings as 'Revolutionary Love Making', and 'Holy Holes', they contained a torrent of advice on masturbation, love making and attitudes to sexual development of children. This was spliced with adulatory support for Colonel Gaddafi and a great deal of anti-semitic and political material.

There were also salacious posters which made their way to the national press. All this was justified, as it still is today, as biblically sound.

Flirty Fishing

Flirty Fishing began in 1973. Jesus said be 'fishers of men'. So that is what they did. The women voluntarily went off seducing men in night clubs and other places, in order to bring them in to find Jesus through sexual attraction.

Marie Christine was one of those 'happy hookers for Jesus'. A devout Roman Catholic girl from Brittany, she was captivated by the Family in Paris in 1975 and, renamed 'Sephorah', remained for five years. Happily married now, to one of the anti-cult group founders in Britain, she has told of the excitement of her first fish in her book *Confessions d'une Enfant de Dieu* (Editions Rochesvignes 1985).

'On the boulevard in San Sebastian, Spain, Sephorah was approached by a devil-ishly distinguished gentleman of about sixty. This was him — the long awaited fish!

'. . .He spoke only English and she tried to start the conversation in the usual way . . . Christians . . . give . . . help. Eddy took five pesetas from his pocket, and so began a conversation. He had retired from his textile business in Manchester and was looking for a beach house in San Sebastian.

'He invited her for a five o'clock tea and she was delighted because he was exactly the sort of man that Mo had described, . . . lonely heart . . . full purse. Over tea Eddy asked her about the movement, its life style, her parents, and then suggested dinner at his club.

'Sephorah, the siren, relaxed, before taking a long, cold shower and putting on her clinging dress and make-up — all set for seduction. She was ready to discover her first man, on God's account.

'At the restaurant she had an aperitif . . . the first for a long time and began to feel sensual. Mo was right to recommend a glass of wine before fishing. She plucked up courage to ask Eddy if he was single. The fruits de mer were swim-ming in white wine; her eyes became even more tender and langorous and Eddy began to lose his phlegmatic Englishness. Touched by her compliments he began to confide, and when she said "I would like us to be friends," he said, "me too." They left the restaurant side by side.

'. . . On the beach her footprints in the sand reminded her of the little Breton child she had been . . . the crescent moon shone over the water . . . they kissed . . . Eddy shivered with desire . . . At that moment Sephorah felt nothing, her actions did not belong to her. She was simply in accord with the thoughts of Mo and the wishes of God. If he became attached to her he would help the community. She must make the enterprise succeed. They lay on the sand between two rocks and his caresses became more and more intimate. His hand moved slowly over her stomach . . . she abandoned her body to masculine desire . . . "you are a strange girl," he said, "you say you love me and yet you don't know me." "God is Love," she replied, "He has breathed a special affection for you into me . . . I don't want to leave you this evening. Come to the community, my room is big enough.

'Persuaded of her sincerity, Eddy accepted . . .

'As a result of his first meeting with the Family and what he learned about their work, Eddy went off to sell his factory and returned later with a large donation. The victorious Sephorah was convinced that she had done the will of God.'

However, Moses felt that Britain was not the best place to develop this method, so he moved with his family to the Canaries and changed the name of the movement to 'The Family of Love'.

The Family of Love had, so far, been for full-time members but now new recruits could remain in their own homes, which attracted professionals, for whom the arrangement was more convenient.

In 1977 the German magazine, *Stern*, published an article which was circulated all over the world; as a result a number of members were arrested and charged with prostitution. David Berg himself disappeared again.

In a message to his people, he wrote: 'They will never stop us, because we are going to scatter into so many countries, in so many ways, that only world government of the Antichrist could organise a world-wide, concerted attack against us.'

In Britain the organisation continued, under cover; in fact things remained so quiet that it was assumed most of the Family had gone off to India and the Far East, where the movement was very strong. But in 1989, after leaving the Philippines due to 'media persecution', they returned to the UK in large numbers.

Today no one — not even members — is sure where David Berg is. He could be dead, but his hypnotic voice can still be heard on the tapes which are distributed everywhere.

There is no central address, and although all official decisions are passed through a PO Box in Switzerland, their destination, and who makes decisions are unknown, certainly to the bulk of members.

The encouragement of sexual activity and ban on contraceptives has meant that there are a great many young children who live in the communities, who have little or no contact with the outside world. Parents do not agree with the anti-God, anti-Bible education offered by school and do not wish to expose their children to the violence and negative influences that are prevalent there, so children are not sent to school but taught at home by specially appointed members within the group.

Typical of the Family hide-outs is a comfortable, Victorian house in South London — rented, as far as the absent landlord believes, to an ordinary couple with their children. Visitors could expect to find a copy of *The Guardian* on the large table in the farmhouse-style kitchen. 'David', his wife and their numerous offspring live there, quietly, with a few friends; it is clean, cared for, relaxed and anonymous.

David himself, in a rare moment of communication, has written some of his personal thoughts about the movement in which he holds a prominent position.

'For myself as an idealistic teen, having just successfully finished a college course, I was in a good job, but still searching for something more, experimenting with drugs and looking for answers in music.

'I found that all the world had to offer, including the many relationships I tried, still failed to satisfy the void and loneliness in my heart. Then one day, while walking the streets, I met someone with real love in their eyes, who I could see had the real peace I desperately needed. This person told me about Jesus's love, and straight away I simply prayed and asked Jesus to come into my heart and I found that He did come in and gave me something to live for.

'Through reading a Bible, and the writings of the Family of Love . . . and seeing how Jesus gave all of His Life for me, I knew I needed to do the same for Him. Not only needed to, wanted to. Since then I have been living for Jesus . . .

'The so-called exposés are stirred up by religious bigots, who are themselves ashamed by our full-time commitment to go to any lengths to obey Jesus's commandment to bring the Good News of God's love to our fellow man.

'We have found that love, beauty, romance and the natural attraction God created between men and women are sometimes an excellent means to help us, initially, interest others in Jesus. Let's face it, almost every business in the world misuses sex to promote and sell their products . . . so why can't the Creator of sex, and His children, use it . . .

'Whilst most of the world engages in extra-marital sex for personal gratification, or for money, we have been willing to do so to try and win others to Jesus and give them Salvation — and it works!'

THE FLIP SIDE

Because the movement is in hiding it is difficult to discuss the situation with its leaders, although written material is made available on almost every subject.

For nearly 20 years, the Family of Love has balanced precariously on the borderlines of prosecution. Everywhere they go, Governments have debated them, local authorities declared war, but they have never been brought to book. Yet the allegations are so serious, and offensive, because they involve not only consenting adults in private but little children.

The national press has interviewed children who have admitted, some happily, having sex with parents, from an early age. Yet neither Home Office, nor the police, feel free to act.

The Family has issued its own answers to these allegations. Here are some excerpts from their 44-page document.

'Jesus Himself had similar problems with the self righteous rulers of His day. Granted, some of these doctrines are shocking but they are Bible-based.'

You have been accused of being pedophiles (sic) and having incestuous relationships with children.

'This is an absurd lie! In fact, we didn't even know what a pedophile was until we heard about it in the news. What about the highly publicised cases in America where Catholic priests have been found guilty of sexually molesting young boys? Sodomy is rampant among the priesthood. *Newsweek* on 23 February 1987 reported that 40 per cent of America's 57,000 Catholic priests are homosexual. Why pick on us for our normal, heterosexual relationships?'

Some male members have more than one wife. Is this true?

'It is against the law to practise polygamy. However, it is true that a few of our heartier male members do live with more than one woman, and according to the Bible, there is certainly nothing wrong in it. Abraham, Moses, Jacob, David all had multiple wives.'

Why is your literature so full of naked, or nearly naked women?

'Why not? That's half the beauty of world-wide classical art . . . we don't believe there is anything wrong with God-created sex or nudity.'

Are such illustrations pornographic?

'By the standards of most Western countries they certainly would not be considered pornographic. Tastefully portrayed, loving, clean romantic nudity is beautiful. The Vatican is full of nude art. We don't promote or portray anything that is gross, coarse, vulgar or unloving . . . thus most of our artwork is beautiful and looks like world-accepted classical art!'

How do you justify illustrations depicting sex acts?

'These are undoubtedly from our private sex educational publications, distributed entirely among adult members within our communities. They are a Heaven-of-a-lot more wholesome than the sickening sexual slop dished out by those who organise sex-tours to Asia to gratify the fantasies of businessmen and the money hungry establishments.'

Why are your publications so sexy?

'It is well known that frigidity, guilt and inhibitions are frequently caused by false religious teaching and they destroy more marriages than anything else. When a marriage goes on the rocks, most frequently the rocks can be found in bed and the Church put them there!'

Do you admit you coerce people into leaving their families?

'No. We don't force anyone into "forsaking all". Only God Himself can do that. When people come to us and express a desire to join us, we try to discourage them, and tell them to go home and think and pray about it and "count the cost" before making such a decision. But, if someone *is* sure God has called them and they want to be a missionary, who are we to tell them not to?'

If women make love with men to whom they are not married does this not break the ten commandments?

'Yes. But they are not sinning. We Christians, who believe in Jesus, are no longer bound by the laws of Moses. This is why the religious leaders were determined to kill Jesus — he continually broke their Mosaic law!'

Is it true you believe the Holy Spirit is a woman?

'What do *you* think the Holy Spirit is? A man? That there are three men up there running everything? God the Father, God the Son and God the male Holy Spirit? We simply believe that God's Holy Spirit, His spirit of love, His comforter, is best represented by a woman, like a mother.'

Why did Father David's own daughter leave the movement and write a book condemning him?

'Deborah did not write the book. It was written by her demon-possessed, drug-addicted, second husband as an attack on us for firing him. She and her first husband were excommunicated for abusing their positions of leadership in South America — they did not want to relinquish the hold they had on people they were supposed to be shepherding.'

REBECCA, FORMER CHILD OF GOD

Rebecca has seven children by different fathers. She is not a prostitute; she is a deeply religious, middle-class, former grammar school girl and she is just 29.

'I was at a girls' school in Kent and when I was 14 I had a wonderful conversion to Christianity. Then, one day, in 1973, the Children of God came to my school. They had recently arrived from America and I was attracted to the hippy life style, with long hair and guitars. They belonged to my generation and I felt "this is fantastic. These people are really dedicated, they are radical and excited about sharing their faith." I could not have conceived they would teach me anything wrong.

'My parents were tolerant and trusted me. I felt God wanted me to be a missionary but I didn't want to upset my parents. Then one day, I told the headmistress I was leaving — two months before my O-levels. I stayed up all night, crying, and my mother said I could go, but not with her blessing.

'I soon went out on the street distributing literature and posters; there was no time to read the Bible or study; all we saw were the Mo-letters.

'I wasn't happy but it never entered my mind to leave. This was for life. I was still a virgin and not interested in sex. But I was lonely and I wanted a partner. Suddenly I had a desire to marry. I didn't love the man and was not attracted to him but we got married. Contraception was forbidden — we were to produce children for Christ. So at 17 I was pregnant. It was all so unloving. I had terrible pregnancies but when we were ill no-one cared for us — we had to be soldiers. The men became lustful and selfish and I am angry at myself now for being tricked. You are terrified of the wrath of God all the time.'

In 1979 her husband threw her out with two of their three children.

'I had had a terrible nervous breakdown; I couldn't cope with all the sharing and I was terribly confused.'

Then she married again. 'He seemed like a knight in shining armour but it was a terrible relationship for eight years. He was violent and made my life hell.'

During this time they went to India, there were more children and more flirty fishing. 'I don't know who their fathers were. I really thought what I was doing was a testimony of my love for God. Before making love we would get into bed and talk about my experiences as a Christian.'

Rebecca could take no more. She returned to Britain in 1987 and went to her parents. The three younger children went to school.

Rebecca has now discovered that her twelve-year-old daughter was sexually abused by, and active with, many men, including her father and, worse still, is missing these relationships. 'David Berg says that as soon as a girl starts periods is the right time.' Her eight-year-old son, who is half coloured, cries himself to sleep because he wishes he were white. Her 14-year-old daughter is still somewhere abroad and she is desperately worried because soon she will go flirty fishing.

'Sometimes I am at the end of my tether,' she says, 'the two year old is so active and I cannot give them all the love I would like. There just isn't time. I cry a lot, although I have joined a new Church and have made friends. I have fallen in love too. I have never had a really loving relationship. It would be so nice.'

In response to this story, the Family says that this is one woman's interpretation of events. Sex with minors is forbidden, violence is excommunicable, and women no longer flirty fish. Rebecca should have reported all this and would have had help.

THE EST TALE

Erhard Seminars Training (EST) –

FOUNDED 1971

HEADQUARTERS: *Britain: 10/14 Macklin Street, London WC2B 5NF*

USA: Contact: 765 California Street, San Francisco, California 94108

ORIGIN: *Not Known*

STATUS: *In Britain: Not Known*

STAR SUPPORTERS: *Not Known*

RESPONSE TO OUR APPROACHES: *'EST' (Erhard Seminars Training), or Forum as it is now called, is not a religious group. There is no membership but the organisation has attracted a huge international following. It teaches a self-improvement technique which was introduced in 1971 by the former Paul Rosenberg, who had changed his name to Werner Erhard in 1960. The courses are intensive and have come under the scrutiny of the cultwatchers because of the number of participants who have been unable to cope with the extremely rigorous, high pressure methods used.*

We met no one from the movement, here or in America, and had no reply to correspondence or phone calls. The only response to our efforts to set the record straight was a solicitor's letter.

This said that 'our clients' (it did not state who their clients are) have no part in a book on cults and that if we wish to know more we should attend a course. Any statements that were defamatory would be taken to court.

THE CHURCH OF CHRIST TALE

The London Church of Christ –
FOUNDED BRITAIN 1982

HEADQUARTERS: *Contact: 2 Park Place, Acton, London W3 8JY for details*

ORIGIN: *Christianity*

STATUS: *In Britain: Registered Charity 289385*

STAR SUPPORTERS: *None Known*

RESPONSE TO OUR APPROACHES: *Initially aggressive because 'we're fed up with the distortions and ruses of the media'. Agreed to meeting and then friendly — but suspicious.*

WE BELIEVE

- The Bible is the inspired word of God . . . Jesus was God in the flesh.

- The Nicene Creed and, implicitly, the doctrine of The Trinity.

- Obedience and not faith alone is necessary for salvation.

- Original sin, promulgated by Augustine, is a wrong concept. Sin comes from within. It is a personal responsibility. A baby cannot sin and therefore should not be baptised.

- There are only two options – repent or perish.

- Christians should be open about their lives, confessing sin to each other.

- To become a Christian [member of the Church of Christ] it is essential to be totally committed before baptism, which signifies the remission of sins and rebirth. There must be a complete break with old ways: drinking, smoking, disco dancing and anything that is not honouring to God are frowned upon and especially lying, pre-marital sex, corruption and deceit.

- The order of events is: hearing the message, believing it, repenting, confessing Jesus as the Lord, baptism by total immersion.

- Ecumenism is misguided.

Once baptised, Church involvement must be woven into everyday life. It is a discipline which makes tremendous demands and calls for a great deal of self-sacrifice. There is no compromise: 'We should honour our parents and love our family and friends but this honour and love should never exceed our love and obedience to God.'

TAKING THE WORLD FOR CHRIST

'Welcome. We're back on line. It's so exciting to have you call and so unexciting not to be here.'

So speaks the answerphone at the home of one of the ministers of the Church of Christ in London. The voice is cheerful — and American. The good humour reflects the confident security of a Church which claims that anyone not yet converted to its particular interpretation of the New Testament is not a true Christian. This rules out Anglicans, Catholics and everyone else leaving the world wide open for the phenomenal evangelising energies of Church of Christ missionaries.

'Denominational groups all over America and the world spend millions of hours in prayer and are not even in communion with God,' they say.

So the Church is all set to take the world for Christ. In 1986 800 million 'lost souls' were 'targeted' in India. In 1988 Australia was the battle ground and in 1990 it will be China.

The reason for such growth? Douglas Jacoby, a minister of the Church of Christ, explains: 'The others teach and don't do. They are happy to have 20 per cent of their congregation active and the rest idle. We would think that a complete failure. We think what the other Churches preach is a watering down of Jesus's teaching . . . we want every single person in the world to spread the word and every person we reach to become a disciple. There is hardly any other Church with that goal.'

The goal is exciting, and in a competitive world it seems to attract intelligent, materially and academically successful people who have lost their spiritual direction.

Central to the teaching is an individual's responsibility to devote time to field work. So, with single-minded zeal, members eagerly collect converts like petrol coupons. The clear cut, Christian fundamentalism, a go-getting sense of direction and sense of personal status, clearly works for the movement is spreading world-wide. There are about 1¾ million members.

There are two confusingly independent and competing Church of Christ organ-isations — the much older Church of Christ and the new Church of Christ, whose cleanly casual young evangelists may well sit next to you on a bus or Tube train and invite you to a party.

Tracing the intricate genealogy of the new Church of Christ is like recalling the plot of *Dallas*. Its origins are claimed to lie within the Baptist movement, which grew in seventeenth-century Britain after the Reformation. According to Douglas Jacoby, there were many petty differences and breakaway congregations at that time. Amongst these was the very first Church of Christ founded at Tottlebank, Kirkby in Yorkshire in 1669

The nineteenth-century Alexander Campbell, a Scottish Presbyterian who later affiliated to the Baptists, took his Baptist tradition with him to America. In 1827 he founded the Christian Association of Washington County, Pennsylvania and denounced denominational divisions in Christendom as a 'horrid evil', proclaiming that the New Testament is sufficient guide for life.

Meanwhile, back in Britain, the first co-operative meeting of the Churches of Christ met in Edinburgh in 1842. New congregations were established in Manchester

(1855), in Birmingham (1858) and, gradually, abroad in Burma, Thailand, South Africa and India. Progress was often slow — it took 2½ years in Burma to win the first baptism.

Today, Douglas Jacoby believes there are still only about 80 congregations overall within the parent group, and 2,000 members — not much above the 1862 figure. This is why new dynamism was needed and why the breakaway Church was born.

Its founder was 43-year-old Charles 'Chuck' H. Lucas, a graduate of Harding College in Searcy, Arkansas. He launched it as the Crossroads Church of Christ in 1967 at Gainesville, Florida.

The Boston Church of Christ, under the leadership of Kip McKean, son of a United States Admiral and a convert of Chuck Lucas, was formed in 1979 as an independent church. Within the next seven years over 3,000 people were baptised there.

This success was due to the 'discipling' methods of recruitment. 'The very minute you meet a non-Christian you are in a discipling mode,' according to Kip McKean. 'There will come a time when some of us will lay down our lives for the cause. That was the key in the first century: Christians loved God so much they were willing to be martyrs. The same price must be paid in the twentieth century if we are to accomplish the same goal — the evangelism of the entire world. The teachings of other Churches are sub-Christian and the only way to bring about change is by insisting on an uncompromising adherence to the New Testament.'

In 1982 two evangelists arrived in South London from America and started the first Church in Britain. There were just eight members. Today around 1,000 turn up for a Sunday morning service and there are centres all over the country: everyone preaches, there is no instrumental music but a great deal of individual participation.

HOW IS IT DONE?

Evangelism comes first. 'We have Christians in Boston who have recently sold houses, condominiums, wedding rings . . . in fact everything they possessed for the sake of evangelism,' declares Kip McKean.

Most members continue with their jobs or studies and go witnessing house to house . . . on buses and Tubes . . . on campus . . . for a few hours every week.

In London 70 per cent of conversions have come this way.

Techniques vary from situation to situation. When the Church organised its HOPE (Heaven's Opportunity Proclaimed Everywhere) Campaigns in 1985 and 1986 it issued strategy guidelines. These are similar in essence to any doorstep sales techniques and can be adapted for single adults, married adults, students on campus and families.

- Be joyful. People will respond more positively (even if they don't they will feel guilty afterwards).

- Be sensitive. Look for a person's need — don't keep a woman at the door if her child is crying in the house.

- Share your life . . . do things together . . . persevere.

- Openness – share your hopes and struggles . . . it will prove natural and interest them.

In his book, *Shining Like Stars*, Douglas Jacoby encourages disciples on their mission. Prayer plays a key part in the recipe for successful evangelism, he says, and suggests a 24-hour, month-long prayer chain in which each participant prays for one hour during campaign time. Regular all night prayer sessions, and a day of praying and fasting, are also important. Disciples are asked to offer friendship and fun to prospective converts, to invite them to a dinner or barbecue, to organise sports and games.

Adult married disciples who may feel they have conflicting loyalties are left in no doubt about priorities.

1. Work out a schedule
(a) Relationship with God. Ensure that regular quiet times are scheduled.
(b) Relationship with family. The married adult's most important earthly relationships are with spouse and children in that order. (c) Relationship with the Church. Schedule Church meetings and group Bible discussions.

2. Evangelism in workplace and neighbourhood
Encourage married adults to see the workplace and neighbourhood as their personal ministry.

3. Encourage an evangelistic life style, inviting people while shopping, travelling on public transport, etc.

4. Group evangelism with singles
Urge married adults to go out (Saturday afternoons) with singles.

5. Bible studies
Always have at least one person they are sharing the Bible with.

This kind of routine can put a great strain on individuals and on families, yet Church elders insist their demands are manageable and that they have a lot of fun.

'We have a passion to make sure that students do well in their exams — sure we encourage discipline but this only helps them get organised. If you are too busy to share your faith you are too busy — you may be gaining the world and losing your own soul!

Douglas Jacoby was brought up with a good spiritual base in an Anglican family.

'At University, in 1977, I was still undecided; I attended the Church of Christ and my parents were a bit alarmed because I suppose I went over the top. They took me off shopping to buy new clothes and I refused, on the basis I should wear my old rags because there are people in the world with no clothes at all. Soon after, I became a Christian [joined the Church], and I took my parents along too; they liked it so much my mother also became a Christian. I completed my degree, took a theology degree and then came to England.

'The greatest test of all for some Church members is the call to mission work abroad, though surprisingly few do, in fact, relocate. In 1989, 20 went to Lagos (18 native Nigerians) and 20 to Manchester, most of whom were from Lancashire. There are 12 million souls living in London alone, "destined to go to Hell". There is no time to waste. No excuses accepted.

'The Church tells its disciples to honour their parents and love family and friends, but this should never exceed love and obedience to God.'

In 1988, the London Church launched a LOVE (Let Our Vision Expand) Campaign, to raise at least £300,000 for poor relief in Bombay, Bangalore, Johannesburg, Kingston, Mexico City and São Paulo. Members were invited to sell possessions and to give as much money as possible.

'There is nothing strange, or new in this dedication . . . it is in keeping with the selfless work of early missionaries — and, of course, the New Testament disciples.'

ORGANISATION

The Church owns no building — using rented accommodation from other organisations. It has no associated businesses.

The world leader is Kip McKean working with a team of seven salaried sector leaders who liaise constantly as friends and colleagues.

Individual Churches in need receive funding from America on a 'twinning' basis. Indianapolis helps Birmingham, England, Boston aids London, and so on.

The Church does not believe in compulsory tithing but in voluntary donations.

Should the commitment prove too much and a member decide to leave the Church, Douglas Jacoby agrees, 'we tell them in no uncertain terms — leave the Church and you walk away from God. Pressure is a loaded word and we don't try to short circuit their free will physically but I would be lying if I said we do not try to get them to stay. If people walk away it is a blow, because they are depriving others in the world from knowing the truth through them. They are compromising spiritually. You must be a committed Christian or Jesus will say "I never knew you".'

THE FLIP SIDE

The London School of Economics, Kings College London, Manchester, Aston and Birmingham Universities have all banned the Church of Christ from campus. The accusation against them is that they are unscrupulous and dishonest and the pressure on their members is often unbearable.

'We are not commenting on their message,' said the Secretary General of Aston University, 'but one person dropping out of a degree course because of the demands of the Church of Christ is one too many. Students most likely to respond to the Church are those already lonely, homesick and unsettled, certainly not strong enough to cope with the arduous life style expected.'

In America the 'multiplying ministries movement', as Church of Christ methods are called, has been under attack for many years. This is because their emphasis is so heavily on individual obligation to seek converts at the expense of everything else, including family life. Some people travel 100 miles to church on a Sunday.

'The unremitting pressure to spend at least eleven hours weekly on church work — prayers, discipling and services, in addition to University studies, causes some students considerable distress. They are driven on by a sense of guilt and the fear of damnation if they should give up.'

This relentless drive is one of the tools of Church of Christ evangelism. Waverers are often harassed by phone calls, or regular visits from disciples, two at a time. Observers in America and London have noted that the relationship between a new church member and the prayer partner has the effect of reproducing identikit disciples who are therefore much easier to control by the revered elders. Their 'advice' is in effect a command. It is the control of the many by the few.

In London, although the church says it receives only £3,000 monthly from donations, it is claimed by critical observers that the income is in fact much higher and that even students give at least £15 weekly and there are rumbling rumours of financial impropriety and missing money. The Church says average weekly contributions are £6.00.

'There is a cynical money motive we had never suspected,' say leaders of the established churches. 'In areas of north London there are nine people in three-bedroomed flats, paying £40 a week to the Church.'

Church leaders says the Church owns *no* flats and rent is never paid to it.

Bibles bought from a charity for £2, on condition they were given away, have been allegedly handed over to passers-by in the street with a request for a voluntary donation of £3.

Such stories, now firmly rooted amongst the cultwatchers, have probably arisen, say leaders, from a single, misguided member being over enthusiastic. 'We would *never* give a Bible to anyone without a really keen interest.'

There is also a growing obsession with dating. 'It is a way of holding young people in the Church,' claims Graham Baldwin, a chaplain to Kings College, London University, who is furious at what he sees as a cynical lack of care by the elders of the church. 'Girls have been asked to stand up at meetings and identify their availability. Everyone is expected to be in a stable relationship within six months. There is a regular "Dating Night" for singles. At a time when young people are developing their relationships towards each other, they are very vulnerable and should not be pressurised by anyone.'

'Rubbish,' says the Church. 'In 1989 — a bumper year, there were five weddings.'

VALERIE IN THE CHURCH OF CHRIST

'I hadn't been particularly religious. Then my husband, who was a policeman, had a heart attack at the age of 35 and had a by-pass operation. There was a lot of pressure on the marriage at that time. He was a difficult man to live with and there were lots of rows. He'd done so many years in the police that he had become hard. Then one day a friend invited us to a Business Men's Fellowship. It was very charismatic and it started us thinking about God. This is my second marriage and I wanted it to work; I wanted him to be fit.

'We moved to Wimbledon, and while we were waiting for our flat we got a leaflet through the door from the Church of Christ. I was quite interested because they seemed to be discussing lots of topics. So, two weeks later we decided to call in on a Wednesday night. It felt really good: there were so many nationalities, old and young and it wasn't charismatic. We both started to study the Bible and I realised that I wasn't right with God and what I had to do. It changed our lives.

'From then we studied and we got baptised together. Now I am pregnant and I am so happy. I also have a teenage son and daughter and my daughter has started coming with us to church because she could see the difference it has made. We had fought and shouted a lot and were at each other's throats all the time. All that changed. My parents are not members of the church. Yet Dad said they can't believe what happened to us.

'You get marriage counselling, in the church, which is really helpful. I've certainly never seen one arranged marriage. There are people I know who have dated for ages and then split up, because they weren't right for each other. I certainly can't imagine an arranged marriage for my daughter — she wouldn't take that. We have been with the church for four years and our relationship has never been better on every level.

'I go to the church on Sunday. Tuesday is a social evening, we bring friends for an hour's Bible discussion over coffee or tea. Wednesday night is house church when we play games, dance, sometimes discuss. We don't want to go home because we have a lot of fun. Sometimes there is a sports night.

'The church is always on my mind, but not exclusively. If you shut yourself off and don't see friends, outside the Church, it is unhealthy. We see all our old friends and go out to dinner sometimes.

'I try to invite people to the Church as I am standing next to them, maybe on a train. I make it a way of life — it's amazing how you soon get used to it. You learn how to witness and if you think that God is expecting you to do it, it is better. We get every sort of response. But many people are seeking, as I was. Peter and I go out together, shopping on Saturday and we tell people who we are.

'There is nothing you can do to stop the media. I don't understand the hostility. I'd much rather my daughter was in the Church than not. There is so much joy being together. Kids give up studies whether or not they are in the Church. I think that parental pressure to do well can be heavy and kids find that pressure is relieved by escaping into a church. We have a lot of teen members who live at home, whose parents don't belong to the Church. It hasn't split the family.

'I'm not very good with money, so sometimes I give nothing. My husband gives more than I do, but no one checks what you do.'

THE JESUS FELLOWSHIP TALE

The Jesus Fellowship, also known as The Jesus Army –

FOUNDED 1969

HEADQUARTERS: *Britain only: Central Office, Nether Heyford, Northamptonshire NN7 3LB*

ORIGIN: *Christian*

STATUS: *In Britain: Inland Revenue reference X 80114. (They are not registered with Charity Commissioners.)*

STAR SUPPORTERS: *None Known*

RESPONSE TO OUR APPROACHES: *'In for a penny' — weary of hostile press but could see nothing to be gained by refusing to see us. Friendly and very hospitable.*

WE BELIEVE

- In one God and in the Trinity – co-equal and consubstantial.

- Jesus Christ is the Son of God second person of the Trinity, begotten and not created of one substance with the father and spirit, born of the Virgin Mary.

- The Holy Spirit is God, third person of the Trinity.

- We believe that angels are the creation of God, to serve him and minister on behalf of the saved ones.

- That Satan is a fallen angel, deceiver of the world who has been totally overthrown by the crucifixion and resurrection of Jesus.

- That demons are cast out of people in the name of Christ . . . and that the regenerate are severed from the evil spirit and the devil or his demons have no power over them.

- Man was created by God in His likeness; through Adam's sin man is fallen away from God's presence and carries the seed of sin and death. Sinful man and the whole world is under the dominion of the evil one and only through God's mercy can man be born anew. Creation will be restored to its perfect state at the final establishment of God's Kingdom on the New Earth.

- That man must be 'born of water and the spirit' to enter the Kingdom of God. Baptism is by immersion, usually with the manifestation of the gift of speaking in tongues, for the remission of sins. We believe that only true Disciples of Christ should be baptised in his name.

- That the unregenerate, or those not holding the pure faith of Christ, cannot be members of His church, and particularly exclude those holding doctrines regarded as heretical when tested by the tenets of the early Christian creeds.

- That the call of Jesus Christ was to renounce all other things to be His disciple, and recognise His prior claim over material possessions, family ties, social ambitions. This does not require the rejection of the nuclear family or any form of strict exclusivity.

- That the regenerate shall, voluntarily, hold all things in common and that the property and income of Covenant Members shall be held and administered communally. This is not a condition of church membership.

- That personal wealth hinders men from serving God.

- That all laws of Government must be obeyed.

- In the heralding of The Kingdom through living witness, church planting and church building.

- That scripture gives authority for the exercise of the disciplines of correction, or of exclusion from the church community should holy standards not be accepted or practised.

- That the Bible is the inspired word of God.

- That the sacrament of Holy Communion, the practice of washing of feet, the anointing of the sick with oil and the laying on of hands should be observed.

- That children living with parent or parents as members of the church are within the Covenant of Grace, though this needs to be reconfirmed by personal regeneration.
That the husband is the head of the household and that wives shall be submissive to their husbands having a gentle and quiet spirit.

- That it is the call of God for some believers to remain celibate.

- That the keeping of special days and seasons (Christmas and Easter) is not warranted by the scripture.

The Elders also issue a social Manifesto which includes:

- The Jesus Army brings the Gospel to the forgotten people, the crowds outside the influence of the Christian religion who have no faith in God and are trapped in the evils of our permissive society.

- The Jesus Army will go where others will not to help the poor and needy.

- The Jesus Army campaigns vigorously against moral and social evils . . .

- The Jesus Army soldiers will receive any training to make victory possible and are committed to sacrifice, hardship and danger to be fully effective in this holy warfare.

- The Jesus Army respects all Christians and churches and will not deliberately compete. The Jesus Army will not, however, allow the necessary all-out offensive to be slowed down, nor the prophetic word silenced because churches are defensive and sensitive.

HOW IT ALL BEGAN

The holes in the elbows of the Rev. Noel Stanton's sweater are at first sight strange on a man who heads a business empire with a turnover in 1988 of £15 m. Paradoxically Noel Stanton also heads a religious community of 600 adults and 200 children, which runs on a common purse, pools personal possessions including clothes, and ploughs the profit from the commercial enterprises into an aggressive campaign to bring the message of Jesus to the poor, the coloured and the needy.

In combat gear, driving double-decker battle buses, circulating a newspaper entitled *Jesus Army*, the Jesus Army, or Jesus People, or Jesus Fellowship, are 'quite happy' to be compared to the early Salvation Army. Their literature is a colourful onslaught on the eye, with banner headlines aiming at full frontal attack on inertia. 'Men! Rise up and fight. God is looking for men today! Men with guts and fight! Men who can lead a Jesus revolution . . . get rid of your boredom, your resentment, your laziness. Show you are a man.'

The Jesus Fellowship, which began in the village of Bugbrooke, Northampton, is the only truly home-grown new religious movement in Britain which has found its way into the top ten 'cults'. The Jesus Army, founded in 1986, is its outreach arm.

They are 'devastated' by the reaction of the media to what they see simply as an early Christian way of sharing. The communal life style, mostly centred in sparsely furnished country mansions, has led to a riot of rumour about strange happenings and about the personality of Noel Stanton himself, who has been accused of being a power mad fanatic.

The then 30-year-old greetings card company director arrived at Bugbrooke in 1957, as lay pastor to the little Baptist Chapel, which had been founded in 1805. For eleven years he lived the life of a village pastor at the Manse.

In 1967 there was an international charismatic renewal. One day in 1969 when Noel was alone in his bedroom he had a mystical experience which he describes as 'being filled with the Holy Spirit'. Things were never the same again. Some members of the congregation began speaking in tongues (claimed to be a divinely inspired but usually unintelligible language) and shifted away from the original congregation.

Fired by Noel Stanton's powerful preaching a new kind of congregation was attracted to the village. They learned to heal through prayer and expressed a desire to reach out to hitherto unreachable people.

The little country village became a focus for hippies and junkies, some of whom were housed in members' properties. Some of those who joined at this time were well-off, professional types, others were destitute. They threw in their lot together. A documentary film in 1974 was entitled 'And the Lord took hold of Bugbrooke'.

By 1974 the congregation had outgrown the tiny chapel and a wall was broken through to create an extension. To further the vision of Christian community, New Creation Hall, a derelict rectory, was purchased from gifts and loans raised by the congregation, who even sold their houses to help the project. There they established the first core community.

This was followed by the acquisition of New Creation Farm with 50 acres of land. Life was primitive, but by this time there were people with a great variety of professional and manual skills within the congregation and they were able to tackle most of the work themselves.

As membership increased a further nine houses were bought and some of the community activities such as building and vehicle repair were put on a commercial footing as businesses. A small health food shop and jeans store were opened in Northampton.

It is impossible to divorce Jesus Fellowship belief from Jesus Fellowship action and during the seventies there was a great deal of local concern at their isolationism.

Noel Stanton's teachings inspired the decision to have no television or radio. Books were largely Christian-based and no music other than gospel music was played within the community. Competitive sport was taboo.

'It is not that all this is necessarily all bad — there is just no time. We are not as strict as some Christian communities have been — you will find *The Guardian* and *The Independent* lying around.' Cooking, cleaning, gardening are shared responsibilities and time is allowed from work for witnessing. Husbands and wives may sleep in separate beds and celibacy is encouraged. Through the early years they evolved the creed upon which, they say, every action is based today.

HOW IT WORKS

Liz Donovan, long-time member and secretary to Noel Stanton, herself came from a close, Irish Roman Catholic family who were very unhappy when she joined the Jesus Fellowship. Her sister had been killed in the Vietnam War and in a fit of bitterness she joined the jet set having a 'wild time'. She was 27 when she met the Jesus People and had a spiritual encounter which made her decide to devote her life to God. Today, she wears the celibate's ring on her wedding finger and is at the hub of the expanding campaign.

The aim is not to poach from other churches. 'We want to break down barriers with them and do not see ourselves as superior. We never say that those who do not believe have no hope. In the last part of the century there will be a revival of many kinds of Christianity. We see ourselves a part of that.

'There have been two main reasons for our success in recent times; first adopting the combat gear, the badges and the banners. It has helped us hold the hearts of the youngsters and made us more accepted on the streets. We are identifiable and open. The second positive move has been our work in London. If you do anything there, you are noticed by the media.'

So the Christian soldiers march on . . . to Liverpool, to Yarmouth, to Glasgow, to Hastings. The Golden Marquee, which takes eleven people three days to erect and seats 1,500 emotionally charged people 'on fire for Jesus', has become the rallying point for mass 'Repentence and renewal. Jubilant, liberated praise. Forgiveness and new birth. Deliverance from evils, habits, fears and oppressions.'

Those who do choose to become rebels for Jesus are allowed to join the church and remain in their own homes if they wish; most however opt for community life. There are now 60 houses of differing sizes, where visitors and relatives from outside are encouraged to call in or to stay. Free short-term exploratory stopovers can be arranged and low cost accommodation is available for up to a year should the curious need more time before making a final commitment.

Even so it *is* hard, especially for the lost and inadequate, not to be overwhelmed and even feel trapped, first by the overload of love and consequently by the fear of the evil world beyond Bugbrooke.

Those who do decide to leave tend to opt out quickly. No one may join under 18 (unless they are with their family) and no one under 21 is allowed to put capital into the Jesus Fellowship Community Trust.

'Far from robbing people of all their worldly goods, we find that very often we are offering shelter to youngsters with huge debts. We pay these off — and what happens? They disappear!' admits Noel Stanton. 'We have also known rich people who have chosen to be struck out of a will and lose an inheritance because our way of life seemed better.'

There are professional people working within and without the community, as there are skilled and unskilled workers. All employees are paid the current prevailing wage levels, and directors are paid exactly the same as non directors.

The Fellowship businesses now include:

The House of Goodness Ltd — a wholesale health food company and a string of health food stores. In 1988, the pre-tax profits were in excess of £1 million.
Skaino Services — a haulage, building, heating and plumbing firm.
Towcester Building Supplies Ltd.
White and Bishop Ltd which took over the Jeans Plus clothing store.

The Elders of the Jesus Fellowship have a long-term dream of taking the battle buses through the Channel Tunnel and on in to Europe. 'If there is going to be an upsurge of Christianity on the Continent in the next ten years it will probably come from Britain. Our main thrust will be in Britain and will be in conjunction with other groups; we will all work together.'

ADMINISTRATION

The Church is divided into Households, with three Elders responsible for ten brothers and sisters each. There are about 100 elders forming the all-male council which runs New Creation Christian Community under Noel Stanton. A community is a portion of the Church — there are about two-thirds of total membership in community at present. 'Shepherds' are appointed to take care for the physical and moral well-being of new members.

In 1979 a Trust Fund was set up, and is still administered by ten Trustees within the community. This was to hold the capital contributions and accounts were to be audited by Coopers and Lybrand. This money was to be used for the purchase of houses and businesses and is not used for day-to-day running.

The Trustees are required to manage the Fund so that the capital contributions of members are invested, rather than expended.

There are separate charitable funds for the Church's running costs and Jesus Army activities such as the Marquee. The community and business activities, which together account for the vast majority of the community's cash flow, are not charitable.

There is a small housing association known as the Jesus Fellowship Housing Association Ltd which is charitable and hoping to establish a nursing home for the elderly.

No one may make any contribution of capital until they have been with the community for a probationary period of between six and 18 months. When money is given it is always allotted to furthering the gospel outreach and not to community life.

Should a member wish to leave, the Trust Deed requires the return of the original capital contribution with a possible allowance for inflation at the Trustees' discretion.

JESUS ARMY CHILDREN

How different again is the approach of the Jesus Fellowship to their children. They admit 'our worst crime is that we are probably 40 years behind the times! We believe that discipline is necessary for children and that being soft is no good for them.'

There is honest support for corporal punishment, in measure, which in the past critics have claimed means rodding even small children. 'We have moved away from caning although we support it in principle. The church now advises the use of the slipper for older children and a smack on the hand for two-year-olds and over. Punishment should never be done in haste and always with love and understanding.'

Most of the Bugbrooke children are at local schools and life is not always easy for them. At 17, Catherine is doing her GCE A-level and studying the flute. She joined the movement ten years ago with her entire family — Dad, Mum and seven brothers and sisters, and is hoping to take medicine at University. 'I do feel a bit weird sometimes at school. But you just accept it; the kids do bait me but my life is more fulfilled than theirs.'

The under fives have their own bright and colourful playgroup with the usual play dough and nursery equipment. But in the community homes, the selection of material available to the Jesus Fellowship children is very different from what their school friends expect in their own homes. Stimulus of a child's creativity or imagination is not considered important.

There is no television, no radio and a conservative attitude towards toys. 'We believe there are some elements of toy play that are destructive — the child does not develop his or her ability to relate. We are not very keen on dolls and would rather see them playing with people. Your will is paramount with a doll — and nothing goes wrong — we don't like this unreal relationship. Nor do we like some of the complex commercial toys. We are very simple people.'

The Fellowship has been attacked because of its stand on Christmas — which is ignored. So banner headlines about the 'children for whom there are no toys' have whipped up anger amongst readers of the national press. But the Fellowship, like the Worldwide Church of God and a number of fundamentalist groups, says that Christmas is a pagan festival and was not part of Jesus's teaching.

This kind of separateness can be hard for the children to cope with at school. They *do* feel different. Their lives are totally God-centred and spiritually motivated, which is acceptable within their community but makes it difficult to face the outside world.

THE FLIP SIDE

The newspaper headlines attacking the Jesus Army are as sensational as those in the Army's own publications attacking the Devil. Some parents see in the Jesus Army a mob, paralysed by religious hysteria and ready to face any kind of persecution or even death at the command of their leader. They fear for their offspring.

The early separation of the Bugbrooke community, and its single-minded determination to establish its own ground rules, led to all manner of horror stories about what was going on behind supposedly closed doors. Some villagers were angry because they felt Noel Stanton had hijacked the Baptist Church, and although some of the congregation remained and developments were supported by the Deacons, there was also genuine concern that his authoritarian style and rigid discipline was causing tremendous distress for some young recruits.

In 1986 the Jesus Army left the Evangelical Alliance (a respected, orthodox, non-exclusive association of evangelical churches with a shared aim of working closely amongst local communities). The press said they had been 'thrown out'; Clive Calver, secretary of the Alliance, puts it differently:

'We are not saying they are not an authentic church,' he says, 'they just didn't fit with our rules . . . We had had complaints that the Jesus Army was not in good standing with local evangelicals. We took a deep breath and investigated — we could neither prove, nor disprove, any charge and we started a lengthy and amicable dialogue with the leaders. They said they were not aware of the value of local involvement and so "we will concur with your request that we resign". But we have never stopped talking with them.'

Liz Donovan has explained: 'We just wanted to do it our way. There came a point when we had to decide whether to spend valuable time chewing the cud with local people or get on with building ourselves up. I wonder if we hadn't done this, if we hadn't cut ourselves off and built our foundations firmly, would we be in the position to help those we do today. There is only so much you can do. Now we have made ourselves secure we are ready to talk with anyone, welcome anyone to preach, go anywhere to preach ourselves.'

The community has also been shaken by the need for inquests into the deaths of four of its members, in 1976, 1978, 1982, 1986. The Coroner recorded verdicts of accidental death on three of these and the fourth received an open verdict.

Even so, much of the anguish felt by the families of the victims has reflected on the Jesus Fellowship. The parents of one of the young men who died wrote: 'We have been very much involved with the Fellowship over a considerable period of time and we can truly say the effect on us has been devastating. What appears to members to be a spirit–given heartease, will always be for us a deep human heartache.'

Their youngest son joined and became inwardly torn between his loyalty to the Christian Baptist parents he loved and his understanding of his commitment to God.

Equally worrying has been the alleged fate of the Bugbrooke children. 'Beaten in the name of Jesus', claimed the *Sunday Mirror* in 1986. Ex-members claim that rods are kept above the bedroom doors for this purpose.

Social workers investigating the charges against the Bugbrooke elders have, so far, been unable to find any evidence of maltreatment.

Ex-members who have broken away from the movement allege that the benign, friendly atmosphere and the comfortable carpet-slipper image projected by Noel Stanton is a front for a formidable man who will not tolerate being crossed. Hell fire, they allege, burns relentlessly in the grates at Bugbrooke and many of its more confused residents are ruled by fear.

The Warden of the local Nightstop, too, is concerned at the lack of expertise and training the Jesus Army 'shepherds' have at their command, when dealing with extremely disturbed young people. Sometimes they wait to meet possible recruits at the hostel as late as 11.45 at night. 'They haul them in off the streets and don't know how to treat them professionally. They can scare the . . . out of an unbalanced kid and all that group praying over them is extremely unnerving. The Salvation Army is much gentler, more diffused.'

LUCY OF BUGBROOKE

Lucy had been married for 35 years when her husband told her: 'I shan't want you with me when I retire.'

'I really prayed. I didn't want to stand back and let it all happen and be torn to shreds. I moved to my son and daughter near Banbury and whilst I was there I went to a meeting in the Chapel. There were so many young people, on fire for the Lord. The love hit me and I knew where I had to be. My husband had never been a church goer, it was a bit of a barrier and he didn't think I'd stick it out. I'm glad he's happy now — he married the other woman. At the age of 65 it is lovely for me to be with a lot of young people — I cook for them, organise the household and feel very peaceful. There is no hypocrisy. My own children come and see me here and I feel very honoured to have a place.'

ISOBEL

Isobel was a normal teenage rebel, who was into most things like drugs but was trying to find a deeper meaning to life than disco dancing. She had been brought up in the Church of England, and even tried witchcraft, but nothing satisfied her.

'I met a boy who had been in the Community and left and I persuaded him to bring me here. It was just what I wanted. The deep bonds of friendship and the sharing touched me. It was what you expect Christianity to be but isn't. My parents were very dubious. The elders of the Community told me to stay living at home and learn to love Mum and Dad like I loved Jesus. Mum said she'd give me six months and in fact it was four years before I finally moved in. I had been training as a dental nurse and now I am working for the Good Health food shops, which is very rewarding. Mum and Dad visit me here and somehow our relationship is much better because I am less self centred.'

FIONA'S TALE

Fiona's tale is constantly used by the cultwatching movements to spotlight the 'evil ways' of the Jesus Fellowship. There are two very different versions of the story.

Fiona's Dad came with a crowbar to break down the door of a Jesus Fellowship house in Daventry, and rescue his daughter. 'What else could any father do, because what happened to her was so gross, so appalling,' he alleges.

Fiona had been approached by a neighbour, she says, when her marriage broke up, leaving her with an 18-month-old daughter.

'He took me to meet the Community and I was surrounded by these kind, helpful people offering me legal and financial help.'

What Fiona alleges happened then, the Jesus Fellowship says, is seriously libellous and most of her very dramatic story totally false and grossly defamatory. In fact, far from taking her money, and persuading her to give up her council house, they say they did their best to stop her joining the community and she left owing them £325.

THE RAJNEESH TALE

Rajneesh –

FOUNDED 1974

HEADQUARTERS: *Britain: Spring House, Spring Place, Kentish Town, London NW5 3BH*

ORIGIN: *Original — with Buddhist undertones*

STATUS: *There is no central organisation but a large number of limited companies sending funds to Poona in India*

STAR SUPPORTER: *Terence Stamp*

RESPONSE TO OUR APPROACHES: *Worried. Distressed by past criticisms. But once assured of, at least, a fair hearing, helpful and efficient. The final comment on this book: 'Osho [Rajneesh] cannot be assessed without experimenting with his techniques, anyone omitting to do so will miss their point completely.'*

WE BELIEVE

Osho's sanyassins say they do not 'believe' . . . they interpret His sayings in a way that is individually appropriate. The concept of a creed does not work for them. Osho will sometimes throw out contradictory messages to stimulate thought.

Osho has said that:

- As things are moving today, the logical conclusion is global suicide. If anything is to be done for the future, now is the time.

- Problems are world-wide. Solutions have also to be world-wide. The United Nations should be converted into a real world government and all nations should surrender their arms and their armies to it. This will change the whole power structure of the world.

- An authentic religiousness needs no prophets, no saviours, no churches, no popes, no priests because religiousness is the flowering of the heart.

- Political power should be in the hands of the intelligentsia, one man one vote being replaced by a 'meritocracy' planned by a network of universities.

- The scientist has unknowingly fallen victim to the politicians. He has to remember not to serve death, whatsoever the cost. Scientists are the most important people for the survival of humanity and should form an independent World Academy.

- Birth control should be an absolute, with medical boards to decide how many new people we need every year, and that, too, should be done by artificial insemination, so there can be a scientific combination of the best sperm with the best egg.

- Genetic engineering can be used for the creation of a golden future on this Earth.

- The family is the root cause of millions of diseases. Love should be the only law between two human beings. Children should belong to the commune, not the parents. Parents have done enough harm.

- Legal systems are nothing but the revenge of society against those who don't fit the system.

- If somebody does something which is harmful to the commune then his mind and his body have to be looked into. There is nobody in the world who is a criminal; everybody is sick and needs sympathy and with a scientific cure most crimes will disappear.

- Miserable people are dangerous . . . they don't care if the world survives or not. If we can make humanity happy there is not going to be any third world war.

In the shimmering heat of an Indian afternoon Osho Rajneesh (known until 1989 as Bhagwan) floats on a wave of mystical music across the stage at his Poona ashram, now known as Rajneeshdam, and sits — the purple satin robes flowing.

The legend above the door — 'Leave your shoes and your minds here' — can be taken two ways. It is either an exciting exhortation to a new way of life, or, if you are a sceptic, it is a clear command to take leave of your senses. Rajneesh would say 'it is your choice'.

This disturbing bushy-bearded man, who resembles Michelangelo's painting of God in 'The Creation', had been spell-binding a daily audience of 5,000 until, in 1989, he announced that ill health would prevent him from talking any more. The honeyed voice, the hypnotic eyes, the chuckle and the hour-long, off-the-cuff discourses, turning the sacred institutions of family, marriage, politics and religion on their heads, have earned him the title 'the most dangerous man since Jesus Christ'. But they had taken a toll of his fragile strength.

Elevating Rajneesh to the status of Jesus Christ is probably wishful thinking on the part of 'His' (capital letters for the personal pronoun) adoring sanyassins (disciples) around the world. Yet even in London's run-down Kentish Town, at the Purnima Rajneesh Centre, 100 or so faithful gather of an evening for meditation, as they do in Amsterdam and in Berlin, in San Francisco and Tokyo. They sit on the floor in front of a large television screen, in peaceful apricot-white surroundings, smiling, swaying and chanting to the words of Osho. The followers of Rajneesh smile a lot. The British audience — professional, *Guardian* types — speak of 'our beloved master', though most of them have never met 'Him' personally. There is a great deal of emotion, touching and togetherness.

Why is this faraway figure, 5'6" tall, diabetic and asthmatic, banned, as he is, by so many Governments?

German, Swiss, Australian and Dutch Governments passed emergency decrees in 1986 that forbade him setting foot in their countries.

England refused to allow him overnight, in transit, when his jet was grounded at Heathrow for eight hours.

Jamaica granted him a ten day visa . . . and then ordered him out after 24 hours. The Vatican requested the banning of his name in Italian newspapers.

No wonder he is chuckling. For, in his eyes, international hostility to him only confirms the strength of his ideas. He condemns puppet masters — those intoxicated with power who destroy individuality — Presidents, Popes, Prime Ministers.

The reason for such universal political anxiety is simple. Rajneesh is preaching rebellion, sedition, heresy; much of what he says, though not new and reaching a comparatively small audience, is strangely compelling stuff.

He says Man is Hell-bent on suicide and he knows how to prevent it. 'My whole effort is to bring authentic religiousness into the world. The whole past is ugly and obscene. I am going to expose all these religions by and by . . . they have been destructive, harmful, a curse to humanity. Only with their death is there a possibility of a new religiousness arising . . . in which there will be no difference between man and woman.'

Until there is a scandal — and there have been plenty, his daily flow of philosophy is largely ignored by the press. No one turned up for the launch of his book *The Greatest Challenge, the Golden Future*, a response to the United Nations World Commission on Environment and Development.

Hunger and war he sees as the result of political games. He has called former President Reagan 'worse than Hitler' and in January 1989 issued a warning to President Gorbachev: 'When you compromise with capitalism it will drown you. If you want to be really revolutionary you will bring spiritualism to your country, not capitalism, which will create a capitalist class again, destroying the sacrifice of millions who died.'

He condemns religion but, since it is human nature to worship, Rajneesh has, ironically, himself become an idol. He emerged from a struggle with this dilemma in January 1989, after a series of contradictory pronouncements about the way his sanyassins should address him.

On 27 December 1988 following a statement by a Japanese Zen prophet, that the soul of the Buddha had found a vehicle in Rajneesh, he said: 'I have been calling myself Bhagwan, just as a challenge . . . it is a very ugly word, but Hindus are not even aware of it. Bhag means women's genital organs. And wan means man's genital organs. The meaning of the word bhagwan is, symbolically, that through his male chauvinist energy the man creates the feminine energy of existence. I hate the word. The joke is over. From now on I am Gautama the Buddha.'

On 31 December, Rajneesh announced he was absolutely finished with all traditions, all ideology. 'I am just myself. You can continue to call me The Buddha but it has nothing to do with Gautama. I am a buddha in my own right. The word simply means "the awakened one". My name should be Shree Rajneesh Zorba the Buddha . . . a synthesis between materialism and spiritualism.'

On 9 January 1989, after the Sri Lankan Ambassador to America had complained of his irreverently linking the name of Zorba to Buddha, Rajneesh declared: 'Zorba The Buddha is my philosophy. If it hurts, I am helpless . . . I don't want to irritate ignorant, blind, unintelligent people . . . I renounce the whole world completely. Shree Rajneesh is enough.'

BELOVED MASTER

Baby Rajneesh was born, the eldest of 13 children, to a cloth merchant and his wife, in 1931 (he is much younger than he appears). He was brought up by doting grandparents as a Jain.

'Those two old persons had no investment — they simply loved me . . . They acted out of a space which parents cannot. They allowed me total freedom to be myself . . . somehow I remained out of the grip of civilisation . . . I became a really strong individualist, hard core . . . by the time I reached my parents, I was almost on my own. I was already flying.'

That's all very well for the flier — but for those with whom he shares his space, life can be difficult. From his toddling days, Rajneesh was an unruly, disruptive boy: 'As far back as I can remember, I loved only one game — to argue. So very few grown up people could stand me. Understanding was out of the question.'

At school he challenged every subject he was taught, every rule that was applied. He turned punishment into a pleasure — by running ten times round the school field, instead of the allotted eight because, he said, the exercise was good for him; by defiantly enjoying the 'fresh air' of the corridor instead of the stuffy atmosphere of the classroom. There's little profit in punishing such a child. He played truant, led gangs of death-defying boys to experiment with danger and, this way, learned that by allowing himself to be sucked into a whirlpool, he could escape its force at the bottom. His relatives saw him as wilful, headstrong, rude and even seditious.

But whereas most mischievous children grow into socially conforming adults, Rajneesh went on to develop his rebelliousness into a philosophy.

As a student he revelled in debate, was banned from philosophy classes for asking too many questions and went on to teach himself, in the University library. In the middle of this period, at the age of 21, Rajneesh experienced enlightenment.

Describing this 'explosion' he recalls: 'Your whole inside becomes full of light, which has no source and no cause or past and once it has happened it remains. It never leaves you for a single moment. Even when you are asleep, the light is inside, and after that moment you can see things in a totally different way.'

Eventually, at the age of 26, he was appointed philosophy teacher at the Sanskrit college of Raipur. 'I was teaching students everything the University prescribed and also showing them in this prescribed teaching how much was bogus.' After nine years he left University and became an itinerant lecturer. 'From the University I moved to the Universe.'

He attacked the revered Gandhi, for furthering India's love affair with poverty by his stand against modern technology. He attacked Mother Teresa for her campaign against birth control, which he said, produced more babies to be saved for Catholicism. He said wealth is a 'must' for salvation because the poor man is too busy surviving to care about his spiritual needs: heretical stuff in a country where poverty is next to saintliness.

By 1969 he had adopted the title 'Bhagwan', and had begun the meditation camps which won him international notoriety. He was attracting huge numbers of Westerners to these gatherings, where he encouraged some bizarre and controversial meditation techniques. His pupils learned to throw off all their neuroses (and often their clothes) in a frenzy of abandoned free expression. The idea was to find the quiet space within. India was outraged.

He moved to the then six-acre Poona ashram in 1974, and by 1978 there were some 2,000 visitors a day, including some of the world's best-known journalists.

Bernard Levin, a tough nut to crack, wrote a long article in *The Times*, and he, like Alan Whicker, like Terence Stamp and many others, was impressed. There was 'something' about Rajneesh.

At this time Prince Wilf of Hanover became a sanyassin, with his wife and little girl. Prince Wilf, or Vilmakirti, as he became, was a cousin of Prince Charles and had been a friend of his when they were at Gordonstoun School in Scotland. Whilst Charles was on a visit to India in 1980, Prince Wilf, in his red robes, journeyed down to Bombay to see him and said afterwards that Charles had expressed sadness at not being able to visit Poona. 'Since Uncle Louis [Lord Mountbatten] was killed,' he is said to have told Vilmakirti, 'I have had no one to turn to for real advice. You are so lucky you have your guru.' Charles then, apparently, gave Vilmakirti a written question for Bhagwan which he tucked into his pocket. Vilmakirti died not long afterwards and his little girl was removed from her mother on the ashram and brought up by relatives in Europe — she was later a bridesmaid at the wedding of Prince Charles and Princess Diana.

In 1981 Rajneesh was ill with a back condition and was taken to the United States for treatment, though there were allegations that he was escaping tax debts in India. It was an ill-fated journey. He was at first refused permanent residential status since the US Government denied he was a religious leader. This decision was revoked, but over the next four years no stone was left unturned in the search for a way to deport him.

During this time, Bhagwan lived on the 126-square mile Big Muddy Ranch in the Oregon desert country of John Wayne movies. His followers had bought it, by fund-raising and by personal investment and sale of family assets, for $6 million. The nearest village, Antelope, 20 miles away, had just 40 residents. As the Mormons had done long ago, in Utah, the Rajneeshees planned to build the ideal community.

Those who lived at Big Muddy worked in conditions which, critics alleged, amounted to slave labour but, for them, it was truly a labour of love. They poured personal, and often family, money into the venture. They created an oasis of green productive land, feeding cattle, growing vegetables and producing wine.

Throughout this time Bhagwan did not utter a word in public. His Indian secretary, Sheela Anbalel Patel, took control demanding more and more money from wealthy sanyassins. Fundraising tours around the world brought in large donations. The Rajneesh organisation was alleged to be on a financial knife edge and yet large sums were being spent on personal indulgence. The outward prosperity of the few began to erode the former happy atmosphere. The free and easy days of Poona were over. There were signs of decay and disillusion.

The inhabitants of Antelope itself felt they were under siege as sanyassins

began opening shops, seeking election to the local council and importing the
infrastructure for an alien way of life. Some older residents felt obliged to leave,
and as they did their houses were bought, at rock bottom prices, by Rajneeshees.
War had been declared. Eventually, attempts to make themselves an independent
unit failed, and Antelope was renamed the City of Rajneesh.

Rajneesh himself acquired his notorious fleet of eleven Rolls-Royces at this
time. He became obsessed with his appearance and, although drugs were totally
forbidden in the City of Rajneesh, according to Hugh Milne, who was his bodyguard for eight years and who wrote *Bhagwan, the God that Failed* (Caliban
Books 1986), their beloved leader was inhaling nitrous oxide, obtained for
'dental treatment', to enhance meditation. 'Suddenly I felt sorry for Bhagwan . . .
it seemed as if the tables had been turned and I was the free spirit while he was
the prisoner of his own creation . . . what was I doing in this hellhole . . . while it
was clear he hated Big Muddy he had sold his freedom for the rewards of the
material world.'

They owned four aircraft, a bus fleet and a weekly newspaper. In July of 1983,
15,000 disciples came for the second Annual World Celebration, buying
souvenirs, stickers and T-shirts saying 'Moses Invests, Jesus Saves, Bhagwan
Spends'.

In 1985, scandal rocked the City of Rajneesh. Some of its top administrators,
including Sheela, disappeared and Rajneesh denounced her 'fascist dictatorship'.
Others have called it 'mutual manipulation'. What was then revealed belongs to
the flip side of the story, for the dream had finally turned sour.

Bhagwan himself was arrested, apparently without warrant, and appeared in
chains in court, before being taken to Oklahoma State Penitentiary. After eight
days he was released, but his lawyers urged him to plead guilty to the minor
immigration violation charges under which they had held him. So he entered an
'Alfred' plea, thereby accepting the contention of guilt whilst maintaining his
innocence. He was fined $4 million and ordered to leave the USA.

He has always alleged that, during this time in prison, he was poisoned.
According to sanyassin Ma Anand Pathika, in the last four years he has suffered
'loss of hair, eyesight impairment, untreatable joint pain and general weakness.
In addition his body has succumbed to one minor illness after another and his
daily discourses have been interrupted by bouts of ill health. A series of tests,
performed at a forensic laboratory in Harley Street, London, have ruled out all
possible diagnoses, except poisoning with a heavy metal, probably thallium,
common ingredient of rat poison.'

Later, US attorney Charles Turner said that Bhagwan had not been charged
with the same offences as his secretary because the Government's top priority
was to get rid of him and not make him a martyr. Besides, there was no evidence
whatsoever to implicate him.

There followed the period in which Bhagwan was shunted from country to
country. December 1985, Nepal. February 1986, Greece. March 1986, Switzerland
. . . England . . . Ireland . . . Uruguay, where he was given permission to stay,
until the President received a call from Washington, apparently, threatening to
withdraw a $6 million loan, if Bhagwan stayed. He flew on to Jamaica and from

there to Madrid and finally back to India — a total of 21 countries had deported him or denied him entry.

On 4 January 1987 he returned to the ashram in Poona.

THE WAY OF THE SANYASSIN

It is not difficult to become a sanyassin: you simply fill in a form wherever you live, complete a course of daily meditation and read as much of Bhagwan's writings as possible. Some people do go to Poona for their acceptance but most are content to receive it, along with their new name, by post.

Sanyassins tend to live in family houses today; the commune days are largely over. Those who join are usually educated, articulate types — doctors, company directors, the questing well-to-do — people like the jet-setting, international computer expert, who, in the early days, wore his orange robes and flowers to work at the office on London's South Bank but, who, with the passing of time, has mellowed into a dark suited executive, mingling with the mighty in the business world.

Former Parliamentary journalist, Peter Waight, became a sanyassin in 1980 and his parents flew out to see him in Poona. His father, ex-naval officer, Monty Waight, and his wife Betty, were not too unhappy with what they saw. 'I must say, the people there were really enjoying their lives,' said Monty. 'I can understand people liking Bhagwan but I can't apply him to any kind of superhuman thing. He's just a man who hit oil.'

So, Rajneesh offers no creed, no doctrine — such formalities are contrary to the spirit of what he preaches. Besides, as author of 530 books in 32 languages, he is constantly throwing down new, often contradictory, challenges. It is for the sanyassins to make of it all what they will — the essence of Rajneesh lies in any one person's individual response to his prolific pronouncements.

'Nowhere in the whole history of mankind has man been given the dignity of a god. I am, for the first time, giving you the dignity of a god and I want you to make a plaything of all the so-called gods, worshipped by humanity.

'The purpose of the priest is to stand between you and God. And the problem is, there is no God, it is their invention. How different, essentially, is the unquestioning belief in the divinity of a cow from the beliefs that send thousands of Arab and Jewish teenagers in waves to die on barren desert ground. How different is clutching a cross in terror from the offering of food to a statue of an elephant?'

To focus attention on what he sees as the absurdity of human superstition, he opened a Museum of Ancient Gods in Poona in 1988 saying: 'It is hilarious that all over the world, in all the temples of so-called gods, people are worshipping toys. My basic function is to take away all this nonsense for you, so you can come out in your full glory, a full moon buddha sufficient unto yourself. I don't teach any prayer, I simply teach exploration of the inner world. The worship of idols, of symbols, and of animals is not simply child's play.

'The only religion is the religion of being conscious. All other religions are simply toys for children.'

Rajneesh's way to consciousness is not by a renunciation of the world: it is, he says, a renunciation of the insanity of the modern mind. There is no dogma or ritual to be found in his teachings, just ways and means of meditation, to enable each individual to discover for himself what is his own potential, what lies buried beneath the conditioning and beliefs imposed on him by others, and to exercise that potential in a creative way in the world.

'Anything that creates bliss in you is sacred. So let bliss be the whole target of your life . . . don't be serious, don't be sad. The universe is a celebration. Participate in the celebration.'

Participation for a Westerner can mean any one of a number of meditations designed by Rajneesh, which tend to evoke what has become jokingly known, in a reference to Poona's most popular form of transport, as 'the rented bicycle syndrome'.

In 1988, for the first time in 14 years, Rajneesh began leading his disciples, personally, in new techniques. Each evening, at the end of his discourse, the drums beat and the audience of maybe 7,000 people let go into gibberish to cleanse the mind of all agonies and inhibitions and leave them with the freshness of a rose flower. On the second beat the uproar gives way to silence. On the third drumbeat everyone falls, silently, to the floor. 'Die so you can be reborn' calls Rajneesh. A few moments later he brings them back to life.

There is a second meditation known as 'The Mystic Rose', which is a fundamental technique. It lasts three weeks and has three stages. (1) Laughing for three hours each day for seven days; (2) Crying for three hours each day for seven days; (3) Becoming a watcher on the hill for three hours a day, for seven days. Sanyassin Swami Satyan Ambhoj, of California, has described his first encounter with the Mystic Rose. 'It was difficult at first. But then I just started going for it. I'd lie down on my back and find different ways to bring up laughter. One way was letting my voice be very high, like a little baby squealing. You have to allow yourself to be totally silly otherwise you dry up.' In the second stage people felt heightened vulnerability. So relaxed, they could hardly walk; others gained insight into how their emotions had been blocked.

The third, silent phase is unexpectedly difficult. 'When you really connect with your inner emptiness, the first thing you want to do is go home, play loud music, smoke a cigarette.'

The existence of Rajneeshdam, in Poona, is still a bitter sweet pill for the Hindu sensibilities of local residents. On the one hand, they are shocked to the core with the stories of happenings on the ashram. How can visitors allow themselves to be 'sniffed' on arrival by attendants, protecting Rajneesh from his alleged, allergic reaction to perfume? What is going on that requires all visitors to produce a medical certificate which justifies Rajneesh's claim to head the only major Aids-free community in the world? But on the other hand, the steady influx of foreigners is a handy source of income to shops and hotels.

Some stay on the ashram, but many do book into accommodation in the town and take part in whichever of the many workshops they feel will be most beneficial. Bodywork, massage, primal therapy and astrology are all on offer. There is a wide range of books published by Rebel Publishing House, plus all Rajneesh's discourses on video and cassettes.

Poona is not, however, the whole story. The *Rajneesh Times International* is a bi-monthly newspaper, published simultaneously in India, USA, Australia, Italy, Japan, Holland, Sweden, Denmark, Norway, Spain and France, where the organisation has a visibly active following. In Germany the Rajneesh-owned discotheques are particularly successful.

ORGANISATION

Every Rajneesh centre or group is autonomous, relying on its own fundraising efforts to support activities.

In Poona, whilst Rajneesh himself is in control, he is supported by a team of professionals responsible for running the ashram on a day-to-day basis, handling publicity and public relations both with the Indian authorities and the rest of the world.

THE RAJNEESH SCHOOL

Thumbing through reports, written with disarming frankness, by the children of the Ko Hsuan School, in Chulmleigh, Devon, responses were much like those of any state school pupil. There is no attempt by teachers to hide honest criticism or unhappiness.

'I liked this term a lot. I had a lot of fun and there were times when I was sad as well. I changed, and have the feeling that I got much more open and so have a lot of people. This term a lot of people have showed their feelings quite a lot. And we had a meeting with the teenies and everybody told everybody what they didn't like and what they'd been hurt about . . .'

'When I heard about the state of the world I was pretty shocked, because I didn't know much about it. The meditations we did in class were really great . . . the discos we had were really great, you can just let your energy out and have fun.'

'I think this term I had more friends. Yasha is much nicer to me. I am awake in class. I like the food a lot . . . the school is messy but I get used to it . . . I am always happy when there is science.'

The Ko Hsuan (the word means chaos) school raises eyebrows because its philosophy, based on the teachings of Osho Rajneesh, does not regard the family as the essential unit. Disagree with this and you disagree with the school. Nevertheless, its educational facilities have been approved by the Ministry of Education.

In his latest book, *The New Child,* Rajneesh says:

'The utility of the family is finished. It has done its work . . . If a few people choose to have a family they should have the freedom to have it. There are families — very rare . . . which are really beautiful, in which growth happens.

'A commune means living in a liquid family . . . children belong to all. If a hundred people live together in a commune there will be many male members, many female members, the child need not be obsessed with one pattern of life . . . he will have a bigger soul.

'Children are fresh entries of divinity into life. Be respectful, be understanding.

'The commune of my vision will have a five dimensional education.'

It is this 5-D curriculum, stressing education for life as well as livelihood, which is the basis of life at Ko Hsuan.

1. The Informative subjects of history, geography, languages, English and the child's mother tongue.

2. The Sciences, including mathematics.

3. The Art of Living. Transforming hate to love and laughter.

4. Art and Creativity. Music, painting, etc.

5. The Art of Dying. Meditation, martial arts, etc., so that you can become aware of the eternal life inside you.

Ko Hsuan was started three years ago to cater for up to 60 children, aged between seven and 14. No child is taken unless he is ready and willing to leave his parents. There are 12 teachers, with varying qualifications, but all are sanyassins and Osho Rajneesh's photograph smiles down from every wall.

Many of the children come from abroad and become bi-lingual; most are from single parent families. The community is seen as compensation for this. A pupil has even been heard to say to a friend: 'You are lucky. You don't know how *difficult* it is having two parents!'

'In an ordinary state school the teacher has his private life,' says headmaster Sharna. 'Here there is not a teacher who has a secret. If we want to cry, we cry. We don't want anyone to have a mask and so we work at grass roots, with total honesty. By the time the kids leave us, we hope they'll have trust in themselves . . . and out of this centredness, we hope there will have grown a sensitivity to others, and a non-serious, zestful approach to life.'

Each day begins with voluntary meditation, adapted from Osho's Mystic Rose Meditation. 'At first, kids can be embarrassed, especially about laughing to order, but those who try soon get caught up. Most of them have been to Poona and seen the adults making fools of themselves, so they get the hang of it and soon understand how good it is.

'At first the school wasn't ready for meditation. It is a luxury, and you need to be settled. We had to cope with daily living first . . . that was followed by the academic side (we are now gearing up for GCSEs), and when we had that foundation there was energy for meditation. Now their inner exploration shines and reinforces the academic.

'We are realistic that you need tools to cope with the outside world — so we have television and computers and go on lots of outings here and on the Continent. They are not shut off at all.

'There are no punishments — they learn through feedback and seeing the hurt they do. Nor is there any religious or moral instruction. There are no ready-made answers and children are taught that there are always other ways of doing things. Humour is a constant. It gives you distance, helps you to deal with situations.'

Ko Hsuan is run as a co-operative, not a democracy. The kids and teachers share cleaning, cooking and clearing up. 'We are learning and have to be open to change. What was right last year may not be relevant now.'

The school is a limited company in which teachers own shares according to their length of service. They take very low salaries but are boarded and fed. There is no outside support at all. Fees are £1,100 a term. There is a school bank and the children are taught to sign cheques and handle their own pocket money from parents.

The major fundraising event, 'the Buddhafield Music Festival', is open to the public so that villagers from around about can see over the premises.

So what of the rumours that brought the local MP and an unannounced press bodyguard on an inspection in 1989?

The children sleep in large airy dormitories — not on the floor. Their own posters and possessions mark each personal patch — much like at home. The views are superb. The building is well worn, tatty in places but undergoes a weekly 'deep-clean'.

Drugs are absolutely taboo. Smoking is forbidden on the premises — but a place is available in the grounds for those who would smoke secretly regardless. Anti-drugs and smoking videos are shown from time to time. There is no alcohol for the kids — though teachers enjoy a drink and often go to the pub. 'We say they must obey the law — but we prefer our kids to grow without fear. Life is a celebration and that is what we want to teach them.'

SERETA, THE SANYASSIN

Ma Sereta was one of the first to reach Poona when the ashram opened in 1973. A fragile girl, cross-legged on a floor cushion in front of a small 'altar' topped by a photo of Rajneesh, she is euphoric.

'I was born in a poverty-stricken ghetto in California. My whole search for meaning was centred on dance because I felt that through the medium of dance I found the essence of life. I had a deep reverence for life and wanted to know what is at its core. That's all that matters. Nothing society tells you to do compared with this.

'So, at a young age, I was studying dance, and since Indian dance felt to me to be nearer to life, I wanted to go to India. I had no money and I hitch-hiked, on my own, overland through Europe into the unknown. When I left, my parents said something very beautiful to me. "We aren't rich but one thing we can give you is our trust." There were seven of us kids. Maybe that's why I was given total freedom and, to me, this is the only real gift a parent can give a child. When you are growing up, people tell you to go to school, to get married, have kids but I wanted to discover who I was on my own. I thought "I'm going to live" first and then I'll do all that. I was scared, but I had this strong inner call.

'I began to be interested in meditation techniques. I had this intense longing to go through life to the source and not to transcend it. I knew nothing about any religions apart from Christianity and I thought I was going mad. I found a little booklet with a picture of Bhagwan and it described him as a man who seduces women yet the words attributed to him were beautiful. So I went to Poona and heard one of his discourses. I was blown out. I knew he had what I was looking for. I felt there must be some catch. It isn't possible for a human being to be so gracious. Next morning I took part in a meditation he was leading: he stood there with his arms out, Christ-like and he said "let go of your passions". People screamed.

'Then he said: "Stop. Allow the divine to enter you, feel the ecstasy." I was astonished by the power of love. Think of love and we think of lust, one way or another; even the love of religion is lusting after heaven. This was love without motive. Here is someone who has found the highest potential in man.'

THE FLIP SIDE

There is a curious ambivalence about reactions to Rajneesh. Perhaps this is the way he likes it, since his philosophy and behaviour is consistently, and purposely, inconsistent. Although he has been banned by so many countries the attitude towards him is, rightly or wrongly, that of an irritating mosquito, a threat to the national exchequer rather than security.

No matter what he says or does, his followers remain fanatical in their devotion and outsiders, though outraged, often appear to suppress an underlying mild envy at the apparent freedom he offers.

The outrage and the envy stem, first and foremost, from his reputation as a 'Sex Guru'.

At heart, Rajneesh's teaching is based on love, and since he teaches that we must work through bodily impulses before we can transcend them, it is not surprising that, for some people, the most obvious and immediate impulse to explore is sex itself. In the heat of Poona, in the seventies, that was not an unattractive option for some and led to the scandalous reputation about Bhagwan's encounter groups.

Certainly the screaming abandonment, the sex therapy sessions, the self hypnosis, happened. But taken in context by independent outsiders who visited the ashram they appeared less threatening than they did when described orgasm by orgasm in the tabloid press.

Bernard Levin once wrote: 'If it is true, and I cannot see how it could not be, that a tree must be known by its fruit, the followers of Bhagwan Shree Rajneesh are in general an exceptionally fine crop, bearing witness to a tree of a choice, rare nature.'

To Bhagwan, all publicity was good publicity. He thrived on the scandals that began to rumble around Poona. He allowed a German film company to film a specially set up encounter group in all its explicit, nude, moaning and writhing. This film has been used time and time again all over the world by anti-cult organisations to reveal Rajneesh in the raw.

Hugh Milne, Rajneesh's former bodyguard, has described the life style and although he eventually left the movement he remembers his time there with nostalgia. 'I was enjoying myself immensely. Here we all were, living in the commune of a truly incredible man . . . It seemed like the eternal Christmas Day, with Bhagwan as Santa Claus. For me the sensation of complete sexual freedom, rather than sexual satisfaction was vital. There was a general awareness that two or three thousand like-minded souls were working together in this place to fulfil Bhagwan's dream. We felt as if we were new people shaping the world. Nobody who arrived in Poona wanted to leave.'

Bhagwan himself conducted what were, perhaps euphemistically, known as 'energy sharing' sessions with selected women sanyassins queuing for the honour.

'As the ashram grew,' says Hugh Milne, "many different groups sprang up, some from the burgeoning human potential movement, others from more Eastern traditions. One of these was the tantra group, where naked people would experiment sexually, changing partners, in full view of everybody else. Looking at some of the pictures of these groups I suppose they might seem pornographic but this was not how they felt to us at the time. We were exploring a new dimension, the sexual one, in a way we had never done before and it was a tremendous liberation.'

The Hindu people of Poona were shocked to the core.

So it seems were the people of Antelope.

The tiny retirement hamlet which had been gradually bought out by the Rajneesh organisation became a commercially ambitious enterprise. Residents sadly sold their houses to sanyassins and moved away from the unwelcome influx of outsiders. What actually happened within the organisation at that time is a matter of dispute but, certainly, Sheela became extremely powerful.

Under her lead political power was being sought and won. Only two weeks residency in a town was required by the State, before it was legal to vote, and so large numbers of sanyassins arrived before election times. Bus loads of homeless people suddenly found shelter in the City of Rajneesh and by 1982 there was a sanyassi Mayor.

But it was the election of 1984 which was the beginning of the end of the community. At Sheela's trial it was stated that salmonella bacteria had been sprinkled over food in the salad bars of Antelope in an attempt to keep the original inhabitants at home in their beds on election day! Sheela was also accused of attempted murder and was imprisoned for 20 years, reduced to four for good behaviour. Rejneesh declared himself the innocent victim of what had happened without his knowledge, behind his back. But he was arrested and after a short time in prison he left America leaving a trail of unanswered allegations, which are still being investigated.

Today there is a small brass plaque at the foot of Antelope's flagpole which bears these words: 'To those staunch and fearless Antelope residents who withstood the insidious Rajneeshee invasion.'

Update Notes
— At the time of going to press, Ko Hsuan School was being investigated by the Department of Education following the death of a pupil in the grounds. An inquest recorded a verdict of accidental death on the 13-year-old boy, who was found hanging from a tree.
— The death of Bhagwan in January 1990 represented a severe blow to the movement, but it is too early to assess what the long-term implications of this may be.

THE NICHIREN SHOSHU (SOKA GAKKAI) TALE

Nichiren Shoshu (Soka Gakkai), Buddhist Society for the Creation of Value –

FOUNDED 1253, REVIVED DURING THE 1930s

HEADQUARTERS: *Britain: Taplow Court, Taplow, Maidenhead, Berkshire SL6 0ER*

USA: Santa Monica, California

ORIGIN: *Buddhism*

STATUS: *In Britain: Registered Charity 268831*

STAR SUPPORTERS: *Tina Turner; Patrick Duffy*

RESPONSE TO OUR APPROACHES: *Open, welcoming, 'nothing to hide' but extremely distressed that Nichiren Shoshu, 'a long established religion . . . recognised by the Japanese authorities for 700 years and more . . . should be classified as a cult'. Apparently completely unaware of the concern of some cultwatching organisations in the West.*

WE BELIEVE

- In the supreme dignity of life, wherever it is found.

- That every form of life possesses the Buddha nature, or inherent enlightenment to the true nature of life.

- Every human being has the fundamental freedom to live in harmony with all that surrounds them and therefore the potential to achieve absolute happiness in this lifetime.

- That Nichiren Daishonin (1222-1282) was the true Buddha for this age – as predicted by Gautama Buddha.

- We can attain the same state of life – Buddhahood – as Nichiren by chanting Nam-Myoho-Renge-Kyo to the Gohonzon – a mandala and object of worship inscribed by Nichiren. Nam means 'return to' and Myoho-Renge-Kyo is the title of the Lotus Sutra expounded by Gautama Buddha 3,000 years ago.

- It is essential to practise (chant) for the happiness of others, our society, nation and the world to achieve personal happiness.

- The Gohonzon is like a mirror reflecting the innate nature within every human being. This mirror is at first, as it were, tarnished and is polished by chanting Nam-Myoho-Renge-Kyo.

- Buddhahood is the essence of life and is experienced by human beings as wisdom, courage, compassion and boundless positive creative energy. It has the power to transform the forces of inherent negativity.

- In the existence of a strict and universal law of cause and effect.

- We are born with the accumulation of the effects of past lifetimes (karma) and our actions are generally predestined by these circumstances.

- These accumulated causes and their effects are stored in the eighth level of consciousness, whereas Buddhahood is in the ninth. Revealing Buddhahood allows one to break the chain of our unhappy karma.

- Hence anyone, regardless of age, ability or circumstance, is free to create the life he or she chooses.

- That the self and the environment are one and inseparable reflections of each other, like a body and its shadow. We can change the environment by changing ourselves.

- That the physical and spiritual aspects of life are also one. Physical suffering causes mental suffering.

- The Middle Way is the way of perfect balance achieved through harmonising our spiritual with our physical life.

- Life is a changeless eternal force and the individual natures of all things pass continuously through its phases of life and death. Just as sleep allows an individual to be refreshed for the coming day, so death allows the life force to renew its energies for re-birth.

- Buddhahood can be achieved by transforming the essential driving force of desire, into enlightenment and wisdom rather than trying to extinguish it.

Richard Causton, the former Lieutenant Colonel in the cricket club blazer, is the very model of old-fashioned British values. Everybody's ideal grandfather.

Mr Causton is, in fact, a pacifist. He is also leader in Britain of a Japanese Buddhist organisation whose lay society, the Soka Gakkai, has, ironically, won for itself a 'red alert' reputation amongst American and European anti-cultists for violence. They accuse it of mafia tactics and heavy-handed missionary activity. The Soka Gakkai was founded in 1930 and is recognised officially by the High Priests of Nichiren Shoshu. It was greatly persecuted before the Second World War because of its refusal to accept Shinto and Emperor worship.

The original accusations arose in the post-war period when Josei Toda was struggling to re-establish Nichiren Shoshu. Many of his new young followers were over zealous. 'It was in the midst of this desolation and distress that these new converts expressed their agony and their desire to save their country and build something out of the chaos that was worthwhile' explains Mr Causton. But both Mr Toda and the current leader Daisaku Ikeda have controlled the zealots and Nichiren Shoshu Buddhism is growing in all parts of the world.

Nichiren Shoshu and the Soka Gakkai now have 12 million Japanese members (in a population of 130 million) and its offshoot — the autonomous Komeito (Clean Government) Party — is the third largest in Japan. The Soka Gakkai are also building a further 200 temples in Japan to meet the needs of membership and to commemorate, in 1990, the 700th anniversary of the founding of the head Temple. Membership in the United States is about 300,000.

In Britain, Mr Causton heads an organisation of some 5,000 members from Taplow Court, an impressive Tudor stately home with an 85-acre estate overlooking the Thames near Maidenhead, Berkshire. The house was bought in 1988 with a £6 million no-interest loan from the parent order in Japan. No wonder other frantically fund raising religious groups with no such fall back are seeking sinister explanations for such good fortune.

THE ART OF LIVING

Nichiren Shoshu Buddhism differs from other forms in a number of ways.

Early Buddhists taught that everything is transient and suffering arises from the desire to cling to what is unstable and impermanent. To attain a state of total selflessness, or nirvana, desire should be eradicated.

Nichiren taught that, to the contrary, earthly desires are essential, as the driving force which sustains life. It is possible to transform negative, earthly desires into positive, enlightened wisdom. Anger, for instance, can become a desire for peace.

The karmic law of cause and effect operates in the past, present and future and it is the karma formed in past lives which accounts for the differences with which we are born. Karma can be changed by purifying our lives and effecting inner change.

The correct practice of Nichiren Shoshu Buddhism consists of twice daily chanting to the Gohonzon. The Gohonzon is a 10″ × 20″ scroll on which are written the names of the enlightened ones, and it represents life itself. It embodies the Law, as inscribed by Nichiren Daishonin on 12 October 1279, and is enshrined at the foot of Mount Fuji in Japan.

Each new member is given a Gohonzon which he keeps in an altar shrine in his home with offerings of fruit and flowers. All Gohonzons are transcriptions by successive High Priests of the original.

There is nothing that cannot be chanted for, and the same chant can be used to ask for anything. Mr Causton has written a book introducing Nichiren Shoshu in which 126 pages are devoted to explaining the deeper shades of meaning of the chant.

Members are also asked to chant in times of distress or doubt.

The introduction to Nichiren Shoshu, *The Art of Living*, says: 'you are not supposed to empty your mind when you chant . . . in fact, at first you won't be able to think about much, other than trying to pronounce the words . . . Usually when people begin to practise they are encouraged to ask for what they want . . . but after a time they find themselves, naturally, starting to dig deeper into their lives . . . or turn outwards. After all, it is easier to be concerned about others when we have the confidence our own lives are expanding . . . and, as we continue, we discover that, by developing compassion for others, we start to tap the power of our greater self.'

The ultimate aim of Nichiren Shoshu is a war-less world, based on respect for the fundamental dignity of all life. The achievement of this goal does not depend on politics but begins and ends with inner reformation brought about by the practice of Nichiren's teachings. So, improving one's personal and family life is the first step on the road to world harmony.

NICHIREN DAISHONIN, THE FOUNDER

Nichiren Daishonin was born on 16 February 1222 in the small fishing village of Kominato. At the age of 12 he entered a temple and was ordained when he was 16.

The boy was distressed by the many confused, conflicting Buddhist sects in Japan. It was a time of terrible natural disasters and people were questioning why they should suffer so. Nichiren set about a course of study into all the variations of Buddha's message. This lasted 16 years and led to his revolutionary statement that the teachings of Siddhartha Gautama (Buddha) contained only partial truths, until, eight years before he died, he preached the Lotus Sutra, which embraced all his other provisional teachings and contained the Ultimate Truth.

In the Lotus Sutra, Siddhartha described his own experience of enlightenment and the existence of the Law of Life; he did not fully define it, nor explain how to attain this enlightenment despite his assurance of its existence within each of us. The time was not yet ripe, nor had ordinary people developed the intellectual capacity to embrace it. The right time would be around 2,000 years later when the great votary of the Lotus Sutra would appear in accordance with his prediction.

Nichiren declared that knowledge of the Lotus Sutra was the only possible route to the true, indestructible state of perfect and absolute freedom — Buddhahood. But whilst Siddharta's Buddhism was that of 'True Effect', Nichiren taught the 'True Cause', which returned to this purest form of Buddhism and offered, in addition, the key to enlightenment, which Gautama Buddha had not yet revealed.

Nichiren's purpose was to bring back order to Buddhism but he was persecuted all his life (he was once saved from execution by a meteorite that terrified his executioners).

In 1253 he declared that everything within the Lotus Sutra was contained, in essence, in its title — Myoho-Renge-Kyo — and that if his followers would recite this title, prefixed by the word 'Nam', night and morning, they would be reciting not only the essence of the teachings of Guatama's Lotus Sutra but of all those provisional teachings which preceded it.

Myoho is the Mystic Law and means unfathomable; renge means the lotus flower which blooms and seeds simultaneously in a muddy pond and so represents cause and effect and the emergence of Buddhahood from the ordinary mortal; kyo means the voice of Buddha, the sound of Buddhahood.

Nichiren died in 1282.

To his followers today, he is the eternal, original Buddha and Siddhartha was his predecessor, a John the Baptist; Nichiren Daishonin went to great length to validate, in his writings, the orthodoxy of his teachings in the direct flow of Buddhism from those of Gautama. His teachings are said to be more than ever relevant to our times.

Some 650 years later — between the two world wars — Japanese Buddhism was again in a parlous state and a number of lay organisations were formed to modernise and reform it. One of these was Soka Kyoiku Gakkai, formed in 1930, by Tsuneburo Makiguchi and Josei Toda.

The increasingly militaristic Japanese Government at the time had issued an edict that all religions must incorporate some aspect of atheistic Shinto (Emperor worship). Makiguchi refused and was sent to prison, where he died.

After the Second World War, Josei Toda rebuilt Soka Gakkai with the purpose of bringing peace and harmony to all. He began a forceful missionary campaign and there was much press hostility to his shakubuku policy (break through and overcome) towards unbelievers. He achieved his aim of 750,000 members within seven years just before he died in 1958. The movement was especially successful with lower middle- and working-class families because it offers the hope of a better spiritual and material life.

Nichiren Shoshu does not deny the value of material benefits. At the time the Japanese economy was in a mess, so its message was in tune with public need.

Japanese politics were very corrupt in the early days of Soka Gakkai and Toda wanted to shape the future with some spiritually grounded politicians, which was why they formed Komeito. Toda's successor, Daisaku Ikeda, who is President today, declared that no politician from Komeito could hold office within Soka Gakkai and there are now more non-Soka Gakkai people supporting Komeito in some places than members. It is a respected political force in Japan.

Japanese immigrants took Soka Gakkai and Nichiren Shoshu Buddhism to the United States, where it has also had tremendous success; in Europe, its seeds were sown in a natural way, through a handful of Japanese artists and students, or by Japanese women who had married Europeans.

The British movement was formalised in 1975 and became a charity with Richard Causton as its first Chairman. He had been in Japan as sales director for a tobacco company. 'What appealed was the idea that ordinary people could transform their own lives without any radical changes in their daily routines, like an unripened green tomato on a sunny window sill.'

Critics, including traditional Buddhists, accused Nichiren Shoshu of materialism: pray and you will receive. 'There are no instant results in spiritual affairs.'

But Richard Causton explains this differently. 'A member may at first chant for what is causing them suffering, or for something they want. If you chant you touch the innate wisdom within and after a time you realise there is something deeper causing unhappiness. If you want a car, you may learn the reason why you don't have one. Even getting a better job may not be the answer to your unhappiness.' Hence a principle of this Buddhism is that you can turn desires into enlightenment by activating your Buddha wisdom through chanting.

Mr Causton's wife is Japanese and came from a Nichiren Shoshu family but she was a rebel, an atheist and refused to join. He tells how, before they met, she was chronically ill and wasting away. One day two friends took her, forcibly, to the Temple. 'The moment she got there and heard the chanting something changed,' he says. 'She joined in and within a year she was cured. This is the kind of situation that has been misinterpreted as heavy-handed proselytising.'

Missionary activity in Britain, as elsewhere in the world, is on a person to person basis, although when requested talks are given in schools and educational institutions. Members are encouraged to establish relationships with their local area organisations. Only recently has the organisation become strong enough to seek ways in which members can give active help in their communities.

Members meet in private houses — for discussion and exchange of views. There is no Temple in Britain, though there are plans to inaugurate centres. New members must practise, for at least three months, before they are allowed to receive the Gohonzon, and leaders go to great lengths to ensure that it will be cared for and treasured. Once a year, priests come over from Japan for the ceremonial Gojukai — receiving the precept.

ORGANISATION

Nichiren Shoshu has been headed by a succession of High Priests since the thirteenth century. World headquarters are Taiseki-ji, near Mount Fuji, where the original Dai-Gohonzon is enshrined. Nichiren Shoshu priests are not celibate, live at home, are equal with the laity and, in Japan, can be seen vigorously bicycling about their business. Their seven-year training is to help them keep the purity of the teachings and guard the treasures and writings of their faith.

The Soka Gakkai, which is a non-governmental organisation affiliated to the United Nations, is also under the High Priest and is run from Tokyo, where it publishes a number of international magazines and periodicals. The lay organisation is headed by the President and Supreme Council for guidance and beneath them are the General Director and Vice Presidents and a Board of Executive Directors. A central council administers policy.

Members of Soka Gakkai International (which is an association, in faith, of the lay organisations established independently according to the laws and customs of each country), are divided into districts of three or four groups. Each of these is headed by four people — a man, a woman (often married) and a younger man and a younger woman. Districts are organised similarly into chapters.

In America the headquarters of the Nichiren Shoshu Academy is in Santa Monica, California and there are six temples centred on Los Angeles.

That Mr Ikeda, as President of Soka Gakkai International recently had tea with The Queen is suggested as a sign of establishment approval. But of course so did Deng Xiaoping before the massacre in Peking.

In Britain, the General Director is responsible to a Board of Trustees, all of whom have to be householders and to have practised for 15 years, and to a Central Committee consisting of lay leaders who are representatives of districts and chapters throughout Britain and Northern Ireland. The leaders have no authority or power; their sole concern is organisation of activities aimed towards the growth in faith of members and the spread of this happiness throughout Britain.

FINANCES

In Britain and America, money is raised partly from publications and the sale of religious paraphernalia, but the karmic law of cause and effect is applied to the giving of donations.

The net income in Britain in 1988 was £233,000 . . . half of which was donated.

Money is never requested. 'If I put pressure on to anyone for funds it would be very bad for me. Similarly, if someone gives but resents the giving, they will reap no karmic benefits from the giving,' explains Mr Causton. Any giving is done in a private way, and probably under half of the members are contributing anything to the organisation. Soka Gakkai owns no businesses, but there are members who do and sometimes this is beneficial, in cash and in kind.

But, overall, if the organisation is used in any way by an individual for selfish purposes, it is thought to be very bad for him in terms of cause and effect.

THE FLIP SIDE

Nichiren Shoshu has been badly affected by the reputation that shrouded the Japanese lay organisation in the 1970s. The fundamental principle of Nichiren Shoshu is that it is the duty of every member to persuade family and friends into converting. But in Britain and America this energetic fundamentalism and exclusivity have been manifest only as high pressure evangelism.

In 1979, President Ikeda was accused of the almost inevitable, sexual improprieties, but the allegations were proved false and those who made them were convicted of libel.

Ideologically, Nichiren Shoshu is criticised for its 'me' philosophy and suggested short cut to happiness, which is contrary to other forms of Buddhism.

THE BAHA'I TALE

The Baha'i Faith –
FOUNDED 23 MAY 1844

HEADQUARTERS: *Britain: 27 Rutland Gate, London SW7 1PT*

USA: 536 Sheridan Road, Willmette, Illinois 60091

ORIGIN: *Islam*

STATUS: *In Britain: Registered Charity 250851*

STAR SUPPORTERS: *Queen Marie of Romania, Tolstoy, Dizzie Gillespie*

RESPONSE TO OUR APPROACHES: *Reluctant to be linked with 'cults' but anxious to have their beliefs correctly explained.*

BAHA'I BELIEF

- There is only one God, who created the world and mankind as an organic unity. No living creature, not even man, can comprehend God's essence or ways.

- It follows, from the doctrine of the unity of God, that there is no such thing as positive evil. There can only be one infinite. Badness is simply undeveloped goodness.

- Life in the flesh is the embryonic stage of human development, escape from the body through death is like a new birth.

- Heaven and Hell are symbolic, not literal, descriptions of being. Heaven is a state of harmony and perfection between an individual and God. The joys of Heaven are spiritual joys, and the pains of Hell, deprivation of such joys.

- The human race is one.

- All religions are essentially one; they form a chain of progressive revelation to which new links may be added.

- Religion, in harmony with science, is the bulwark for the protection of all peoples and nations. As a bird needs two wings so religion and science must complement each other for a proper understanding of God's purpose. Religious belief which is not conformable with scientific proof is superstition. True science is reason and reality; religion is reality and pure reason, the two must correspond.

- The founders of all religions are messengers of God, mirrors of His image, bringing the people guidance appropriate to their particular time. Adam, Abraham, Moses, Jesus, Muhammad were such prophets.

- Baha'u'llah is God's mouthpiece for our age, he is the Great Educator who will carry on the work of the prophets and bring it to fruition. He is not viewed as the final messenger of God.

- We are living in a time which is as dawn after darkness, spring after winter. The world is stirring with new life, thrilling with new ideals and hopes. Things that but a few years ago seemed impossible dreams are now accomplished facts.

- The cause of this sudden awakening throughout the world is due to a great outpouring of the Holy Spirit through Baha'u'llah.

- The ages of the infancy and childhood of the human race are past: the convulsions associated with adolescence are slowly and painfully heralding the Age of Ages when swords will be beaten into ploughshares. God's purpose is not to destroy, on the Day of Judgement, but to fulfil the Revelations of the past, to reconcile, rather than accentuate, the divergencies of the conflicting creeds, which disrupt present day society.

BAHA'U'LLAH TAUGHT

- All men and women have been created equally to carry forward an ever advancing civilisation.

- Men and women have equal rights but different tasks.

- Marriage is a monogamous state to be agreed between two people and their parents.

- There must be no monasticism.

- Every human being must provide for himself and his family with the well-being of all mankind in mind. Drink and drugs must be avoided.

- Violence and the use of force are forbidden.

- It is the duty of every Baha'i to demonstrate their unquestioned loyalty and obedience to whatever is the considered judgement of their respective governments.

- The aim is lasting peaceful co-operation. Prejudice of all kinds must be abolished.

- The need is for the evolution of a World Parliament, in whose favour all nations will cede every claim to make war, rights to impose taxation and all rights to maintain armaments, except for maintenance of internal order.

- A Supreme Tribunal should be established for the adjudication of disputes between nations.

- Tariff barriers should be abolished and the interdependence of labour and capital recognised.

- An auxiliary universal language should be adopted.

THE BAHA'I FAITH

On 18 June 1983, 17-year-old Mona Mahmudnizhad was forced to watch the hang-ing of ten of her girl friends in Shiraz, Iran. Then she, too, was taken to the gallows. Like all Baha'is in Iran after the 1978 revolution, Mona had been denied a formal education herself and so had tried to organise school classes for the youngest chil-dren in her town. She was arrested, imprisoned, tortured and finally killed. The 300,000 Baha'is in Iran are said, by the Shi'ite Muslims, to be a subversive heretical cult 'a cancer which must be eliminated'.

The Baha'i Faith was founded by Husayn Ali, born in Teheran in 1817, son of a wealthy family, who eventually assumed the title Baha'u'llah, meaning 'Glory of God'. He declared that he was the Promised One, foretold by all previous prophets but the Shi'ites said he was an impostor, and his followers have been imprisoned, executed, harassed and tortured ever since.

Thirteen hundred years ago, after the death of Muhammad, the Shi'ites them-selves had broken away from what they saw, then, as the 'repression and violence' of the majority. But this has not made it easier for them to show tolerance towards the Baha'is.

In Iran, the only country in which Shia is the official religion, the peaceful Baha'is have been accused of all manner of moral, political and religious turpitude.

Western Muslims do not regard Baha'ism as a religion at all but are, traditionally, more tolerant in their response. Despite, or maybe because of, this the movement spread.

Denis MacEoin, university lecturer in Arabic and Islamic studies, has said: 'If one had to put money on a new religion likely to emerge from the 1980s, unscathed, and in a position to take on increasingly challenging roles, it would have to be Baha'ism.'

The Baha'i movement has matured from being an obscure oriental sect to a world religion, with 5 million believers.

The philosophy of Baha'ism has been expressively explained. 'Unification of the whole of mankind is the hallmark of the stage which human society is now approaching. Unity of family, of tribe, of city state and nation have been successively attempted and fully established.

'World unity is the goal towards which a harassed humanity is striving. Nation building has come to an end. The anarchy inherent in state sovereignty is moving towards a climax. A world growing to maturity must abandon this fetish, recognise the oneness and wholeness of human relationships and establish once and for all the machinery that can best incarnate this fundamental principle of its life.'

That machinery is to be the Baha'i Faith.

Some evangelical Christian groups also rank Baha'ism as a heretical cult — though they do not suggest eradication as the antidote! Other Western cult-monitoring organisations are less concerned, since they have, at no time, received complaints about Baha'is infringing civil liberties in any way. The growth of the Baha'i Faith has been a gradual and organic process.

But just as recruitment for the Moonies or Hare Krishna rises when there is publicity, whether it is favourable or unfavourable, so it has been for the Baha'is. But, unlike publicity for the other New Religious Movements, that for the Baha'is is almost invariably positive. There are about 6,000 in Britain; over 100,000 in the United States. The world is aware, more than ever before, that they exist — even if it is not sure who they are.

Abdu'l Baha, the eldest son of the founder, who made a sensationally successful visit to London in 1912, said: 'The man who lives his life according to the teachings of Baha'u'llah is already a Baha'i. On the other hand a man may call himself a Baha'i for 50 years and if he does not live the life, he is not a Baha'i. An ugly man may call himself handsome but he deceives no one, and a black man may call himself white yet he deceives no one, not even himself.'

It is a movement with compassionate ideals that attract a great variety of followers; since its teachings stress the equal value of secular and spiritual affairs, they point the way from words to deeds. 'Work performed in the spirit of service is worship.'

It is a religion offering a complete and practical life plan, though not until the 1980s, when the movement was considered to be internally strong, did it begin to apply its philosophies externally and politically.

Today, Baha'i social and economic development programmes, especially in the Third World, are seen as a reinforcement of the missionary teaching, a vehicle for carrying the Baha'i message. Over 1,600 ethnic groups and tribes are represented within the movement, and its writings have been translated into 700 languages and dialects. The movement has been accredited as an international Non Government Organisation with the United Nations since 1948, and has formal links with UNESCO and the World Health Organisation.

The Baha'i Calendar is based on a solar year and has 19 months of 19 days each (361 days in all). There are also four intercalary days, in an ordinary year, five in a leap year, between the eighteenth and nineteenth months. Months are named after God's attributes: Splendour, Glory, Beauty, Grandeur, and so on. The New Year begins at the Spring equinox.

The very positive message of the Baha'i movement is reflected in the large number of feast days they enjoy, which are celebrated as family and community gatherings with much music and praying. Fasting, like feasting, is considered a symbol of closeness to God.

Houses of Worship are circular buildings with nine entrances, open to anyone. Visitors are as likely to hear passages from the Bible and the Koran as they are the writings of The Bab or Baha'u'llah, but there is no ritual and no sermon. So far, there are Houses of Worship in Chicago, Panama City, Kampala, Frankfurt, Sydney and Western Samoa, and in India an exquisitely beautiful lotus-flower building. Where there is no House of Worship meetings are held in any appropriate building.

BAHA'I BEGINNINGS

The appearance of Baha'u'llah, like that of Jesus Christ, was preceded by a messenger who prepared the way for His coming: Mirza Ali Muhammad was born in Southern Persia in 1819. His father was a well-known merchant, a Siyyid, or descendant of Muhammad, and all through His early life He was noted for His piety and nobility of character. On 23 May 1844 He declared that God had exalted Him to the status of 'Babhood' — The Gate, herald of the new era.

The Bab appointed 18 disciples (one of them a woman) to take the news of His coming to Persia and Turkestan. He wrote prolifically, spoke eloquently and preached reform, which excited hatred amongst orthodox Shi'ite Muslims. Eventually, after several years of persecution during which His followers of both sexes were beheaded, burnt, hacked to pieces or even blown from cannons, the Bab Himself was martyred.

It is His teachings, the basis of Babism, which were to become the inspiration of the Baha'i Faith which followed.

Amongst The Bab's followers from the early days was Husayn Ali, who had taken over the care of the family estates at the age of 22 when His father died. In 1852 the Babis, as they were still called, were held responsible for an attempt on the life of the Shah. Husayn Ali was imprisoned and then exiled to Baghdad. For two years He withdrew, alone, to the wilderness after which time His fame spread. His teachings were bringing people from far away and so both Persian and Turkish Governments agreed they had to stamp out the new religion, which was a threat to Islam. It was during this time, after lone walks along the banks of the Tigris, that the young prophet wrote most of His best known book, the *Hidden Words*. Its lyrical wisdom has 'brought help and healing to thousands of aching and troubled hearts'.

In 1863, Husayn Ali was summoned to Constantinople by the Turkish Government. But during the 12-day period when a caravan was being prepared for the 4-month journey, He declared to His followers that He was the One whose coming had been foretold by the Bab. The garden where this took place is known to Baha'is today as the Garden of Ridvan and the time Baha'u'llah spent there is commemorated annually by feasting.

For the next few years Baha'u'llah was incarcerated with His family in various parts of Turkey, but his following increased. By this time most of the Babis — followers of the Bab — had joined Him and eventually, in 1868, the Government banished Him and all Baha'is, as they were now called, to Cyprus and Palestine.

Around this time Baha'u'llah wrote, pleading the cause of the Baha'is to the Pope and all the crowned heads of Europe, including Queen Victoria. She, alone, replied.

For two years, Baha'u'llah and 63 followers were imprisoned under appalling conditions in Acre. There were no beds, no water, dysentery was rife, children cried and no visitors were allowed. They were eventually released and Baha'u'llah's final years were spent in contemplation, writing, receiving pilgrims in the nearby villa of Bahji. Sometimes He wrote in Persian, sometimes in Arabic; His language could be simple but very often it was lyrical and rich in poetic imagery.

Baha'u'llah died in 1892 after a fever, at the age of 75. In His will, His son, Abbas Effendi, who assumed the title Abdu'l Baha (servant of Baha), was appointed His father's representative and followers were instructed to obey Him.

As a child the boy had suffered greatly because of the persecution of His father and as a young man He became His closest friend and follower. When His father died, He was a happily married man with four children.

According to His father's wishes, He began the building of a tomb for the remains of the Bab, on Mount Carmel outside Haifa, but rumours were spread that this was to be a fort which the Baha'is intended to make a garrison and eventually take over Syria. So for seven years He and His family were confined within the city.

It was not time lost. With the help of His four daughters, Abdu'l Baha began a correspondence with people from America, Britain and Europe. The doors of His house were open to all and it seemed as though the entire world wanted to see Him. One such visitor described how 'within its doors the rigid castes of India melted away, the racial prejudices of Christian, Jew and Moslem became less than a memory . . . It was like a King Arthur and the Round Table, but an Arthur who knighted women as well as men and sent them away, not with the sword but with the Word.'

Between 1904 and 1907 commissions were set up by the Turkish Government, which Abdu'l Baha knew could lead to his execution. Despite offers by the Italian Consul of a free passage to anywhere He chose, He refused to run away. In 1908 He was released and in 1911 made His first visit to the West.

It was an extraordinary tour. He breakfasted with the Lord Mayor of London, addressed the congregation of the City Temple, and the Salvation Army, before going on to America. There He spent nine months speaking at meetings of Mormons, Jews, agnostics, Peace Groups and New Thought movements. He went on to Germany and to Egypt, revisited Britain, returning to Haifa in 1913, worn out. He was then 70 years old.

Throughout the war, He organised agricultural and relief projects and when, eventually, in 1918, Haifa was occupied by the British they responded warmly to His benign gentleness. He was awarded the KBE in 1920 for His efforts towards peace. On 28 November 1921, He died quietly and His Oxford undergraduate grandson, Shoghi Effendi, assumed the role of Guardian of the Baha'i faith.

Shogi Effendi was an administrator, and it was largely due to Him that the machinery of the movement, which had survived so much, was streamlined, modernised and made able to take its place as an independent religion. He translated the writings of Baha'u'llah and Abdu'l Baha into English and cut some of the final links − such as Friday prayers − with Islam. He set about planning a world administrative centre for the Baha'is in Haifa and establishing the Universal

House of Justice — the seat of the supreme body of the faith.

That centre, where the Bab and Abdu'l Baha are now buried, is a golden domed shrine, set amongst acres of landscaped gardens and is a place of international pilgrimage. Baha'u'llah is buried in Bahji, also amongst beautiful gardens.

When Shogi Effendi died, suddenly, in London in 1957 the Baha'i Faith was well enough established to cope peacefully with His succession, although He had no children and had left no will. The concept of a divinely inspired, hereditary leadership foundered and it was decided to hand the movement into the care of the House of Justice.

BAHA'I ADMINISTRATION

There are neither clergy nor personal leadership.

It is governed by an Administrative Order, outlined by the Founder of the Faith. In every village, town or city where there are nine or more adult Baha'is a local Spiritual Assembly is elected annually. The election is based on spiritual principles — there is no nomination or electioneering and voting is carried out by a secret ballot.

The National Spiritual Assembly governing the affairs of each country is elected annually.

The Universal House of Justice, the supreme administrative and spiritual body, is elected once every five years.

There is a Fund to which only Baha'is are allowed to contribute. Donations are voluntary and private and no form of coercion is permitted.

THE JEWISH RESPONSE

'Jesus made me Kosher.'

T-SHIRTS BEARING THIS MESSAGE are on sale in many parts of the world. They are part of a continuing onslaught by Christian missionaries which has caused the Jewish community world-wide to close ranks.

They claim that 'cultish' American groups, such as Jews for Jesus, are helping mainstream church organisations such as the Churches Ministry Amongst the Jews (Patron the Archbishop of Canterbury). They assert that aggressive, bargain-basement offers are being made to young Jews who, like youth everywhere, long to rebel against rat-race materialism.

The Jewish experience touches the heart of the cult problem . . . it focuses on the controversy over conversion. It echoes the international surge in fundamentalism of all kinds. But it puts evangelical Christianity in the dock.

Angry Jewish leaders claim that the Church is spending huge sums of money on brainwashing potential converts and so threatening much-prized family life, in exactly the same way as Scientology, ISKCON and the rest. They estimate that, in America, every Jewish conversion costs the Church about $500,000.

Rabbi Arkush, who founded a defence organisation, Operation Judaism, at 95 Willows Road, Birmingham, with the backing of the Office of the Chief Rabbi, the Board of Deputies of British Jews and the Lubavitch Foundation, has said: 'It is my duty to warn our people that not everyone with a smile on their face is doing it out of love. The Jewish community is susceptible to friendship — it needs friends.'

Rabbi Dr J. Immanuel Shochet is a world authority on missionaries and he is appalled by the latest methods. 'There is a 2,000-year-old tradition of the sword and the cross', he says. 'The Crusades, the Inquisition, the Pogroms and the Holocaust were the direct result of the Christian teaching that the end justifies the means. The Moonies call it Heavenly Deception. Now we are being told *not* to convert. To remain a Jew but put salt and pepper on it and become a complete, fulfilled Jew.'

These missionaries find young people in a low emotional state and they blackmail them by saying they can retain their Jewish faith *and* worship Jesus.

'You cannot be Jewish and Christian. It is a square circle. A Jew who believes in Jesus is idolatrous. Interfaith dialogue is espoused to find a point of common contact — but there is none. We must all learn to live together anyway, whoever we are,' he says.

'Why must we all be the same? Can't we show respect for a Zulu because he is a human being? The minute you say you have to understand his religion, his way of life, you have created barriers. The minute you believe "no Man cometh to the Father but by Me", and that consequently you, as a Christian, have a duty to target those in need, you build the way towards the need to eliminate the non-believer. The New Testament makes Mein Kampf look like a nursery rhyme.

'Judaism is the only world faith that believes in the immorality of saying that you can go anywhere, do anything to spread your own version of truth.

'I have even heard it said that to keep the news of Jesus from the Jews would be anti-semitic!

'At the World Council of Churches Conference, in Lausanne, the question was asked "How is it that the Jews, who rejected salvation, were granted the State of Israel?" The answer given was "God has gathered Jews into one place to make evangelism easier." This is appalling arrogance.'

In Britain, there are now some 8,000 Messianic Jews — as those who believe in both Judaism *and* Christianity are called. There may be 100,000 in America and 2,000 in Israel itself. The Rabbis in black hats and beards look traditional enough; but though the cherished Friday family night begins with candles and songs it moves on to the New Testament; blessings carry the name of Jesus. The New Testament itself has been adapted with Jewish phraseology.

Rabbi Arkush has written a handbook aimed at such congregations and at liberal Jews or those apostates who have abandoned their family religion and are seeking a new way. In its unequivocal denunciation of Christianity as 'the celebration of 2,000 years of failure' — of Jesus to achieve what the Messiah was promised to do — it is a poignant reminder of the message in *Alice's Adventures Through the Looking Glass* — that any situation has, almost always, another point of view.

Of the beginnings of Christianity he says:

'Life was so hard that thousands of Jews thought they were living through the birth pangs of the Messianic age . . . and sure enough Messiahs appeared . . . There were 24 religious sects . . . some very large and influential . . . Each taught a slightly different interpretation of the Torah . . . And each believed it alone had the Truth.

'The Nazarenes were so called because the founder of their sect came from Nazareth. In fact we know of five messiahs of that period.

'Each sect maintained it had the true interpretation of Judaism . . . but members had to be able to prove it to win new converts. This was achieved by interpreting the words of the ancient prophets (which *all* Jews accepted). Nazarene literature abounds with quotations from the prophets which are made to refer to Jesus . . . In this way they gave expression to the idea of having a new covenant through Jesus and, through usage, the terms "Old" and "New" Testament became institutionalised.

'With the destruction of the state and Temple, in the year AD70, the sects disappeared from the stage of history. The Nazarenes ceased to attract Jews to the messiahship of a man 40 years dead, and Paul and Barnabas had already laid the foundations of a new religion by extending the sect's teachings to non-Jews.

'Nazarene writings do have their value. They are as important as the Dead Sea Scrolls for understanding the religious history of the first and second centuries. But what Jew (today) would allow his observance of G-d's* commandments to be influenced by the teachings of an ancient Jewish sect, nearly 2,000 years defunct . . .?'

Footnote: The name of God may not be written in Judaism.

Rabbi Arkush — for whom, of course, Judaism *is* the spoken word of God and for whom Christian evangelism is little better than any other cult activity, claims that the anti-cult movement is on the wrong tack.

'The cult problem is *not* a question of civil liberties. That's a waste of time and is ducking the facts. It all comes back to religion. Most people are pulled into a new faith because they are looking for some kind of spirituality. I am worried because there is no one that is really independently qualified to give such spiritual guidance.'

James Richardson, of the Department of Sociology, University of Nevada, Reno, has studied the Jewish dilemma in the USA where young Jews seem particularly vulnerable to all forms of missionary activity.

'Children of Jewish families have been caught in a tension. On the one hand (American) society appears somewhat open to them, encouraging them to move away from their cultural and religious heritage. This has been further encouraged by parents who, themselves, appear more interested in assimilation than maintaining traditional Jewish life.'

'Yet the lessons of history remind Jews to proceed with caution . . . thus leaders of Jewish religious and cultural organisations have not embraced fully the invitation to join the greater society. This counter-pressure has been felt by many Jewish young people.'

Rabbi Maurice Davis in America has claimed that though Jews form only 3 per cent of the total population there, over 10 per cent of the Unification Church, are Jewish. Equally, young Jews are over-represented in Krishna and EST.

'Any emotive-led response is a cult,' claims Rabbi Arkush. 'I have yet to find anyone converted out of intellectual conviction. If someone intellectually analyses Judaism and decides against it, then this is a sad, but acceptable, decision.

'Judaism has such an intellectual heritage and wealth it requires study for years, but all our educational system was destroyed by the Holocaust. We must rebuild and teach our children the fundamental truths of the Jewish experience, which is one of the longest and deepest of all.'

James Richardson says the roots of the current Jewish identity crisis lie much further back than this generation of students. The counter-culture may have some effect on Jewish students whilst they are in high school but the primary source of their identification as Jews, or lack thereof, is family socialisation.

So the orthodox Jewish response to erosion is not to weigh in on any infringement of civil liberties by Christian or cult brainwashing groups. It is to see what is happening more as a potentially anti-semitic witch-hunt. Such religious intolerance points the way to Auschwitz.

Therefore it is vital for Jewish families to stop the rot by knowing and understanding their religion and communicating the value of its unchanged tradition to the next generation.

Many Jewish schools do have a cult programme built into their curriculum. Before you buy a car, go to a cookery class or join a cult, check it out.

In a high-security office, 6506 Wilshire Boulevard, overlooking the San Fernando Valley, the Cult Clinic and the Jewish Federation Council of Greater Los Angeles are lovingly nurtured by Rachel Andres, whose book *Cults and Consequences* was published in 1988.

Rachel is young herself and she believes that Jews are brought up with a fundamental belief that they must repair the world — it is called Tikun Olam. Because of this, any group that offers a better chance for the world will appeal. It is not necessarily a weakening of their faith. Also, 89 per cent of Jewish teenagers go on to college, so they are accessible.

'Holiday times at the Cult Clinic are very painful,' she says. 'Whether a child is not coming home for Christmas or for Passover, everyone is feeling the same. It's a kind of double whammy. It is not only that they have rejected Judaism, but they have accepted some set of ideals we have found to be destructive.'

The Task Force on Cults and Missionaries was started in 1973 to counter the 'extra-points-if-you-convert-a-Jew' movement. Today, the organisation acts as a support group for parents, keeping communications open where possible, and through the Cult Clinic offering therapy and counsel to ex-cultists who find themselves homeless and without a job.

'Most people leave cults of their own accord,' says Rachel, who does not support kidnapping. She blames brilliant recruiting, not family failure, for Jewish attraction to cults and Christianity. 'In LA there is superb Jewish education and any level of observance we need, but the cult groups are always there when others aren't . . . when you are walking home after an exam, working on revision in the park. It is powerful.'

At the root of the Jewish response are the Seven Noahlide Laws, which they say were given to *all* mankind by the sons of Noah in the Old Testament, and which forbid one group to attempt the conversion of another. Judaism is not exclusive. At the revelation of God on Mount Sinai 613 laws were given to Jews, seven to gentile nations.

THE JEWISH LAD

Benjamin died under a train after the turmoil his conversion to Christianity caused within him. He was a student in London, on his own and lonely, so that when he was invited to Hanneke parties by a group of Jewish Christians he accepted.

He began attending meetings. Many were at night, when he was tired and he was also persuaded to pray through the night. He was told he could keep his Judaism and still worship Jesus.

His parents kept in touch, even after he was baptised but were really worried about his behaviour: he was laughing one minute and getting distressed the next. 'We realised something was amiss.'

Eventually Benjamin was admitted to hospital where his Mum and Dad met the missionaries. 'We pleaded with them to leave him alone. But they said he should ignore us and follow the path of Jesus.'

'When he left hospital Benjamin found a job, but he did not turn up for work. Then we had a phone call to say he was in Worcester and was not coming back. We both panicked. "Dad, I can't face it," he said. He couldn't. He was found where he had lain down — on the railway line.'

Tragically Benjamin's story is typical of what can happen when any religion goes wrong. It could be repeated in any chapter of this book.

NOT ONLY BUT ALSO

THERE ARE SAID TO BE ABOUT 600 movements in Britain, 3,000 in America. Some are famous, some less well known. Their names have at one time or another made news. This is a cross-section of a handful of those we had no time to meet. For help or information about others, whether out of interest or concern, the safest route is, initially, via one of the cultwatching organisations.

JEHOVAH'S WITNESSES,
The Watchtower Bible and Tract Society,
Pennsylvania, The Ridgeway, London NW7 1RN

The Jehovah's Witnesses are a theocracy, under the direct rule of Jehovah through Christ. Their government is modelled on those of first-century Christianity. There is a President and Governing Body of 17 members who have direct control of the entire organisation.

The first leader and President was Charles Taze Russell (1852–1916).

Jehovah's Witnesses are Bible believing followers of Christ. They regard the Bible as the infallible source of truth, every detail therein being true. They reject some mainstream Christian concepts such as the Trinity, the Incarnation of Christ and traditional ideas of Heaven and Hell. They believe he died on a stake, not a cross.

Blood transfusions are opposed because of biblical warnings against drinking blood. They do not celebrate birthdays, Christmas or Easter because of their pagan origins. They also refuse military service, to vote or give allegiance to any country or flag.

Central to their belief is the imminent end of the world, the bloodiest battle of all time and the annihilation of all, except Jehovah's Witnesses, to be followed by a millennium which culminates in Satan testing the saved to see that they are still faithful to Jehovah. The survivors of this test will inherit everlasting life, most here on Earth, but an elite 144,000 with Jehovah in Heaven.

They believe they are called by God to prepare people for this future, which is why so many of their resources are poured into door to door work and vast quantities of literature. Their statistics are said to indicate that 740 house calls are needed to recruit one member. 200,000 join each year world-wide.

The failed end-of-the-world prediction of 1975 caused many people to leave and there is controversy, even within the movement, over blood transfusions and pacifism.

Funds are from voluntary donations.

They claim a membership of more than 3 million, in 200 countries.

THE EXCLUSIVE BRETHREN,
96 Green Lane, Hounslow, Middlesex TW4 6BW

The Brethren were formed in Dublin in 1825 by a group of young men who had become impatient with ecclesiastical barriers and preferred the ideal of full inter-communion. They were joined by Lord Nelson's godson, John Nelson Darby (1800–1882), and his energy helped them to expand activities to Britain and Europe. However his authoritarian attitude caused a split between his followers 'The Exclusive Brethren' and the others known as 'The Open Brethren'.

The Brethren (known more widely, to their dismay, as Plymouth Brethren) are Protestant, orthodox and evangelical, with a strong emphasis on missionary work. Sunday services are unstructured and centre around Holy Communion. All are welcome.

The Brethren are strongly against all forms of entertainment — television, radio and films, and also any occupation that involves Sunday work. Their children are excluded from shared worship with others at school and, in 1989, they issued a letter to education authorities which attacked the use of computers and asked that their children be removed from any lessons making use of new technology.

The Exclusive Brethren are tightly-knit and centrally controlled, whereas each local congregation of the Open Brethren is autonomous.

Financing is by voluntary and systematic donation.

THE SALVATION ARMY,
Queen Victoria Street, London EC4P 4EP

The Army was founded in 1865 by William and Catherine Booth and from the beginning women have had equality in status and ministry. It is a denomination within mainstream Christianity and William Booth had no intention of starting a new movement. He had been a minister in the New Methodist Connection but he left to take the gospel into the poorest, most neglected areas of London. His revivalist style and militant evangelism were backed by a genuine concern for the conditions of those he preached to. His Salvation Army was determined to improve the day-to-day life of the people, as a stepping stone to improving their minds.

In their striking uniforms and bonnets, 'the Hallelujah Lasses' became familiar figures first in the pubs of the East End of London, and eventually amongst the down and outs in the toughest quarters of cities around the world. The Army set up a wide sweeping programme of social reform and care which included rescue homes for fallen women, cheap food depots, summer outings and a missing persons bureau. This, together with their vigorous, militant evangelism to music — 'why should the Devil have the best tunes?' asked William Booth, made them immediately popular. But it also brought a great deal of persecution: many Salvationists were assaulted and they were imprisoned for public order offences. In Switzerland Catherine Booth was herself gaoled.

Even so, the movement thrived and spread.

In worship it is non-liturgical and there are no sacramental ceremonies. In organisation it is quasi-military and authoritarian with about 17,000 full-time 'officers', or ministers, led by the General who is elected by a High Council.

THE SEVENTH-DAY ADVENTISTS,
Stanborough Park, Watford, Herts WD2 6JB

The Seventh-Day Adventist movement was started in North America in 1863. It is a branch of mainstream Christianity with its theological roots in the Great Advent Awakening of the 1830s and the European Reformation 200 years before.

The church believes in the authority of the Bible. Baptism is by total immersion. The essential oneness of the human personality is emphasised and the dualistic concept of body and soul rejected. They believe that we have a responsibility, in this life, to care for our bodies which are seen as Temples of the Spirit: so there is to be no consumption of alcohol, narcotics, tobacco, unclean animal flesh or irresponsible drug use.

The SDA Sabbath is Saturday and their worship is free and non-liturgical. The church practises tithing.

The church believes in the separation of church and state but encourages members to take a full part in the responsibilities of citizenship, such as voting.

Members are encouraged to be active in witnessing and faith sharing, but coercion is frowned on. The church has extensive publishing interests and runs some 160 hospitals.

Current membership is about 4.5 million world-wide.

THE CHURCH OF CHRIST SCIENTIST, (CHRISTIAN SCIENCE),
108 Palace Gardens, London W8 4RT

The Church was founded in Boston in 1879 by Mrs Mary Baker Eddy (1821–1910).

The basic belief is that matter and evil are unreal, that God is the only Reality and is available to everyone as Healer. Christ himself showed the way to salvation by healing the sick and overcoming sin and death. Healing and spiritual and bodily health are central ideas. Some members are accredited by the Church in healing and most believers prefer their treatment to that of orthodox practitioners.

The Church also accredits hospitals where Christian Science treatment is available, and trains nurses and practitioners. It runs a publishing organisation which produces the famous international daily newspaper, *The Christian Science Monitor*.

The Sunday service is the same throughout the world. Passages from the Bible and interpretative texts from Mary Baker Eddy's own *Science and Health* are read. Members are expected to be actively involved in the Church and to lead moral lives.

Financing is by endowment and voluntary contribution.

Authority is invested in a five-person Board of Directors of the Mother Church in Boston which has direct control of the Mother Church congregation, church agencies, teachers and practitioners. Each congregation is democratic, electing its own officers, who must be members of the Mother Church. Each congregation is also responsible for at least one of the now famous Reading Rooms.

The Church is attacked on theological and medical grounds and has been blamed for the deaths of members who refused orthodox help. It balances these stories with others of members who have been healed.

SUFISM,
21 Lancaster Road, London W11

Sufism probably emerged in Turkey from one of the more devout, mystical branches of Islam in about the eighth century AD — but it also contains elements of Christianity.

The orthodox Muslim is content to submit to the will of Allah, whereas the Sufi seeks immediate knowledge of Him. This is achieved through meditation and ritual. Some, who became known as the 'Whirling Dervishes', gain this experience of oneness with God by performing an hour-long twirling dance. For this they wear high felt hats and white cloaks symbolising a tomb stone and a shroud. It is considered that the cloaks might have been inspired by those of Christian monks — Sufi means 'wearer of wool'.

The theology is pantheistic, with a spiritual hierarchy of saints. The Qutb, the Pole of the World, is the chief of these and the creator of the material world, subordinate to the Supreme Being. Love and fear are equally strong motivating forces.

The Sufi 'path' (progress through the 'stations' of worldly renunciation) and the 'states' of spiritual gifts conferred by God (for example, nearness to Him) are the means of achieving real communion with God.

Omar Kayyam, the Persian astronomer, was a Sufi.

Sufism flourishes in many parts of the world but is banned in Turkey.

SUBUD,
Sherland Road, London W9

This is one of the movements that grew from the teachings of the extraordinary George Ivanovich Gurdjieff, who was born in Armenia about 1870 and died in 1949.

Gurdjieff exercised a profound influence on mystical thought. During his extensive travels he observed many spiritual and occult faiths, including Sufism.

He established the Institute for the Harmonious Development of Man at Fontainbleau, France in 1922. The core of his teachings, which became known as 'esoteric Christianity', lies in seeking to open up man's consciousness of higher planes of awareness. His path, known as 'The Fourth Way', stressed the need for change in attitude to life, not in life style. Sacred dances also form a part of the teachings — described sometimes as 'yoga in motion'.

In one of his books, *All and Everything*, he referred to the Ashiata Shiemash, a future Prophet of Consciousness. His followers today believe that a former Javanese local government official, Muhammed Subuh (born 1901), is that Prophet.

Muhammed Subuh (now known as Bapak — Father) had been enlightened in 1925 when he surrendered to God's power, and in 1933 he formed the Subuh movement which spread throughout Java. But it was not till 1956 that a group of Gurdjieff's disciples invited him to England and the movement was established here through the Institute for the Comparative Study of History, Philosophy and the Sciences.

He had developed a process for submitting to God's will, known as Latihan. Latihan is a group activity taking place twice a week in two darkened rooms, one each for males and females. When the power enters followers they moan or scream and move spontaneously. Subud believes the original power given to Bapak is transmitted by personal contact.

The movement is fast growing but information is difficult to come by, since literature is mostly available only to members and there is a sharp distinction between outsiders and those who have experienced Latihan.

THE AETHERIUS SOCIETY,
757 Fulham Road, London SW6 5UU

This is probably the best known of what are sometimes called the UFO groups (unidentified flying objects — flying saucer). The most commonly accepted theory of the origins of UFOs is that they are ETIs (Extra Terrestrial Intelligences).

The Aetherius Society was founded in 1954 by His Eminence Sir George King DSc, who received a message from the 'Cosmic Brotherhood' of 'Space Masters'. Master Aetherius of Venus was the ETI chief spokesman and Dr King had been chosen as the main terrestrial channel for their communication because of his supreme understanding of yoga. The ETI aim is to enlist our support in their battle with 'black magicians' living on Earth and to encourage members to be channels through which ETIs direct their energy.

Members of the Society believe we are far less advanced than the inhabitants of other planets, at stages of evolution both lower and higher than ours. Members also believe in reincarnation, which is seen as an opportunity to learn and evolve to a higher planet. Eventually everyone will become a Master. How long this takes will depend how closely an individual lives by the teachings of

Masters such as Jesus, Buddha (who both came from Venus) or Shri Krishna (who came from Saturn). Cosmic Masters come to Earth to guide our preparations for the New World and the millennium of peace. Some already live here but shortly, Another will come, on a flying saucer.

ROSICRUCIANS,
Greenwood Gate, Forest Row, Sussex

There are several different orders of Rosicrucians who have adopted the occult symbol of the rose juxtaposed with a cross. The Order is reputed to have been started in Germany in 1378 by Christian Rosenkreuz who had studied occult arts in Egypt, Morocco and Damascus.

During the seventeenth century Rosicrucianism spread throughout Europe, emerging from Freemasonry — which also used the symbol of the rose/cross. AMORC — Ancient and Mystical Order of Rosae Crucis — one of the offshoots of Rosicrucianism, was started in America in 1915.

The Rosicrucians are a world-wide, non-sectarian fraternal order. Their philosophy is based on the ideal of everyone living in harmony with cosmic forces, thus leading to health, happiness and peace. They emphasise that they are *not* a religion and that the acquisition of knowledge is all important. But their teachings are available only to members and are obtained through correspondence courses on a loan basis. If a member leaves they must return the teachings. By no means all members join a Lodge or participate in ceremonial. There are 3,400 members in Britain but all money goes to the Grand Lodge in America. In France they own a 24-hour-a-day radio station.

Rosicrucians have remained free from scandal — there are stories of strange rituals and links with the occult and with Freemasonry but these have not led to any major outcry.

The headquarters, at San Jose, California, with the Planetarium and Egyptian Museum are an international tourist centre.

DIVINE LIGHT MISSION
(Elan Vital), PO Box 398, London SW6 2LW

Maharaji assumed the role of Perfect Master of the Divine Light Mission in 1966 when he was eight years old. He inherited the title from his father Shri Hanns Maharj Ji who formed the organisation in 1960 in Northern India. In 1971, when he was 13 years old, Maharaji announced plans to expand to the West and an American headquarters was established in Denver, Colorado (since closed). By 1973 they had tens of thousands of 'premies', or followers but things went sour when the much heralded 'Millennium '73' failed. Few people attended and the Divine Light Mission was left with a debt of $600,000. Six months later Maharaji married his 24-year-old American secretary, Marolyn Johnson, and declared her a reincarnation of the Goddess Durga. The couple moved to a luxury estate in Malibu, bought by the premies.

Maharaji's mother disapproved of his playboy life style and declared that he had broken his spiritual disciplines. She took control of the movement in India, after a legal battle, and there Maharaji's brother is recognised as its head.

Beliefs follow a monistic Hindu tradition with no personal God and belief that, ultimately, all reality is One — pure and beyond all reason. Divine Light is said to be an experience of God as eternal energy rather than a religion. Four techniques are taught which give premies the knowledge to find God. This knowledge is a form of meditation which must be kept strictly secret (sometimes for this reason it is performed under a blanket) and enables followers to experience Divine Light, Divine Music, Divine Nectar and the Divine Word. The Mission also has less spiritual concerns and encourages the ideals of world peace, unity and better social and educational services.

Recruits are attracted by large festivals or personal contact. Income is generated from the fees to these festivals and a 'love present'. Tithes are extracted from married members and the wage packets of young unmarried premies living in ashrams are handed in.

There have been many serious difficulties with the Divine Light Mission since it discourages rational thinking. Experience and feeling are paramount and moral or intellectual issues should be forgotten. 'Give your mind to me' (Maharaji). Critics say that this produces a robotic submission to Maharaji himself through a series of ceremonies which include the activating of the third eye and hyperventilation which lead to being 'blissed out'. Membership in Britain is between 10,000 and 12,000.

THE WAY INTERNATIONAL

The Way International developed from 'Vesper chimes' radio ministry in the United States. This was founded in 1942 by Victor Paul Wierwille (1916–1985), when pastor of the Evangelical and Reformed Church in Paine, Ohio.

His interpretation of the Bible is regarded as *the* Word and his church can be defined as a Pentecostal Ultra-dispensational Christian Group.

He denied the Trinity and the Divinity of Christ and taught that Christ was resurrected on Saturday and that four, rather than two, were crucified next to him. He rejected water baptism believing in baptism by the holy spirit (no capitals) accompanied by speaking in tongues.

The organisation is based on the formation of a tree: 'roots' are made up of establishments such as its International Headquarters at New Knoxville, Ohio; 'trunks' are countries; 'limbs' are states; 'branches' are large cities; while 'twigs' are local community fellowships; and 'leaves' are individual members.

Aspiring members pay a fee and can then take the initial course named 'Power for Abundant Living'. This consists of 33 hours of tape and video recordings of

Wierwille's teachings. It is followed by more advanced courses.

Critics have alleged that Wierwille's teachings lead to loose living and violence. Once a man is saved, he no longer sins 'in his spirit' even if he sins in his body. It has also been said that members are taught the use of guns as a means of defending the faith but this is justified as a method of self-protection. In the 1980s The Way replaced the Unification Church as a prime target for deprogrammers.

Membership figures are unreliable but The Way is believed to be one of the largest of the new religious groups.

SOME PARENTS' TALES

'I WOULD RATHER MY DAUGHTER HAD been raped than to have her mind raped by a cult. If she had been physically raped we could have obtained professional help and kept her from further contact with the rapist, but with her mind raped there is so little we can do.'
Parent of cultist.

Dorothy Johnston was 72 years old when she enrolled as a lady's companion — in an attempt to raise the money to pay for a private detective, who would find her graduate teacher son. Donald walked out of her life, five years ago, after a terrible row over the Divine Light Mission, and she has not seen or heard from him since.

'All our problems were because of that evil cult', she says. 'But now I only want to make it up — I shan't go on for ever and I can't bear this rift between us.'

Donald was a confirmed Anglican, at Oxford, when he met the Divine Light Mission. He went to India and when he returned his Mother was uneasy about the change. 'He would sit meditating under a blanket and although he continued to come home, he was always attacking me verbally for my materialistic life style. I almost dreaded the visits. He kept asking me not to hassle him. It was like a gramophone record. He really believed Maharaji was God.'

In 1975 Donald's father became ill and died. Donald did not go to the funeral but he did keep in touch. For a while he even stayed with some Divine Light friends at Dorothy's pretty bungalow in Kent. All this time he was doing casual work, moving from place to place. Then she heard he was likely to go to America. 'I had heard so many awful things about what happens to people in these cults once they go abroad that I panicked and I did something that I now regret bitterly.

'I wrote to the American Embassy and asked them not to give him a visa because he had not enough money. Donald found that letter, and in a fit of terrible rage he hit me and knocked me down. He had never done anything like that before and I know I had made him very angry. I didn't know what to do — and I made another dreadful mistake. I reported the incident to the police and there was a court case. I can see him now, leaving the court; I wish to God it had never happened. I have been to the Salvation Army and to the DHSS but there is no trace; I dearly want to see him, after all he is my son, no matter what.'

Four times a year, about 70 to 80 people, like Dorothy, gather over a picnic lunch and cups of tea in a South London church hall. They are parents, and grandparents, sharing a mutual heartbreak — they have all experienced the loss of a loved one to the 'cults'. Each meeting includes representatives from most of the anti-cult network. You will find their counterparts in France, in Sweden, in the United States, in towns and in villages, meeting to compare notes, shed tears and comfort each other.

They are mostly articulate, intelligent and very, very angry. These are the lobbyists, the militants, ready to fight for their cause at the Home Office, in Parliament, with Congress, with the law, and with the EEC.

They feel that the authorities, almost without exception, are being weak-willed and lily-livered in the face of possible litigation by powerfully wealthy movements who have 'stolen' their offspring. What's more, they suspect corruption in high places, especially in the United States. Outsiders are regarded with caution since most parents wish to remain anonymous for fear of reprisals, and all fear intimidation by the 'cults'.

Ex-diplomat, David Turner, has a son, Stuart, who was head boy of his public school, a rugby blue and member of the SAS branch of the Territorial Army. His childhood was affluent, happy, within a caring family. Friends described the lad as an 'establishment man'. He had always been interested in religion, so his mother and father were not over worried when they came down to breakfast one day to find him eating bacon and eggs and reading scriptures with a newly found friend from the Church of Christ. They even went along to one or two of the services, and, though it was all too emotional for them, it seemed innocuous and there was really nothing, at first, to be afraid of.

Today, clearly shattered by lost hopes for Stuart, the dreams unfulfilled, they live in dread of the day he agrees to an arranged 'coupling' within the church and is sent far away as a missionary. One of his new friends was recently married to a girl from Barbados, who was ten years older. For them, the likely prospect of a mixed race marriage is horrific, one which they feel sure any prospective bride's family would view with equal concern.

Stuart gave up his job, moved from home into a communal flat in Kilburn and was supported by the church for a year so that he had time to devote to its relentless demands.

'He used to have a lot of friends but he doesn't see them any more. We could sense at the beginning, after having been very close, he suddenly thought we were evil. That was devastating. He has a time table which orders every minute of his day and he has absolutely no time for music, culture or any of the finer aspects of life.

'We decided the only way to react was with reason. I have written several letters explaining our concern but it made no difference at all. I managed to keep my temper and we have always left the door open to him to return. He does come back, from time to time, but conversation is difficult now because there is so little we can talk about. We are constantly looking for the key to help him out.'

The Turners' experience is well known. Mrs Jill Baldwin has been a widow for some years. She too is comfortably off, living in a mews house in London. Her son David was at Bristol University when 'the nicest man' he'd ever known stopped him in the street — and so off he went to join the Family of Love.

Like the Turners, Mrs Baldwin tried to be positive; she went along to meetings and, although she became very irritated, kept quiet whilst David opted in and out of the movement, received dozens of phone calls from his shepherd, pressing him to make up his mind. Then, eventually, he used some inheritance money to go off to Thailand with the movement. 'He was not brainwashed,' she says. 'It was entirely voluntary.'

But when she realised that David had begun teaching little children and he had accepted Moses David's interpretation of the Bible she became very concerned. The greatest hurt was to David's brother, Tim. He diverted a business trip to see him. They made an appointment to meet but David didn't show up. After several days hanging around, Tim had only five minutes conversation with the brother with whom he had been so close.

Marc Toms dropped his own career in television in order to go to America to find the son who had disappeared. But he lost his daughter in the process, because she could not understand how her father could do such a thing. 'No one has studied what happens to families *after* their sons or daughters have come out of a cult,' he observes. 'So much effort is put into saving one, that the rest may feel neglected and suffer too.'

There are parents all over the world who share this kind of pain. They usually lay the blame, squarely, at the door of the underhand, dishonest recruitment techniques which sap logic and common sense,. No one can *choose* to join a cult, they say. Therefore, hidden pressure must have been used. Until that day, when a son or daughter turned a back on family life, most parents feel all was well and the relationship warm and sound. What happened was not their fault and they are powerless to put the clock back.

Parents whose pain is given vent at support meetings, or in the press, are re-inforced by others — a more silent body of bewildered people who do not know where to turn for help. There are as many reactions to the threat as there are young seekers being lured into the cultweb.

The father of a girl who became a Moonie, and was found hanging from a country signpost, stormed from a court in 1988 claiming his daughter had been murdered.

The parents of a young Scientologist who tried twice to have her 'kidnapped' found themselves under threat of legal action by their daughter.

A Muslim boy who joined the Church of Christ was symbolically 'buried' by his family as though he were dead. He has no work permit, no visas and his brothers are hunting for him.

Many parents find comfort clinging together and sharing the problem: by putting their energies into organisations which run on much the same lines as those offering back-up for families contending with addiction in whatever form it takes — anorexia, drink, drugs or work.

For them, the leaders of the groups who lace the nightly cocoa with an intox-icating religious elixir are little better than pushers or ponces.

Very few parents realise how irresistible is the appeal of strong belief and fresh ideals, for which to work, or even fight, within the security of a well-ordered framework. Youth especially needs the buzz of new ways rather than the mellower comfort of parents' values.

Besides, is it always the acknowledged 'cults' that cause such distress? Jewish parents have held 'shiva' (a funeral wake) for offspring 'lost' by marriage to non-Jews, regardless of their faith. In the British House of Lords there is a non-Catholic Peer, whose son announced at the age of 17 that he would not go to agricultural college and had chosen, instead, to become a monk. Even his Roman Catholic mother was devastated. 'He was far too young and had seen nothing of the world. But there was little we could do.' Remember Archbishop Fisher's remark: 'There is no unreasonable argument that cannot be proved reasonable by reason.'

Opus Dei, sometimes known as 'Octopus Dei' or 'The Holy Mafia', is an orthodox order, recognised by the Pope, within the Roman Catholic Church. It was founded in 1928 in Madrid by Monsignor Josemaria Escriva. He believed that anyone — ice cream man, bank manager or kitchen hand — can be called to Sainthood and that every act performed should be an act of praise for God.

It has become an enormously wealthy political force, an alleged spiritual Militant Tendency, surroundd by rumour and intrigue. Certain members of the order are pledged to self mortification, wear a spiked metal belt around the thigh and practise flagellation.

Father Vladimir Feltzman was a member of Opus Dei for many years and he sees the movement to which he belonged as comparable, in its character, with many of the new religious movements.

The borderline that exists between the behaviour of the cult-establishment feared by most parents and the mainstream-establishment is dangerously ill-defined.

'Opus Dei is like a fire; it will warm you but once you are in you will get burned. Very often movements that are born in persecution acquire delusions of grandeur and paranoia; the world becomes an enemy. In the end, because they believe their ideas are infallible, the end justifies the means. Even the warmly offered friendship is just a hook to bring in converts.'

Susan Foster was a 19-year-old, at Domestic Science College, when she was recruited and told her mother she would not be coming home. She was, apparently, never allowed to spend the night at home again and was even driven to and from a family wedding to prevent her doing so. From a happy teenager she became a cold, withdrawn stranger; but she seemed to think she was doing God's will. Even now her experiences are too painful for the family to talk about.

Some families react to this kind of rejection as though it is worse than death. The body of their child is still around but without the spirit — because so often this is what appears to happen. They see a son or daughter who was a gifted student, or musician on the road to a great career, lost to the service of an organisation, concerned only with feathering its own nest.

These parents are prepared to go to any lengths, even putting their distraught and sometimes hysterical offspring through tremendous psychological battering, in an attempt to break the ties with the cult.

The English peer, Lord Rodney, is adamant. 'I do not see how it is possible to be neutral about cults,' he says. 'Helpless people are being exploited by these

monsters and parents are at the sharp end. This is not an intellectual exercise.'
Lord Rodney employed a professional kidnapper to bring his own daughter from
one of the lesser-known cultic groups.

In America, where de-programming is legal in certain States, the threat to
Jewish children prompted a thriving business in professional kidnapping.
Spurred on by the desperation of parents, Chasidic Rabbi Shea Hecht wrote, in
his *Confessions of a Jewish Cultbuster*: 'According to Jewish Law a parent has an
obligation to take his child away from any cult and de-programme him. And I've
got news for you. It is an obligation incumbent on any Jew . . . as a Jew, as an
American, I am convinced that grabbing a kid, breaking him out of a cult religion
is the greatest service I can perform for my people and my country.'

The foreword of his book is by the notorious Ted Patrick, who has served
several terms in gaol for his long-standing campaign against what he sees as
mind control. Of himself, he says, 'I'm a tenth grade drop-out with a PhD in
common sense.' Of his tactics: 'It is like turning on a light in a darkened room or
bringing a person back from the dead. It is a beautiful thing . . . like seeing a
werewolf turn into a man.'

Parents love him and have paid him huge sums of money to rescue their
offspring, often with force. Since he first began his 'Godly' crusade in 1971, Ted
Patrick has been condemned by almost everyone — even anti-cultists — for
methods which are much more overtly aggressive and controversial even than
those of his 'enemies'. His language is raw. His tactics designed to jerk members
from their trance-like allegiance, through intense psychological pressure. This has
often meant solitary confinement, abuse of cult leaders, lack of sleep, lack of
food, interrogation.

The net result is to wear down the resistance, through physical and emotional
fatigue, humiliation and guilt. 'Girl, you're a bitch. You're sitting there looking
more like a man than your two brothers. You are in a cult that took a beautiful
girl and made a lesbian out of her. You take orders from that no good, son of a
bitch. You will eat his shit.'

Parents in America who were prepared to put their kids through a Patrick de-
programming were, indeed, desperate. It worked about 50 per cent of the time;
for the rest, families found themselves faced with counselling fees for essential
rehabilitation therapy to offset the effect of the de-programming trauma. Sometimes the patient 'floats' for two or three days, sometimes it is weeks; a few may
never recover.

Such ruthless determination can easily run amok. In America one of the first
anti-cult organisations to practise commercial de-programming eventually turned
its attentions on Born Again Christians, Catholics, Baptists and even lesbians. It
seemed they would do battle with any group targeted by disapproving parents.

In Britain, on the other hand, kidnapping is still illegal and de-programmers, at
£3,000–5,000 a time, a rare and expensive breed. Cecil Harrison was a de-
programmer who left his wife and children behind in Scientology, became an
undercover kidnapper and he claims was marked down as 'Fair Game' by the
Church. He was arrested in Spain, caught in a legal battle in Germany and all the
time was convinced he was being watched and framed. All in all, he helped some

250 parents, before emigrating to Australia to forget it all. 'I've done my bit.'

Sometimes in a knee jerk reaction, ex-cultists turn de-programmers themselves — but it is a dangerous world to enter. John Thompson, a young English convert from Krishna, took on a spot of freelance kidnapping and went off to Munich at the request of a German mother who was offering £3,000, for the recovery of her daughter from Scientology. A safe house was prepared for the process, but John found himself dealing with a hysterical girl who threw herself on the floor, cut her wrists, kicked her mother and spattered blood all over the walls and floor.

Life is a prison of anger and despair for Lily Ezra, whose late husband, and son, Peter, had nervous breakdowns after her 35-year-old daughter committed suicide. She feels trapped, whilst an uncaring world walks by and those who destroyed her once-happy family go free. They were broken, she believes, on the rack of The Church of Scientology. Peter has fought ceaselessly, since 1987, to expose what he sees as the real cause of his sister's tragic suicide — the teachings and method of the movement to which she belonged. No one will listen.

On the May Bank Holiday Monday, in 1987, Jennifer Ezra wrote to her parents 'thank you for all you have done', walked to the garage of her Sussex home and died there, alone, of carbon monoxide poisoning. When her husband phoned the Ezras to tell them of the tragedy, they could hear the heartrending screams of their 11-year-old granddaughter in the background.

Jennifer was 19 when she filled in the personality test at the Tottenham Court Road, London showrooms of Scientology. Her answers revealed, of course, that Dianetics could help her find a new lease of life, so she signed up. Three years later she met her husband, who was also in the organisation, they married and, eventually, went to live in Sussex near the East Grinstead headquarters.

Jennifer had previously suffered from depression and renewed anorexia which led to a first, failed suicide attempt. Her doctors recommended psychiatric treatment, which she did not undergo because The Church of Scientology believes such treatment to be harmful.

Whatever really happened in those 15 years before she died, Jennifer's mother and brother will never cease from fighting to expose what they feel is the hidden story behind the 'evil' teachings of The Church of Scientology.

Scientology leaders have collated copious documentary evidence — inquest transcripts, correspondence, and media reports to defend their name. The inquest verdict was suicide. Jennifer's involvement with the Church was not blamed. Despite this, the Ezras remain, in their eyes, 'gagged'. They genuinely believe they are helpless and utterly broken by an organisation of whom, they say, the authorities are afraid.

THE CULTWATCHERS' TALE

MARGARET THALER SINGER, at Berkeley University, on the outskirts of San Francisco has bought a paper shredding machine. She was convinced that her garbage bins had been raided for personal correspondence, and poison pen letters then sent to her friends.

The offices of FAIR (Family Information Action and Rescue) in the East London suburb of Leytonstone, have been infiltrated and the girls running Cultists Anonymous in Britain do so under assumed names, from a box number address, for fear of reprisals. It is also whispered that conferences of the international cultwatching organisations have been plagued by uninvited moles from various 'cults'.

The battle still rages.

World-wide anger at the growing danger of cults today is backed, say the protesters, by evidence of repeated skulduggery. No one attempting to put a brake on events is safe, so they believe, from the sabotage of the cults.

It was the activities of the Children of God that prompted the formation of the first anti-cult group, FREECOG, on the West Coast of America in 1972 although there had been active opposition long before this.

FREECOG was new because it was tackling, for the first time, what parents saw as the threat to civil liberties.

Historically, in Britain and in America, the response to new and unpopular soul-searching minority groups had been orchestrated from the high moral ground of the Church itself.

In America, for every revolutionary regional religion or quasi-religion that rolled up to the state fair or the rodeo, set up its stand and preached its own variation on the theme of Christianity, there also emerged a protest group. Often, these were encouraged by the Evangelical Church, taking action against what were called 'Christian aberrations'. Jehovah's Witnesses, Mormons, Christian Scientists, for instance, were each graced by their own personal protest group.

When, eventually, this reaction was formalised it developed in two ways. There were those who fought heresy and were, very often, not personally threatened by the individual 'cult' or sect under fire; and there were those who were defending their Constitutional rights and those of their family, usually as a result of a direct collision with one of the new groups.

Christians had been warned as long ago as 1917, by William C. Irvine who wrote the very first counter-cult book *Timely Warnings*. The Jehovah's Witnesses bore the brunt of his attack then.

But after the Second World War the gradual escalation of concern was brought to a head by the noisy 'Jesus People' Christian revival in Berkeley, California. This spawned all manner of strange offshoots.

CITIZENS FREEDOM FOUNDATION
(now CAN – Cult Awareness Network), 2421 West Pratt Blvd, Suite 1173, Chicago, Illinois 60465

The FREECOG founders soon became aware that they were far from alone in their anger about CoG. There was, indeed, a need for a national organisation which could be a rallying point for parents and, in 1974, they founded the Citizens' Freedom Foundation. The CFF promoted a series of hearings on the new menace, led by Senator Robert Dole in Washington, and its credentials were established.

CFF soon set up shop in most of the 50 States of America, as a 'national organisation of anti-cult citizens'. Its declared goals were:

* To legislate a federal law to be copied by all 50 States that will make coercive mind control a felony. A felony that upon conviction will guarantee a minimum five years (no parole) prison and a minimum fine of at least $50,000.

* to legislate a federal law that will require all existing cult members to submit to a complete physical and mental examination by accredited, non-cult physicians. And at the option of these medical people to require cult members to spend at least 90 days in a medical facility, not under cult domination.

The Cult Awareness Network, as it is now called, is against de-programming, but supports what is known as 'exit counselling' – a directed procedure which aims to help a cult member to forsake the cult in question.

It describes itself as a 'non-profit corporation founded to educate the public about the harmful effects of mind control, as used by destructive cults'. It is run by volunteers in 25 States and confines its concerns to unethical or illegal practices, passing no judgement on doctrine or belief. It is funded entirely by voluntary contributions.

The leading lights in CAN are also concerned by what they see as the political ambitions of most cult groups. An anti-Communist, anti-abortion, pro-nuclear cult platform has been created by the religious right, they say, backed by the fundamentalist churches. There is no compensating left-wing biased cult – the New Age Groups might have taken that direction but have formed no political muscle.

SPIRITUAL COUNTERFEITS PROJECTS,
Box 4308, Berkeley, California, CA 94704

Spiritual Counterfeits began life in San Francisco, as a result of the personal conversion of its founders who had, like so many others, been dabbling in meditation and Eastern Mysticism. They had trodden the hippy trail to India and returned unsatisfied. The first time the public knew of the existence of Spiritual Counterfeits was in 1975, during their campaign to prove that Transcendental Meditation was, in fact, a religion and the public should be wary of its infiltrating into secular organisations. This campaign resulted in legal recognition of the claim (upheld on appeal in 1979).

The purposes of SCP are:

- **To understand the significance of the spiritual turmoil and pluralism in our culture.**

- **To research the effects and influence of the new religions, particularly those based on Eastern philosophies.**

- **To provide a biblical perspective on the new significant religions and other movements so that the church can respond appropriately.**

- **To produce accurate and attractive resources, through which to bring the good news of Jesus Christ to individuals and society.**

The base line is an assumption that any group under the SCP microscope is guilty until proved innocent and that there is no smoke without fire. The mushrooming of New Age thought, self-expression groups and fringe religions are 'a symptom of corporate decay and a threat to individuals and to society'. Joining such a group, they say, is spiritual death.

Spiritual Counterfeits' main mission, today, is to inform — through publications, and it claims a mailing list of 37,000 for its *Newsletter*. The *SCP Journal* is an annual, scholarly magazine, addressing the broader trends of Eastern infiltration. It is run by a Board of Trustees, relies on voluntary subscriptions and works with a team of researchers who supply up-to-date news about 'cult' activity. There is also a hotline and referral service which links callers with some 250 counsellors nation-wide.

DEO GLORIA OUTREACH,
Selsdon House, 212-220 Addington Road, South Croydon, Surrey CR2 8LD, 01-651 6246

Meanwhile, over in Britain it was, once again, the arrival of The Children of God which was to be the catalyst for protest — in respectable Bromley, Kent.

It was here that a property developer, Leslie Frampton, decided to set aside one-tenth of a legacy from his wealthy father to set up a Christian Trust. Deo Gloria was born in 1965, at the same time as 'Billy's Back' proclaimed the arrival of Billy Graham.

Mr Frampton's original aim was not centred on cults. As a good Christian he was worried about the guru image of Billy Graham — after all, he was only a *man*. So, through Deo Gloria, he initiated his own campaign which reminded the public to 'Thank God for Jesus'.

The Billy Graham Campaign was really a part of the same Jesus Revolution which spawned the Children of God. So when CoG first came to Britain they appeared under the same banner, and there was no hint of the scandals that were already rippling around the western States.

Kenneth Frampton offered them premises, and two of his five sons joined the movement. This initial support was withdrawn by 1972, when Mr Frampton became aware that all was not as it had appeared to be (see The Family of Love's Tale).

His Deo Gloria Trust has three main objectives, one of which is concerned solely with 'cults'. The aim of the Trust is: 'to expose the nature and demonic source of the spiritual deception as seen in many forms of current ideologies and mystic and cultish philosophies'. The other aims are: 'to present, assert and promote the truth of the unique Christian message; to encourage and stimulate Christians to witness boldly.'

Deo Gloria seeks to educate those interested in learning more about the 'cults' from information on over 100 groups in Britain. Their library and extensive literature are available to the public, as is specialist help for families and for ex-members of cults.

The horror of Guyana seemed to prove to the public that the anti-cultists had been right. There really was something evil eating at the roots of society. Professionals of all kinds — psychologists, sociologists, theologians began to polarise. Some declared their colours behind the anti-cult movement and the message was given added credibility. The American Family Foundation, which operates throughout the USA, was formed, and began issuing the first scholarly reports. It works side by side with FAIR in Britain; these are the two most extensive, secular anti-cult organisations.

AMERICAN FAMILY FOUNDATION,
PO Box 336, Weston, Mass 02193

This is a 'non-profit making, tax-exempt, research and educational organisation, dedicated to understanding and exposing damaging cultic practices and other forms of unethical social influence.' It also helps individuals and families who have been harmed by these processes and educates society, so that it can deal effectively with a pervasive problem that has affected nearly 5 million Americans.

It has an impressive advisory board of eminent psychologists, psychiatrists, medical doctors, lawyers, scholars, clergy and educators and is staffed by professionals.

This is the academic face of protest.

In 1988 its programmes covered six main areas, with a total budget of some $179,000. These areas included law, ethics, education, research and production of information and scholarly journals, so helping families with immediate practical help on such matters as local, state and federal prosecution of cults.

AFF has also organised a number of international conferences on cultism, and issues referral lists of experts, world-wide, on specific aspects of cult behaviour.

FAIR (Family Action Information Rescue), BCM Box 3535, PO Box 12, London WC1N 3XX, 01-539 3940

In 1975, Labour MP Paul Rose tried to have the Unification Church banned from Britain by Parliament and in 1976 he formed FAIR to help distressed relatives and friends of the new young Moonies. But his efforts backfired and Mr Rose was faced with a libel action, which he lost. He resigned from FAIR in 1977. Today FAIR watches some 100 cult groups in the UK and, working on a shoe-string budget with voluntary staff, produces an extremely detailed newsletter with a circulation of 800, including 100 foreign subscribers.

The organisation is run by a central committee with regional branches. FAIR:

- Is committed to working with families and individuals who have been adversely affected by cult involvement. An individual's decision to leave such a group must, however, remain his/her own.

- Supplies speakers with specialist cult knowledge.

- Alerts government departments, media and public bodies to the dangers posed by cults.

- Provides information and fact sheets on cults and their characteristics.

- Offers counselling, with their consent, for cult members. FAIR does not advocate coercive de-programming, or illegal rescue techniques, nor does it recommend 'professional' freelance de-programmers.

DIALOGCENTRE, Katrinebjergvej 46, DK-8200 Aarhus, N Denmark

All over Europe organisations such as Dialogcentre, in Denmark, also established a kind of spiritual Interpol.

Dialogcentre was founded by Dr Johannes Aagaard at Aarhus in 1973. 'We live in a world which largely rejects Christianity . . . all too often this rejection has brought tragedy,' he says. 'How can we respond? Aggressive antagonism, always sub-Christian, is now also ineffective, leading to isolation. Compromise is anti-Christian, as well as irrational . . . Some Christians have sought, from the start . . . the way of honest, responsible dialogue with participants in the new religions . . . Confrontation in love.'

Gradually movements in other parts of the world began to co-operate and a quarterly journal is now published in English. But Dialogcentre has specialised in understanding Indian religions, with a view to reaching young 'refugees from the West who stream in to the sub-Continent in a sometimes aimless and destructive way'.

There is a British branch (BM Dialogcentre, London WC1N 3XX) whose aims are:

- To give assistance to those in Britain experiencing difficulties through cult involvement.

- To establish inter-faith dialogue.

- To educate the public about NRMs in a preventative and corrective way.

- To inform groups wishing to pray for, contribute to or participate in the work of Dialogcentre UK.

- To promote the Christian mission to Western youth.

- To offer a training programme and literature and promote a deepening renewal in Christian life by diligence in evangelising members of new religions.

CULTISTS ANONYMOUS
PO Box BM 1407, London WC1M 3XX. Tel: Hull (0482) 443104

Cultists Anonymous is one of the newest groups — formed in 1985. The founding members were all parents who felt there was need for more than tea and sympathy. 'We are the other end of the spectrum,' they claim. 'We never, ever rest. Because we are so worried we man our phone all the time, day and night, and are, every one of us, personally involved. We have become so knowledgeable it almost hurts . . . and yet there is so little we can do. The only way, effectively, to persuade a cult member to leave, is for them to express doubts themselves, from within. How do you tell a mother what to say, in a letter to her child, which will sow the seeds of that doubt?

'We believe strongly in exit-counselling though not in kidnapping. Some ex-cultists who have been successfully de-programmed might never have been saved any other way.'

Cultists Anonymous is run by volunteers and one of its functions is to refer callers to other specialist advice.

CULT INFORMATION CENTRE,
BCM Cults, London WC1N 3XX, 01-651 3322

After helping establish organisations in the cult-awareness field in Canada and the United States, former cultist Ian Haworth returned to his native Britain to set up the Cult Information Centre.

The Centre employs two people — Ian and a secretary, and is helped by a small team of volunteers.

The main focus is on education and Ian Haworth gives talks warning schools, colleges, universities, churches, local authorities and clubs about cults. He also works closely with the media.

He says: 'Innocent people are psychologically coerced from their traditional life styles and beliefs by cult methods which represent a violation of freedom of choice and religion.'

CHRISTIAN INFORMATION OUTREACH
92 The Street, Boughton, Faversham, Kent ME13 9AD, (0227) 751489

This is a husband/wife partnership. Eric and Jean Clarke have travelled the country, over many years, speaking on religious extremes — especially Jehovah's Witnesses and the Mormons. They have an extensive library of tracts, books, leaflets, cassettes and videos for hire on subjects as wide-ranging as *From witchcraft to Christ* and *Islam the anti-Christ.*

There is a nationwide contact team sending information to 17 countries and a quarterly journal-cum-teaching-aid called *Awareness.* The Clarkes are adamant, despite their Christian mission, that no person who has been eased out of a cult should be re-introduced to their original religion for at least six months, or the sense of betrayal would be too acute.

HOUSETOP,
39 Homer Street, London W1H 1HL 01-402 9679

Housetop is, to date, the only Roman Catholic family advice centre in Britain specialising in cults. Director John Wijngaards says: 'any centre providing information to pastors and parents about the new religious movements resembles a small dispensary, where wounds are bandaged and medicine prescribed.'

'Members of NRMs are ordinary people, not significantly different from everyone else. Good people, who joined with honourable motivations. What helps families best is a constructive approach to try and understand why their son or daughter is attracted to a particular cult. The NRMs challenge us to reach out to them, in Christian love . . . and this can, at times, best be done by joining others in common prayer. I am not proposing that we should compromise our Christian faith, but so often members of NRMs sing, pray or meditate. Since we, too, are praying people what is more natural for us than to join in? Not only have I found temples and meditation halls conducive to prayer, it has helped me establish meaningful spiritual contact. Sitting

cross-legged, on a floor before a lighted candle, would probably be branded
as bizarre . . . I like to think this is how Christ prayed.'

Just as there are so many second and third tier cults, so are there dozens of
counter-cult organisations. Possibly the best known of the energetic street
protesters are the workers of the Upper Room Tract, prolific publishers of leaflets
against Catholics, Jews, vegetarians. The Tract also offers to tell 'the truth' about:
the Royal Family, children's games (warning of Superman and Superted as
Satan's 'substitutes for Jesus Christ') and rock music (the heavy metal beat was
apparently used by Druids during human sacrifice).

Individually, they have lobbied the political leaders of their respective countries, together they have pressurised Governments, legislators and the EEC.

There have been attempts to curb missionary activity in public places, to give
parents temporary guardianship of grown-up offspring and to enforce publication of doctrinal beliefs and practices.

Official reactions have been varied but, on the whole, low key. Surprisingly,
few Americans who were aware of Rev. Moon's much publicised stay in jail are
aware he is again living in New York. In France, an official blind eye is turned on
de-programming. On the other hand Germany imprisoned the British anti-cult
hero, Martin Faiers, in 1989, for his kidnapping of a Krishna devotee. Spain took
action for a similar offence there.

To avoid trouble, a number of countries, such as Indonesia, have refused overt
cult members immigration visas.

Very few of the numerous bills which have been brought before US State
Committees by indignant individuals have even reached the newspapers. The
courts have been slow to clamp down, too, and where damages have been
awarded against cults they have usually been reversed on appeal.

In America every legal case involving Scientology has been 'sealed' for lack of
evidence; almost every word written for, or by, the movement is copyright, as are
many of the business 'secrets'; the State and the law seem to have been effectively gagged.

But there have been cases in which one or other of the cults has been found
guilty. The Rev. Moon's imprisonment for tax evasion was one such, as was the
Daily Mail's winning of the Moonie action for libel against them — when the
anti-cult movement was able to use its international strength to bring in a team of
impressive witnesses from America.

In Britain there have been many Parliamentary debates on the cult issue — it
was one of these which led to Prime Minister James Callaghan's ban on Scientologists in 1968. Various MPs have seen votes in such a popular cause, but responsibility for NRMs has fallen between a number of departmental stools.
Increasingly, the Home Office, with its concern for charities and its role as
Church of England/State mediator, has been involved.

It was through the Home Office that a start-up grant of £120,000, over three
years, was raised in 1988. This was for the setting up of an independent organisation, which would provide help and information and offer, for the first time,
dialogue with the controversial groups. 'This does not mean we accept, or

believe, everything we are told,' they say. Called INFORM, far from being welcomed by the anti-cult groups, its arrival was greeted with grave suspicion and it has ben the subject of BBC radio and television investigations.

INFORM,
Lionel Robbins Building, 10 Portugal Street, London
WC2A 2HD 01-831 4990

INFORM makes no bones about its wish to remain objective. There is to be no pre-judgement of any individual group or any particular situation. The brochure states: 'INFORM's policy of maintaining direct contact, wherever possible, with new religions does not imply that INFORM agrees with, or approves of, any of the movements in question . . . INFORM . . . does not accept money from any of the new religious movements or any organisation that might wish to prejudge the outcome of its research.'

INFORM's Patrons include the Archbishop of Canterbury, the Moderator of the Free Church Council, Roman Catholic Bishop John Crowley and Professor Sir Ralph Dahrendorf, Dean of St Anthony's College, Oxford.

On its Board of governors are, amongst others, Dr Eileen Barker (Hon. Director and Chairman), Dr John Wijngaards, Director of Housetop and nominee of the Westminster RC Diocese Trust, Mrs Fiona Palmer, British Association of Counselling and George Cohn, former chairman of an independent association of parents of Unification Church members.

There is one full-time paid member of staff, one part-time, Dr Barker's involvement is voluntary.

To date, the organisation has given information to hundreds of anxious parents, referred them to counselling services and compiled a huge data-list about new movements world-wide, establishing links with academics and field workers and setting up a networking relationship with professional organisations, churches and Government. If parents ask they will try, where appropriate, to make contact with the 'cult'.

There are four main reasons why there is so much hostility to INFORM amongst those who have been beavering away, unpaid, for so many years to focus attention on the plight of unhappy parents.

1. Financial. The Government grant has been resented.

2. Policy. There is a fear of appeasement, and accusations that the members of INFORM are too academic, living in an ivory tower. 'No attempt is made to define too precisely the term "new religious movement", which is merely used to provide a common sense starting point to cover what others have called non-conventional religions, alternative religions, self religions or "cults"', they say.

3. Personal. There is a vendetta against the Hon. Director, who has been criticised for her contact with the Moonies during sociological research. She is, they claim, too close for comfort.

4. Historical. The 'cults' have, on the whole, welcomed INFORM.

INFORM's response to critics is to say: that Government funding was available to anyone able to justify it; that one way of monitoring or changing a movement is through direct contact and not through confrontation; that any involvement with the Moonies or any such group has always been on the basis of fundamental research.

The aim is to 'INFORM' with accurate, unemotional material but its three staff members also have many years of personal and professional experience of new movements and related fields, and are very sympathetic to the anxiety of the hundreds of callers. The Home Office remains committed to INFORM and is unconcerned by the controversy.

THE ANTI-ANTI-CULT MOVEMENT

The anti-cult movement and its support network of professionals is offset by an equally articulate network of sociologists and psychologists who do not see cults as a single body, with failings in common and who believe the confrontational approach is wrong. Never shall the twain meet. The professional jealousies between them have meant that there is seldom any public debate for neither group is welcome at the other's meetings. FAIR accuses INFORM of being a fellow traveller with the cult movement. INFORM claims that much anti-cult advice frightens parents unnecessarily. Ask anyone from Cultists Anonymous if they will discuss the disagreements with INFORM and the answer is 'no way!'

In America there are, on balance, more 'neutral' and detached academics treading the anti-witchhunt trail than otherwise, but rarely are they heard in the popular press. Many of them are sound and informative. All are prolific — there is no shortage of reading material for the confused parent. The words you will hear in these circles to describe their counterparts on the other side are 'hysteria', 'faith-breakers' and 'misinformation'.

This does *not* mean unqualified support for the new religions but it does mean a tendency to be more selective in their criticisms and, like INFORM, consider the use of 'cult' as far too sweeping a description of a thousand and one individual movements, each with its own character.

They accuse the anti-cult movement of having good but misguided intentions and terrifying parents, unnecessarily, with scare stories.

Casey McCann, a master at a Kent public school, was once on the committee of FAIR. He says: 'In the early days the anti-cult movement did a good job — they pushed the cults into open ground and provided a haven for parents. But I accuse them of profound intellectual dishonesty. They are re-living misery, whipping up fear and encouraging parents to feed on their own unhappiness. It is vengeance and not positive thinking.

'As a teacher I see too many parents unwilling to let their children grow up. The art of a parent is like that of the potter . . . take your hands away at the right time and you have a pot, leave them there too long and you achieve nothing.

'The anti-cult movement is not interested in the undoubted good that is done by some cults. I don't see any harm in cults presenting a financially healthy front. Jesus would need to be a mega-millionaire today to get his message across. The anti-cult movement is like a cult itself, practising the same techniques of coercion and terror.'

Some of the most eminent anti-cult psychiatrists have also been accused of using the cult vehicle to make a name for themselves, and of conducting careless and laundered research to support their theories.

It is often said that there is almost no scholarly written material presenting the anti-cult case, and that none of the academics supporting it has actually spent time with any of the major movements they attack.

Professor Jolyon West, and his colleague Margaret Thaler Singer, have had a particularly rough ride because they have spoken of 'cults, quacks and non-professional psychotherapies'. Dr West says that the public image of cult is either 'Utopian' or 'Infernal'. In the first instance they would appear to offer self-fulfilment to a band of kindred spirits; in the second he quotes Dante's *Inferno* where men, women and children are bound to a Satanic master and 'loud wailings resound through the starless air', making us weep in sympathy.

He speaks of an epidemic of cult-related damage in America and suggests 'social medications' that would kill malignant cells and spare the healthy. 'Many people in cults are at risk. Some are already dead, some are dying. A public health strategy is called for.'

Attempts have been made, many times, to discredit them both with the American Psychological Association. 'Jolly' West warns anyone embarking on research into the 'cult' world: 'you had better be aware what you are getting into. These people don't hesitate to threaten and use any sanctions they think will work.'

He speaks with anger about the way in which even children suffer because of the *laissez-faire* attitude of authority, and recalls a pseudo-Christian cult in Philadelphia. The leader was, he says, cooking women and feeding them to members. No outside agency would go into his house because he had called it a church.

'We must protect the public from these predators — we are talking about a growth industry.'

OUR TALE

THERE IS A RUMOUR THAT I HAVE JOINED The Family of Love. I do hope God has a sense of humour.

Not for one fleeting moment on the journey have I been tempted to linger longer. There has been a lot to like; I have been surprised to meet so many ordinary, everyday people and it is easy now to see why so many do find comfort in the friendship of the fringe. But neither have I been tempted by much that orthodox religion has to offer. I prefer spiritual independence.

I would like to learn to meditate; I fancy being freed of inhibitions by Osho's Mystic Rose, I would like to live in a community — and, on a lighter note, I must remember to ask for the Hare Krishna recipe for sweetmeats.

But it was also easy to see why an impressionable student, or a lonely soul seeker, could become confused, isolated and perhaps frightened — and why parents fear for their children's well-being. In most cases I was sure that the best advice would be: 'it could be worse . . . leave them alone and they'll come home . . .'

When I was invited to undertake this pilgrimage I was warned my phone would be tapped, my children threatened and my house watched. I was urged not to visit any 'cult' alone.

My chosen companion, Sally Evemy, and I, felt we were bravely venturing in search of some undiscovered bourne from which no traveller returns. We arranged for visiting cards that identified only our publisher's address, in order to put up a smoke screen and prevent word-processor piracy.

In a mood of open-minded curiosity we wrote identical letters to everyone we hoped to see, and their response (or not) was what shaped the course of this book.

Our most dangerous adventure turned out to be a wild ride on the Matterhorn roller-coaster in Disneyland. Though we had a flat tyre in the fog, 50 miles from anywhere on the Big Sur, and lunch to the sound of gun fire at the Police Academy in Los Angeles, at no time was anyone really gunning for us!

Far from it. We were mildly love-bombed, though never brainwashed. Seeking evidence for the prosecution we ate afternoon tea in the House of Lords and drank sherry in the Commons. Seeking evidence for the defence we had cream scones with Scientology and macaroni cheese with the Jesus Fellowship.

Clearly, in some cases we saw what we were meant to see. All our chosen groups were given an opportunity to sing their own praises and some were more polished performers than others. But there was a great deal of trust — on both sides. We were given free access to 'black books' of critical press cuttings. We went unexpectedly to a Moonie camp. I took my daughter on a Moonie weekend and she was unimpressed. There was no reason for any of those involved to assume we were honest, or benign; all have suffered at the hands of the press.

We met a large number of people of all ages finding happiness in a variety of, to us, strange beliefs. They were happy and not too concerned by the rumours around them. We heard of some horrific individual acts by some groups and some amazing cultural contributions to society by others.

We found most ready and willing to listen to ideas for change and improvement; for softening the recruitment techniques and increasing pastoral care that are the cause of most concern. Whether, of course, they would act accordingly remains to be seen.

There may well be dark secrets of which we were unaware. The corridors of religious and political power are dimly lit at the best of times. There have undoubtedly been tragic happenings.

Our journey, from Skelmersdale to deepest Devon, from Fifth Avenue, New York to Venice Beach, Los Angeles was an attempt to look at the local hands-on operation of a few but representative groups. We wanted to meet as many people as possible who have been affected by their activities. We were not looking for trouble but we were anxious to identify and spotlight the problem areas which have been responsible for so much pain. For pain there undoubtedly is.

As we moved between camps, we were continually told stories to discredit the other side which, on investigation, proved totally untrue. Hearsay, rumour and sensationalism are not the prerogative of the press. Truth is a forgotten virtue.

At the root of much of the problem is religious fundamentalism which is bubbling, dangerously near to explosion, in many parts of the world. It is the natural reaction to the ecumenism and the easy-going tolerance of the Age of Aquarius.

The Archbishop of Canterbury, whose soft-centred Church of England is in tune with this mood of togetherness, has made a strong attack on such fundamentalism. Not surprisingly he is regarded with suspicion by more militant Christians for he called it 'ecclesiastical apartheid' and condemned it as one of the most disturbing features of the late 1980s. He said that in religions and cultures all over the world there is a growing intolerance of others and a refusal by many communities to accept the legitimacy of any point of view other than their own. 'Where toleration is in peril, persecution stalks not far behind,' he warned. He would not wish to enter the Kingdom of Intolerance.

Like all explorers, there have been times when we have been physically exhausted and emotionally bewildered. We have located the Garden of Eden, variously, in Mesopotamia, in Missouri and in Africa. We understand that the salvation of the world is, in fact, in the hands of a Korean, an Indian, an Iranian and an Englishman. The Chosen People, confusingly, seem to be American, Jewish or Korean. Jesus, we were told, will return on a flying saucer.

This seems possible.

Twenty million homes in Britain are now in a position to pick up satellite stations from outer space. By the turn of the century God's share of prime-time could match the situation in the States where a religious company runs the fourth largest national television network. There, billions of dollars are spent buying time to sell the Christian message.

It is not the established churches who will be able to afford the luxury of telecommunication by satellite. It will be the independent, entrepreneurial 'High Priests of the Electronic Church' as Peter Elvy calls them in his entertaining book, *Buying Time*, who will rule the space waves. The American tele-evangelists own and operate independent businesses — and this may well become the pattern for Europe. Not for nothing did the controversial Oral Roberts sign off his tele-show with the blessing:

'May God bless you in your bodies, in your spirits and in your finances.' The safe-guards, at present, would seem to ensure that Britain will be protected from the worst excesses which were forecast in the horrific film, *The Vision*, starring Dirk Bogarde. In this a sinister religious organisation is set, by bribery and blackmail, to beam the galactic gospel into every home and eventually take over the world.

So far, of our chosen few, only the Worldwide Church of God has a foot on this particular celestial ladder and this has been achieved by skilful understatement in its television programmes, and a great deal of expense.

The cultwatching movement is passionately sincere, but divided and indulges in in-fighting. Vigilance is vital. But witchhunting is not.

If, indeed, there really is Anyone out there, He must be exasperated. His limitless, inexplicable, unknowable Universe is in danger of being diminished by too many God-grabbing spiritual bargain hunters, with a desire to monopolise the road over the rainbow. In the crush, many vulnerable people and their families are hurt.

The situation is not new. It is as old as religion itself. If God does not have a sense of humour, He must, surely, have a headache.

BIBLIOGRAPHY

The Koran
The Old Testament
The New Testament
The Tao Te Ching
Bhagavad Gita
The Lotus Sutra
The Divine Principle. The Rev. Sun Myung Moon
Allegro, John, *Lost Gods* (Michael Joseph 1977)
Allen, John, *Shopping for a God* (Inter Varsity Press 1986)
Andres, Rachel and Lane, James R., *Cults and Consequences* (Commission on Cults and Missionaries 1988)
Ballard, Marin, *Who Am I?* (Hutchinson Educational)
Barker, Eileen, *The Making of a Moonie* (Blackwell 1986), *New Religious Movements. A practical introduction* (H.M.S.O. 1990)
Beckford, James A., *Cult Controversies* (Tavistock Press)
Bishop and Darton (eds.), *The Encyclopedia of World Faiths* (Macdonald Orbis 1987)
Brockway, Allan R. and Rajashekar, Paul (eds.), *New Religious Movements and the Churches* (WCC Publications, Geneva 1986)
Bromley, David D., *Strange Gods* (Beacon Press 1981). 'Required' reading.
Bronowski, J., *The Ascent of Man* (BBC 1973)
Brown, Alan Calvert, *Techniques of Persuasion* (Pelican)
Choquette, Diane, *New Religious Movements in the U.S. and Canada* (Greenwood Press 1985). An annotated bibliography
Conway, Flo and Siegleman, Jim, *Snapping* (Delta Books 1976)
Cunningham, Loren, *Is That Really You Lord? The Story of Youth With a Mission* (Kingsway Publications 1984)
Davies, Russell, *The Bare Faced Messiah. The True Story of L. Ron Hubbard* (Michael Joseph 1987)
Davis, Deborah, *The Children of God* (Zondervan Books, Grand Rapids, Michigan 1984)
Eco, Umberto, *The Name of the Rose* (Picador 1980)
Elkins, Chris, *Heavenly Deception* (Kingsway 1982)
Enroth, Ron and Melton, Gordon, *Why Cults Succeed Where the Church Fails* (Brethren Press, Illinois 1985)
Forbes, Cheryl, *Religion of Power* (Marc Europe 1986)
Gaustad, Edwin S. (ed.), *A Documentary History of Religion in America* (William B. Eerdmans Publishing Company, Grand Rapids, Michigan 1983)
Gorman, George H., *Introducing Quakers* (Quaker Home Service 1981)
Gratus, Jack, *The False Messiahs* (Gollancz 1975)
Gurdjieff, George Ivanovich, *All and Everything* (Routledge & Kegan Paul 1950)
Hecht, Shea and Clorfene, Chaim, *Confessions of a Jewish Cultbuster* (Empire Press,

Brooklyn, New York 1985)

Hounam, Peter, *The Secret Cult* (Lion)

Hubbard, L. Ron, *Dianetics, the Modern Science of Mental Health* (Church of Scientology)

Huxley, Aldous, *Collected Works. The Doors of Perception* (Chatto & Windus 1954)

Irvine, William C., *Timely Warnings* (1917)

Jacoby, Douglas, *Shining Like Stars* (London Central Church of Christ 1987)

Kennedy, Alex (Dharmachari Subhuti), *Buddhism for Today* (Element Books 1983)

Knight, Stephen, *The Brotherhood* (Grafton 1985)

Knott, Kim, *My Sweet Lord* (The Aquarian Press 1986)

Larson, Bob, *Larson's Book of Cults* (Tundale House, Illinois 1982). A good popular overview from a Christian viewpoint

MacCollam, Joel, *Carnival of Souls* (Sebury Press, New York)

Marie Christine, *Confessions d'une enfant de Dieu* (Editions Rochesvignes, Paris 1985)

Melton, J. Gordon, *The Cults Experience* (Pilgrim Press, New York 1982). One of the best books so far

——, *The Encyclopedia of American Religions* (Gale)

——, *The Encyclopedic Handbook of Cults in America* (Gale 1989)

Milne, Hugh, *Bhagwan. The God That Failed* (Caliban Books 1986)

Murray, David Christie, *A History of Heresy* (New English Library 1976)

Naifeh, Stephen and Smith, Gregory White, *The Mormon Murders* (Weidenfeld & Nicholson 1988)

Parrinder, Geoffrey, *Mysticism in the World's Religions* (Sheldon Press)

Sargeant, William, *The Battle for the Mind* (Harper & Row 1957)

Saxby, Trevor, *Pilgrims of a Common Life* (Herald Press, Ontario 1987)

Shoshu, Nichiren, *The Art of Living* (NSUK 1986)

van Baalem, Dr K., *The Chaos of the Cults* (Eerdemans 1960)

Webb, James, *The Flight from Reason* (American Library Association 1975)

Wells, H.G., *A Short History of the World* (Penguin 1970)

Yallop, David, *In God's Name* (Corgi 1985)

Yanoff, Morris, *Where is Joey?* (Ohio University Press 1981)

INDEX